Cartelisation, Convergence or Increasing Similarities?

ECPR Press

The ECPR Press is published by the European Consortium for Political Research. It publishes original research from leading political scientists and the best among early career researchers in the discipline. Its scope extends to all fields of political science, international relations and political thought, without restriction in either approach or regional focus. It is also open to interdisciplinary work with a predominant political dimension.

ECPR Press Editors

Editors

Peter Kennealy is Deputy Director of the European University Institute library in Florence, Italy.

Alexandra Segerberg is Associate Professor at the University of Stockholm, Sweden.

Associate Editors

Ian O'Flynn is Senior Lecturer in Political Theory at Newcastle University, UK.

Laura Sudulich is Senior Lecturer in Politics and International Relations at the University of Kent, UK. She is also affiliated to Cevipol (Centre d'Étude de la vie Politique) at the Université libre de Bruxelles.

Cartelisation, Convergence or Increasing Similarities?

Lessons from Parties in Parliament

Edited by
Henrik Enroth and Magnus Hagevi

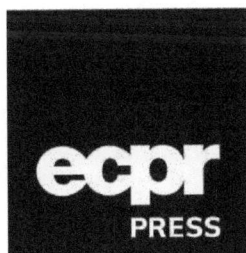

ecpr
PRESS

Published by the European Consortium for Political Research, Harbour House, 6-8
Hythe Quay, Colchester, CO2 8JF, United Kingdom

Copyright © 2018 by Henrik Enroth and Magnus Hagevi

British Library Cataloguing in Publication Data
A catalogue record for this book is available from the British Library

ISBN: HB 978-1-78552-254-3 PB 978-1-78661-311-0

Library of Congress Cataloging-in-Publication Data Available

ISBN 978-1-78552-254-3 (cloth)
ISBN 978-1-78661-311-0 (paperback)
ISBN 978-1-78660-530-6 (electronic)

ecpr.eu/shop

Contents

Acknowledgements   vii

Parties and Abbreviations   ix

Cartels and Competition: An Introduction   1
Herbert Kitschelt

1   Cartelisation in Sweden?   15
    Magnus Hagevi and Henrik Enroth

2   On the Concept of a Cartel Party   27
    Henrik Enroth

3   Are the Predictions of the Cartel Party Thesis Supported in the
    Swedish Case?   43
    Magnus Hagevi and Karl Loxbo

4   Professional Politicians as Representatives   71
    Magnus Hagevi

5   Cartelisation and Europeanisation?   97
    Karl Loxbo

6   Homogenisation or Fragmentation? Perceptions of Mediatisation
    Among Finnish and Swedish Parliamentarians   119
    Douglas Brommesson and Ann-Marie Ekengren

7   Party Cartelisation or Gender Politicisation?   143
    Helena Olofsdotter Stensöta and Anna Högmark

8 Party Culture and Cartelisation: Exploring the Inner Life of the Parliamentary Party   159
Katarina Barrling

9 Democracy and the Cartel Party   189
Henrik Enroth and Mats Sjölin

10 Conclusions   205
Magnus Hagevi and Henrik Enroth

References   215

Index   237

About the Contributors   245

Acknowledgements

As editors and authors we would like to express our gratitude to the MPs in the Swedish Riksdag who so generously let themselves be interviewed for the research project 'Party Government in Flux'. The project would have been impossible without your readiness to share your experiences of and insightful thoughts on the workings of the Riksdag. We hope that you find the results useful. Special thanks are due to Herbert Kitschelt for making time for this project in spite of a forbidding schedule. We are also pleased to record our gratitude to Riksbankens Jubileumsfond – The Swedish Foundation for Humanities and Social Sciences – and to the Crafoord Foundation for generous financial support for the research project.

Parties and Abbreviations

POLITICAL PARTIES IN THIS BOOK: NAMES IN ENGLISH AND SWEDISH, ABBREVIATION, POLITICAL BLOC AND PARTY FAMILY

Swedish Parties

Name in English	Name in Swedish	Abbreviation	Party Family
Right-wing parties			
Centre Party	*Centerpartiet*	C	Agrarian
Christian Democrats	*Kristdemokraterna*	CD	Christian Democratic
Liberals	*Liberalerna*	L	Liberal
Moderates	*Moderaterna*	M	Conservative
Left-wing parties			
Greens	*Miljöpartiet*	G	Green
Left Party	*Vänsterpartiet*	LP	Left Socialistic
Social Democrats	*Socialdemokraterna*	S	Social Democratic
No bloc affiliation			
Sweden Democrats	*Sverigedemokraterna*	SD	Radical right populistic

Finnish Parties

Name in English	Name in Swedish	Abbreviation	Party Family
Centre Party	*Centerpartiet*	C	Agrarian
Christian Democrats	*Kristdemokraterna*	CD	Christian Democratic
Social Democrats	*Socialdemokraterna*	SDP	Social Democratic
National Coalition Party	*Samlingspartiet*	NCP	Conservative
Swedish People's Party	*Svenska folkpartiet*	SPP	Ethnic

Source: Adapted from Gallager et al. (2011).

Cartels and Competition

An Introduction

Herbert Kitschelt

This Introduction is an opportunity to highlight key themes at the core of the debate about cartelisation and party system change in post-industrial democracies that is taken up in this book, as applied to the Swedish case. But it will also contribute a few considerations that pertain to the cartelisation debate more broadly. The cartelisation debate quickly gained prominence after the publication of Katz and Mair's original 1995 article. By the time of writing, this article had attracted more than 2,800 Google Scholar citations; the 2009 follow-up by the same authors already has more than 350. Yet the subject has given rise to relatively little close, systematic empirical examination, in spite of its prominence in political science literature. Neither cross-national analyses nor longitudinal investigations within individual polities have been particularly numerous. For this reason, we should be particularly grateful to the organisers of the present book on Sweden, which investigates the validity of the cartelisation argument by examining dynamic change over time in a single polity.

The motivating intuition underlying the cartelisation debate goes at least as far back as Otto Kirchheimer's (1966) claim that parties transform themselves from being representatives of socio-economic constituencies with distinct class or group interests, to 'catch-all' parties venturing to scoop up a diverse, incoherent mass of voters around vague and malleable political appeals. He foresaw that principled opposition to structural social injustices would decay along the way and be sidelined by a centripetal competitive dynamic in which all parties essentially affirm slight modifications of the existing order. Tracing the historical lineage of this argument, one could go back at least as far as Robert Michels's study of political parties, published in German in 1911 under the title *Zur Soziologie des Parteiwesens in der modernen Demokratie*. Under the umbrella of a general theory of political organisation that attributes agency and strategic capacity only to small cores of elites, the historical claim here is that early-twentieth-century leaders of socialist parties and labour unions refused to sustain the revolutionary zeal of their constituencies. Instead, political leaders prioritised their own political survival in office and therefore preferred assimilation into the national political elite, embracing the existing social order by committing to incremental reform within the broad parameters of the status quo, rather than advancing their followers' yearning for revolution.

The current cartelisation debate triggered by Katz and Mair is theoretically complicated, if not muddled, by the presence and interaction of multiple arguments. Michels and Kirchheimer, however, anticipated two of the three major strands that have become staples of a critique of current Western democracies from the left (and at times from the perspective of a populist extreme right as well). As a first analytical strand, there is Michels's claim of a fundamental rift between a party's principals, its electoral constituencies and the active membership, and its agents, the leaders in party office and elected legislatures (and cabinet representatives, if the party participates in the executive). The former want policy; the latter cherish office and sacrifice policy. Michels tacitly assumes cartelisation or monopolisation, with parties rendered as 'closed' systems: the idea that dissidents could exit and form their own new and 'pure' party, if they were dissatisfied with the 'accommodationist' tactics adopted by leaders of their original political vehicle, is not seriously considered. Ironically, in historical reality, such an exit and organisational division happened just a handful of years after the original publication of Michels's book, when, on the outbreak of World War I, German socialist legislators divided over the German empire's plan to finance the war effort against the French–English–Russian coalition. Both party elite and electorate split right through the middle: contrary to Michels's hypothesis, however, the divide was not so much an elite–mass division but one between different factions, currents and even regions.

With the second analytical strand, Kirchheimer moves the debate from the individual party level to the systemic level but, once again, has a propensity to brush aside the significance of competition as a mechanism for establishing elite accountability to principals. In fact, in the spirit of Downs's (1957) median voter theorem, Kirchheimer asserts that office-seeking political leaders aim to appeal not to 'core' partisan constituencies but to 'swing' voters close to the median in the policy-preference distribution; alternatively, they attempt to cobble together a heterogeneous, precarious coalition of voters with superficially held, disjointed preferences. Overall, party strategists favour a 'catch-all' approach to heterogeneous voter-groups that eliminate a 'principled opposition' to the status quo and leaves many core constituencies dissatisfied and without representation.

Katz and Mair's cartelisation theory is the logical continuation of the trail Michels and Kirchheimer had previously blazed. At the individual party level, leaders find ways to silence opponents of the status quo by disempowering them through organisational rules and by public party finance that removes the political leverage card-carrying, dues-paying members and amateur activists might wield, if they held the power of the purse. At the systemic level, cartelisation emerges out of co-operation between leaders across established parties in finding ways and means to prevent new competitors challenging the centripetal dynamic of party competition stipulated by the 'catch-all' thesis.

In an revision of their cartelisation thesis, Katz and Mair (2009) add a third analytical strand with a political-economic claim about democratic disempowerment not quite anticipated by Michels and Kirchheimer: contemporary democracy cannot deliver on popular demands, because, at the national level of political democracy, politicians' 'room to manoeuvre' is constrained by the effects of the globalisation of trade and finance as well as by the abdication of national sovereignty to the supranational governance, without democratic accountability, of bodies such as the key institutions of the European Union.

Before considering some arguments of the cartel party theory more closely, however, let us build on the political economy theme and highlight the exogenous triggers that increased the salience of these arguments in each of the respective historical periods in which each of the three analytical strands became prominent.

- In the early twentieth century, Michels wrote his treatise in the midst of a spectacular run of economic growth and globalisation in the Western hemisphere, as real industrial wages noticeably increased for the first time since the Industrial Revolution and the living conditions of the working class improved. These developments enabled 'reformists' to become more vocal in European Marxist and socialist labour movements, but this substitution of reform for revolution was fiercely opposed, especially by party intellectuals. Nevertheless, an increasing number of socialists embraced the idea of a piecemeal, incremental shift from capitalism to socialism, through policy innovation, rather than an outright rupture with capitalism and its replacement by a socialist Dictatorship of the Proletariat. The Russian Revolution cemented this split in the labour movement irreversibly. Radicals attributed the unwillingness of Social Democrats to embrace the revolution to their fear of loss of political office and its perks and privileges, rather than to changing economic realities.
- About fifty years later, Kirchheimer wrote his 'catch-all' argument during another spectacular run of economic recovery, after World War II (the 'Golden Age'), and in the context of the Cold War between communism and capitalism. Both developments stifled what was left of the popular appeal

of Marxian socialism in advanced capitalist democracies and turned European social-democracy towards a reformist strategy of improving rather than replacing capitalism. This strategic shift was epitomised by the post–World War II universalistic social-policy agenda of Scandinavian social-democracy, highlighted, for example, by the 1958 Swedish superannuation pension fund legislation as well as by the German Social Democrats' 1959 Bad Godesberg Congress, which approved a new, reformist programme, stripped of references to Marxism, that prompted fierce resistance from the party's left wing and ultimately helped to launch an 'extra-parliamentary opposition' in Germany in the 1960s. Similar New Left, non-communist, but militantly socialist movements sprang up across the Western hemisphere, where socialists had adopted social-democratic approaches to remedy the ills of capitalism, but these new dissidents remained marginal forces. Social Democrats, by contrast, succeeded in wooing critical segments of the white-collar salariat to their side and made their parties critical contenders, if not hegemonic forces, in national party competition almost everywhere in the advanced industrial world.

• Now, another fifty years later, in the early twenty-first century, the current cartelisation debate takes place during another fundamental political-economic and global shift. Communism has collapsed and national security questions focus on complicated cultural and identity divides across the globe. At the same time, occupational and technological change has precipitated the economic and political atrophying of the old blue-collar working class and simple low-skilled salariat, creating a broad mass of economic, social and cultural losers but also strong groups of winners, primarily among high-skilled managerial, technical and socio-cultural professionals, to say nothing about the top one per cent working primarily in finance and technological innovation. The now ongoing debate about political accountability is a symptom of the current political-economic situation but mischaracterises the politics of it as one between 'elite' and 'mass' rather than identifying the new political alignments it brings to the fore. But before I return to this subject, let us briefly preview why, as this book argues with Swedish evidence, the first two (Michels-and-Kirchheimer-grounded) claims of the cartelisation thesis are not borne out.

With regard to Michels's claim at the level of individual parties as closed systems, the study of Sweden in this book will show that some phenomena identified by the cartelisation argument are certainly empirically confirmed. There are fewer members and activists in political parties and, undoubtedly, those are socio-demographically more homogeneous in terms of their higher education and social status, when compared to members in the past or the general population. But these data are also consistent with a host of rival arguments. Just consider that in a time before the automobile and the television, let alone the internet, social disposable time for interaction was much more concentrated in a small set of opportunities in one's close neighbourhood and its public spaces (gardens, pubs), and much of it revolved around political parties. Most people joined parties for social and cultural reasons rather than for political ones. The core cadre of political activists with policy and career aspirations was always small. Over the decades, the attractiveness of programmatic party activism to young people may have marginally shrunk as well, as political participation became differentiated across a myriad of social movements and interest groups focusing on specific purposes rather than generic, general-purpose partisan ideologies (see Kitschelt 2003). But the big loss of party membership and low-level diffuse social participation is among those social groups which, in previous generations, treated party membership as a source of social entertainment and cultural comfort.

The critical core hypothesis of the Michelsian face of the Katz-Mair cartelisation hypothesis, however, concerns the principal–agent question. Are leaders nowadays more detached, in terms of their preferences, from voters and from policy-oriented party activists than before? Have they managed to silence intra-party debates and established their supremacy over the wishes of their followers? There were always reasons to doubt that hypothesis, particularly in democracies with low barriers to the entry of new parties, enabling dissatisfied political entrepreneurs to create their own new venues of partisan claims-making. But the contributions to this book give an empirically grounded confirmation that, for Sweden, the cartelisation thesis is incorrect. Intra-party debates are alive and well, even though their substantive focus may have shifted.

Also, more general comparative studies of political representation yield disconfirming evidence with regard to the claim that voters and politicians have drifted apart (cf. Dalton et al. 2011; Kitschelt and Rehm 2015). This does not mean, however, that all is sweetness and light from the perspective of parties' democratic performance (as we will see later on). Moreover, rough representativeness of parties, viewed in a cross-sectional analysis, certainly is consistent with dynamic processes in which shocks cause disequilibria between public opinion and party positions that, in turn, can generate party system innovations. There will always be emerging issues in society that established parties have difficulty mapping on to their existing policy profiles and partisan constituencies (think of EU monetary integration or immigration recently). Established parties will then be forced to calculate how deeply incorporation of electorally advantageous positions on these novel issues will divide their existing constituencies and how many erstwhile supporters this will cause to defect.

When anticipating that adoption of a position on the new issue (dimension) will lead to a grave loss of votes among existing supporters, as the position cross-cuts an existing inter-party alignment, party strategists might well take a pass, hoping that (1) the new issue might fade away again or (2) that it will generate only a feeble political entrepreneurship that is unable to get a new party off the ground. In case of deep and persistent social divides, however, these hopes will be disappointed, as the rise of radical right-wing parties in Western Europe has proven most recently. *Ex ante*, party strategists may have a tendency to discount the net future cost of entry by new parties and therefore be slow to adjust to new issue priorities, generating a disparity between public opinion and party representation. If political entrepreneurs manage to address the resulting dissatisfaction through new party entry, established parties will incur heavy net loss of electoral support.[1] *Ex post*, the damage to an established party is clear, but even then it is questionable whether it would have been preferable, from a vote-seeking perspective, to make policy adjustments earlier.

The dynamics of partisan misrepresentation and re-equilibration I have sketched out involve a great deal of voter dissatisfaction. These dynamics are, however, far removed from what the cartelisation thesis claims. While I propose that dissatisfaction involves a transitional process of disequilibrium, the cartelisation argument postulates a static, persistent state of representational disparity between political parties and public opinion.

The dynamic disequilibrium argument also does not deny that resourceful members of society – in terms of capital or skill – have more leverage over the political process than those who are deprived. In Marxist language, inherent in a capitalist market economy is a structural asymmetry of political leverage that favours capital owners, by way of the latter using investment decisions to endorse or withhold approval from democratic majority preferences (Therborn 1978; Przeworski and Wallerstein 1988). Differential voter turnout, based on citizens' unequal resources and networks, further slants the political playing field, particularly when political elites face high costs for mobilising disadvantaged citizens (Anderson and Beramendi 2012). Nevertheless, while muted by economic asymmetries, shifts in public opinion, even among deprived electoral groups, tend to result in changes in political representation as well as in policy-making.[2]

Let us turn next to the Katz and Mair cartelisation arguments that build on Kirchheimer and extend the party system argument that established parties fail to represent citizens adequately. They claim that as cartelisation institutionalises mechanisms to make the entry of new competitors difficult, the established parties are wont to gravitate towards defence of the political status quo, expressed in vague, uninformative, centrist 'catch-all' appeals; competing merely on the valence grounds of competence and style. However, in regard to this convergence thesis, readers of the current book will see that the balance of the evidence for this is negative. On many, though not all, policy issues there are continued and renewed inter-party disagreements even among the established political parties, particularly when it comes to gender issues and social policy. Within the bounds of what mass publics find plausible, parties still offer distinctive visions of the future and at least those voters who process a modicum of political information appear to line up with these partisan alternatives.

Have established parties managed to restrict the competitive political partisan space and thus prevented the entry of new competitors that break with the 'catch-all' convergence of the establishment, as the cartelisation thesis holds? And does public party finance help established parties to maintain their grip on their electoral shares? There is probably no aspect of the cartelisation argument that has failed more spectacularly in empirical terms and Sweden is a showpiece case for demonstrating this.

Particularly in countries with high levels of public party and campaign finance, the established parties have shed substantial shares of their voters over the past thirty years and had to tolerate the successful entry of new parties into increasingly complicated party systems. Sweden is a perfect exemplar of this dynamic. Its traditional five-party system – consisting of a left of Social Democrats and communists, a centre (formerly agrarian) party and an urban-liberal as well as a more rural-conservative party on the centre-right – has had to endure the addition of at least three new party formations, all of which look set to persist for some time to come. First, there was the appearance of a Christian Democratic party; then the rise of left-libertarian environmentalists, now possibly supplemented by a feminist libertarian party; and, finally, the recent advent of the right-wing 'populist' Sweden Democrats, whose take-off was fuelled by the immigration/multiculturalism controversy.

More recently (2009), Katz and Mair have claimed that the rise of radical right-wing parties is a consequence of cartelisation, expressing voter frustration with the established choices. But they cannot have it both ways. *Either* there is cartelisation and it cuts off the possibility of the rise of alternative parties *or* new partisan alternatives indeed respond to unmet voter demands, a process that clearly demonstrates the failure of cartelisation. What is then left to explain is why established parties do not jump on to the bandwagon of new issues. As I suggested above, this may well have to do with the complicated electoral trade-offs between retaining established voters and winning new ones that existing parties have to manage when considering strategic shifts. The 'issue yields' of adopting new policy positions may well be negative (De Sio and Weber 2014).

This leads me to introduce the third and most recent iteration of the cartelisation argument, that responsible partisan governments are left with 'vanishing room to manoeuvre' as international constraints of trade, capital flows and regional integration into the European Union remove partisan alternatives. Many policies that voters prefer have ceased to be part of the set of feasible choices that parties can credibly offer to voters. Hence, parties opt for policy convergence, abandoning voter preferences and generating disaffection and alienation from the polity among voters. In Katz and Mair's 2009 article, this argument emerged as a fallback position, as their earlier claims – the Michels-based individual party principal–agent setup and the Kirchheimer-extending systemic claims about centripetal party competition and entry-prevention – had become less plausible. In contrast to the earlier cartelisation thesis, the convergence of parties was now no longer said to be generated by *endogenous* processes of partisan competition but by *exogenous* constraints (open economies, European integration), even though these might themselves result from conscious partisan government policies at earlier points in time intended to bind the hands of successors by eliminating options from the domestic democratic political choice set through globalisation and European integration.

The simple and direct response to the new exogenous cartelisation thesis is, of course, to identify the rather impressive range of partisan choices that national governments are still left with, even once common constraints and trends are taken into account. Thus, a number of economic and technological processes may have increased income inequality everywhere in advanced post-industrial capitalist democracies but the levels reached, extent of change and pace of this process varied substantially (cf. Huber and Stephens 2014). The extreme escalation of income and wealth inequality in the Anglo-Saxon countries, for example, cannot be accounted for without the explicit policies of ideological, programmatic, right-wing partisan governments (Huber, Huo and Stephens 2016). Similar arguments about the continuing vitality of partisan government have been made about key aspects of social-policy reform, whether they concern the retrenchment of welfare state generosity (Finseraas and Vernby 2011; Giger and Nelson 2010); the modalities of introducing competition and privatisation in health care (Gingrich 2011); or the trajectories of higher education reform (Ansell 2010). Overall, partisan differences on a whole range of socio-economic policies continue to be substantial and incorporate new divides, such as the conflict between an emphasis on a social-investment- or a social-consumption-oriented transformation of the welfare state (Beramendi et al. 2015). Even in many non-economic policy areas, such as law-and-order policy (see, for example, Wenzelburger 2014), partisan imprints on public policy are starkly contoured. Partisan effects, of course, are not without limit and occur within the boundaries of economic, fiscal and institutional constraints.

The cartelisation thesis interprets European integration, particularly within the single European currency area, as a force of discipline and convergence that blocks the degrees of freedom sought by domestic partisan governments. While this might have been the intended effect of the original regional agreements, the EU integration crisis since 2010 illustrates that, in fact, little convergence has been achieved within the European Union. Across countries, differences in the institutions ('varieties') of capitalism manifested by different eurozone countries stubbornly resist levelling, even though the economically dominant Northern Europeans have made mighty – but in many ways futile, if not self-deluding – efforts to make their 'model' of capitalism dominant over the whole euro currency zone, especially in the most recalcitrant Mediterranean Member-States (cf. Beramendi et al. 2015; Hall 2014; Iversen, Soskice and Hope 2016). Moreover, within individual countries, the stalemate of the EU integration process has fuelled unprecedented partisan polarisation that has often paralysed governments for extended periods of time. Add to this the refugee crisis since 2015 and its partisan politicisation of migration issues. In light of all these developments, it is obvious that cartelisation does not provide a meaningful theoretical frame to account for the dynamics of party competition in much of Western Europe.

But let us go beyond a simple and direct response to the cartelisation argument and make some concessions. There are, in fact, new long-term constraints imposed on partisan politics in contemporary capitalism that have asserted themselves mightily over the past few decades and are likely to intensify their hold on post-industrial economies in the future. Globalisation, however, is a comparatively feeble force in terms of imposing economic dislocation, uncertainty and hardship when compared to other developments: farmers in the twentieth century and blue-collar manufacturing workers over the past generation have not, for the most part, lost their jobs to workers in foreign countries but to technology, that is, machines and, more recently, to the unstoppable rise of 'IT code'. In the same vein, the supreme challenge in the next fifty years and beyond will be that most of the remaining technical-manufacturing jobs, as well as a large proportion of administrative-service jobs, will vanish due to IT advances (Frey and Osborne 2013). The only areas left for employment growth will be: first, low-skilled localised services of personal care and maintenance and, second and foremost, high-skilled non-routine occupations requiring a sophisticated, situation-specific capacity for judgement against a broad and deep professional background, based on both overt, teachable knowledge and tacit, experiential knowledge.

A second major challenge and impending further crisis is that in many Western democracies, demographic reproduction rates have fallen way below the levels needed for labour force replacement. These countries face intensifying imbalances between a shrinking working-age population and a growing retiree population that requires upkeep and comprehensive medical care. Moreover, more immigration is not a costless and instant solution to this challenge, as immigrants, just like domestic offspring, have to go through a costly and time-consuming process of instruction before they become productive members of a complex post-industrial society.

Taking both challenges together, the first challenge – technological innovation through 'code' – calls for an intensification of human-capital investment, to enable young labour market entrants to practise occupations for which it is hard to substitute automation for human workers and also to increase their ability to learn and adapt to ever-changing technological conditions. As automation progresses, the second challenge of the impending demographic crisis, in contrast, raises the imperative to spend more resources on 'consumption' to maintain the standard of living of increasingly large cohorts of retirees and to boost their life expectancy with ever more sophisticated medical technologies. Between the millstones of social and political imperatives to invest more in the young and to spend more on the old, current party systems face contradictory demands for expenditure as well as new forms of political governance that are unprecedented and that are likely to grind up existing political-economic voter alignments. The emerging divides are only partially captured in terms of familiar class and sectoral distributive divides. Moreover, they have cultural implications that compel large segments of the population, even in advanced post-industrial polities and particularly among the less well educated and culturally more traditional groups, to reconceive their visions of the good life and the social appropriateness of conduct and aspirations.

No incumbent politician or outside political entrepreneur can currently seriously claim to have a convincing answer to resolve the dilemma of how to address rapidly growing demands for social investment while simultaneously both increasing social consumption and managing profound cultural transformation. If we revisit the situation encountered by citizens and politicians in the Great Depression, then the political-economic challenges of the day were pretty obvious: most clearly, the need to do something about high unemployment and low investment (Gourevitch 1986). But the answers to the question of how to do this were not. No politician – not Franklin D. Roosevelt in the United States, Per Albin Hansson in Sweden or, for that matter, Adolf Hitler in Germany – could invoke well-considered, theoretically reasoned and empirically grounded policy plans to lead their countries out of their respective economic crises. Depending on regime and partisan configurations, different problem-solving strategies emerged incrementally out of the protracted interplay of conflicting political forces (cf. Luebbert 1991). The ultimate outcomes were not willed, intended or even anticipated by their protagonists.

Likewise, today, different constellations of interests advance rival problem-solving strategies to cope with the increasing demands for social investment and social consumption that threaten to tear apart post-industrial societies (cf. Beramendi et al. 2015). Politicians are compelled to pursue any of these strategies in trial-and-error fashion in a prospective horizon of profound uncertainty. Citizens have only vague preferences, if any, and politicians do not know the payoffs of alternative strategies. This situation is bound to generate tremendous anxiety and dissatisfaction, both at the mass and the elite level of politics.

By contrast, there is no place for policy and preference uncertainty in the cartelisation theory. Here, the counterfactual claim is that people, for the most part, subscribe to a popular social demand function X, with clear policy and institutional prescriptions, that would, with some certainty, address the new challenges of investment and consumption. For the cartelisation thesis, the critical claim is that politicians, generically conceived as a 'class' of electoral office-holders regardless of partisan stripes, do not want to implement these popular policy priorities. They systematically subvert the pursuit of such priorities, as 'doing the right thing' would undermine the chances of the political establishment surviving in political office.

Quite to the contrary, in fact, partisan democratic politicians are likely to feel electoral pressures very much as powerful incentives to identify successful solutions to the impending dilemmas of production and consumption, if for no other reason than to lock in their partisan hegemony for the future. This is essentially what leaders in 'hard times' delivered before: Roosevelt and Hansson were able to secure the hegemony of their respective political parties for generations beyond the Great Depression. *Ex ante*, however, it is the thick fog of uncertainty over viable solutions that disempowers politicians and that creates uncertainty and dissatisfaction among mass publics. This situation of profound ambiguity and indeterminacy, often yielding timid, incremental, trial-and-error muddling-through in policy-making or sometimes even paralysis of the entire policy process as veto-players create persistent stalemates, suffices to explain current public dissatisfaction with democratic politics, including intermittent yearnings for strong leaders who claim that they can cut through the complexity of our times and offer simple solutions. No conspiracy theories about selfish leaders organising political cartels in order to prevent equitable, efficient and appropriate government strategies are needed to account for the political anxiety of our time.

As an indirect empirical point of reference for the claim that it is the absence of programmatic solution concepts, and not the thwarting of 'correct' concepts by obstructionist elites motivated by the defence of the political status quo, that is at the heart of current voter malaise in post-industrial democracies, consider voting patterns since the financial crisis of 2008.

Starting with the European elections in 2009, and with the exception of a few recent elections in Mediterranean countries, the post-crisis conditions have, in most countries, not rewarded left and centre-left opposition parties. Instead, when electorates had a chance to reward an oppositional social-democratic or socialist party, and especially when there were quite radical social-democratic or socialist visions on offer, voters have, for the most part, stayed away from them or only fuelled a tepid recovery of left-wing parties' electoral fortunes.[3] Among several reasons for Social Democrats' disappointing electoral fortunes, I would nominate a scepticism shared widely within mass electorates that welfare state policy solutions that worked in the past can be crisis-coping strategies applicable to the present; rather, voters believe that pursuing more of the same policies delivered during the Golden Age of post-war capitalist economic recovery and democracies will be counterproductive for current political-economic performance.

Anxiety breeds status-quo orientation. Most Europeans strongly support their welfare states and public services but they are sceptical that further expansion will do more good than harm. Their appetite for supporting dissident parties that would change the status quo is limited. In fact, the new parties successfully establishing themselves in Western party systems are, for the most part, about fighting change and preserving the status quo, or even returning to an imagined better past. This applies most clearly to the new radical right in its fight against multiculturalism and immigration, but left-libertarian parties, inasmuch as they oppose what they see as harmful new technologies and threats to the environment, do much the same. None of these agendas really confront the new challenges of technological innovation and demographic transition.

If it is *not* anxiety about political-economic uncertainty that unsettles current party systems, but rather systematic elite subversion of popular demands, as implied by the cartelisation thesis, its advocates had better come clean and identify those political appeals that would crystallise better democratic representation, if not thwarted by cartelisation. The immediate response might be to claim that the current left-populist movements in Southern Europe – from Syriza in Greece to Podemos in Spain – are standard-bearers of a new democratic vision of political-economic reform. But it is telling that even in countries most profoundly ravaged by high youth unemployment and economic dislocation, the appeal of such parties is limited and their programmatic grasp of the political-economic landscape is feeble.

Even the proponents of the party (system) cartelisation thesis, therefore, may have a difficult time identifying political forces and programmatic strategies that would constitute the core of a new popular political platform able to overcome what they diagnose to be the poor representation of electorates by contemporary parties. This applies most clearly to Northern Europe, where the only emerging alternatives are racist and xenophobic radical-right parties. But it also is plausible for Mediterranean Europe, where the crisis of politics is even deeper than in the North, since these countries are mired in rampant corruption, clientelism and bad governance. Even here, leftist protest parties have excelled at negative demands but offered few, if any, constructive policy proposals that look better than taking voters on a trip back to the past. It is anxiety about the absence of unambiguous policy solutions in the face of profound and evolving structural crises that creates scepticism towards democratic politics. And it will take different conceptual and theoretical means to analyse that situation from those offered by cartelisation theory.

NOTES

1. This does not rule out that policy-issue leadership, when applied tenaciously over time, can enable established parties to change the minds of some of their voters on a new issue, convince them to adopt policy preferences consistent with whatever position the party adopts on the new issue and thus retain voters' continued allegiance to their traditional party preference.

2. To modify Schattschneider (1960), the heavenly choir of politics sings with an upper-class voice, but it varies its modulation depending on shifts in the upper class, and these tend to be correlated with shifts in general public opinion. Thus, as Erikson (2015) shows, the preferences of the disadvantaged leave some imprint on this dynamic process.

3. Even in Greece, when Syriza caved in to Northern European fiscal policy and reform demands in spring of 2015 and part of its core cadre founded a new party to pursue a promising alternative to the EU's structural-administrative-fiscal austerity programme, only a miniscule group of voters supported the new alternative.

Chapter 1

Cartelisation in Sweden?

Magnus Hagevi and Henrik Enroth

On Saturday, 27 December 2014, six people called an urgent press conference. They were the party leaders of the main adversaries in Swedish politics – the Social Democrats on the left and the Moderates on the right – and their respective allied party leaders in the competing left- and right-wing blocs. They announced their agreement to form what amounted to a cartel, the so-called December Agreement (Bäck and Hellström 2015).[1] Because of the success of the populist radical-right Sweden Democrats in the general election earlier that year, neither of the two political blocs had gained a majority of the parliamentary seats. The main intention of the agreement was to exclude the Sweden Democrats from political influence and to maintain the two-bloc system as the basis for cabinet-formation (Bäck and Hellström 2015: 272). The agreement had little of substance to offer except this: the largest established political blocs would form the government and the government budget bills would win the final vote in Parliament.

Given the collaboration between the established parties and the lack of policy substance in the resulting agreement, this unprecedented event might seem an open-and-shut case of party cartelisation, as stipulated by the influential yet contested cartel party theory of Richard Katz and Peter Mair (Katz and Mair 1995) – albeit that, in this case, the point of the cartel was not so much to reduce party competition *tout court* (cf. Mair 2007) as to ensure continued bipolar competition in the Swedish multi-party system (Bäck and Hellström 2015).[2] However, as critics of the cartel party theory have pointed out, cartels in general are inherently unstable and vulnerable to defection by those who have the least to gain from staying in the cartel (Kitschelt 2000: 168; cf. Blyth and Katz 2005: 39; see also Chapter 2 of this book). Indeed, in a delegate rebellion against party leadership, the smallest right-wing party, the Christian Democrats, voted down the December Agreement during a party congress in 2015, setting off a domino effect that led the other right-wing parties to swiftly defect from the agreement as well.

Far from supporting the cartel party theory, then, in point of fact this cataclysmic event in Swedish politics constituted a high-profile cartel failure, one that calls into question Katz and Mair's claim that the Swedish political system would be especially conducive to cartelisation (1995: 17). If anything, the break-up of the December Agreement suggests the need for a systematic assessment of the cartel party theory, empirically, theoretically and normatively. This book seeks to provide such an assessment.

For two decades, the cartel party theory has been a strong and controversial presence in the field of party research. According to the theory, political parties in Western democracies have come to function ever less as channels into the state for constellations of interest and identity in society and ever more as professional organisations in the state whose prime interest is organisational survival. Rather than bridging the gap between state and society, Katz and Mair suggest that political parties have, instead, widened the distance between them to a point where the party as an organisational form has been incorporated into the state.

The cartel party theory consists of two interrelated hypotheses (Katz and Mair 2009: 756–7). The first hypothesis is that parties are becoming increasingly removed from civil society and instead are converging with the state (Mair 1994: 7–8), which encourages or forces them to co-operate with one another. This change is leading to parties becoming dependent on public party subventions, effectively making the parties a part of the state (Katz and Mair 1995: 15, 2009: 754–5, 759), while party members, as representatives of civil society, are in practice becoming rationalised out of existence (Mair 1997: 113–4; Katz 2001; Katz and Mair 2002; see also Panebianco 1988: 220–35). The second hypothesis is that the parties are developing common, similar and sharply constrained policies (see Blyth and Katz 2005). The most significant change is said to be that parties are becoming increasingly alike. The pressure to transform should, according to these scholars, entail the levelling-out of differences between how parties manage the polity.

Even as the originators of the cartel party thesis were calling for studies to test their ideas (Katz and Mair 2009), other scholars were scrutinising the same ideas and criticising the thesis as vague and difficult to confirm (Koole 1996; Widfeldt 1997; Kitschelt 2000; Hopkin 2004; Detterbeck 2005; Scarrow 2006; Loxbo 2013, 2014a; Kitschelt and Rehm 2014; Enroth 2014, 2017; Hagevi 2014c). Despite the lack of empirical studies of cartel parties and cartelisation, the notion of the cartel party as a typological successor to the 'catch-all' party – a type of party seeking to appeal to a large and diverse segment of voters by way of general and vague policies (Kirchheimer 1966) – seems dominant in current party research. The engines of change, according to the cartel party thesis, are parties' increasing dependence on state party subsidies to pursue and manage the polity (Pierre, Svåsand and Widfeldt 2000; Gidlund and Koole 2001; cf. Koß 2011); dependence on the mass media for political communication (Strömbäck 2009); and social changes, primarily economic globalisation (cf. Loxbo 2014a). As a result of these, according to the theory, parties perceive their latitude to pursue policy and engage in representation is shrinking (Blyth and Katz 2005; Katz and Mair 2009; Mair 2009, 2013; Katz 2014).

While the cartel party theory has been the target of a good deal of critical commentary in academic journals since it first burst on to the scene, the theory has not yet been subjected to systematic empirical and normative assessment in a single book. Such attention is long overdue, as the theory remains dominant in research on parties and party systems and its authors have continued to work on and defend it. Most recently, Peter Mair's posthumously published *Ruling the Void* (2013) reiterates the basic tenets of the cartel party theory. The present book is based on an extensive empirical investigation of the Swedish case, which the authors of the cartel party theory have themselves presented as a critical test: if cartelisation is going to happen anywhere, the theory suggests, it should be evident in the Swedish party system (see Katz and Mair 1995; cf. Blyth and Katz 2005). By the same token, to the extent that this is not the case, it is less likely that cartelisation would be found in other political systems with circumstances relatively less favourable to it.

The aim of this book, therefore, is to assess the cartel party theory based on a study of the Swedish party system, specifically, the party groups in the unicameral Swedish Parliament (the Riksdag). Attending to a range of factors, we ask whether or not the party groups in the Riksdag have increasingly come to resemble one another in the period from the late twentieth century to the first decade of the twenty-first century. This is an important and original contribution to current research on changes in parties and party systems. Most existing studies are comparative surveys of general trends, whereas this book investigates the causal mechanisms that are expected to foster cartelisation, through a critical case study. Our study focuses on everyday parliamentary politics, not extraordinary events such as the December Agreement. Our data were systematically collected during the period when the proponents of the cartel party theory claim that cartel parties emerged (Katz and Mair 1995). Before we turn to the contents of the subsequent chapters, let us take a closer look at the Swedish case as a testing ground for the cartel party theory.

THE SWEDISH CASE

In Swedish politics, the originators of the cartel party thesis and their followers have noted a number of characteristics that, they argue, would facilitate cartelisation. Sweden has been a stable democracy since the 1920s (Möller

2015). Scholars regard political parties as strong and pivotal actors in the Swedish political system, including in Parliament (Isberg 1999; Hagevi 2000a; Detterbeck 2005). As in all proportional electoral systems, Swedish voters focus on parties (Oscarsson and Holmberg 2013; Hagevi 2015a). The parties are vital in the careers of politicians (Petersson et al. 1997; Hagevi 2003; Öhberg 2011; Isaksson 2006; see also Chapter 4 of this book); they suppress alternative ways of aggregating interests in society (Hermansson 1993); and they are becoming increasingly important in the public sector (Wallin et al. 1999). Several studies report that public party subsidies are replacing both the financial and internal democratic significance of party membership (Katz and Mair 2002; Borchert 2003; cf. Pettersson et al. 1997; Isaksson 2006; Hagevi 2014b; see Chapter 3 of this book). Also, Swedish parties have received substantial party subsidies for a very long time, in an allocation system that they control themselves (Gidlund 1983, 1985; Wiberg 1991; Gidlund and Koole 2001; Hagevi 2003; Koß 2011). Swedish politics has also long been characterised by consensus-seeking actors in a system in which agreement and compromise are embedded in the political culture (Tingsten 1966; Uddhammar 1993; Hadenius 2008; Möller 2015; cf. Arthur 2010), conditions expected in the theory to facilitate cartelisation.

With respect to distinctive national characteristics, several scholars have linked the cartel party thesis to the greater political dependence of individual countries on international conditions (Blyth and Katz 2005; Katz and Mair 2009). Here as well, the Swedish case favours cartelisation, because Sweden has been a member of the EU since 1995 and the Swedish economy has been strongly internationalised for a very long time (Ekholm 2000; Sandelin 2005).

The Swedish population is ten million. Politically, Sweden is a unitary parliamentary state with general elections (by proportional representation) held every fourth year (between 1970 and 1994, every third year). At the same time as parliamentary elections, citizens also elect representatives to 21 regional and 290 local (municipal) assemblies. A large proportion of welfare state policies are implemented at the regional and local level. As well as the Swedish Parliament, the municipalities and regions also have the right to levy income tax. As is the case with all EU Member States, elections to the European Parliament are held every fifth year.

The Swedish party system was long entrenched as a typical Scandinavian five-party system (Lipset and Rokkan 1967). However, previously strong social cleavages and party identification have now weakened considerably among Swedish voters (Oscarsson and Holmberg 2013: 69–103). Since 1988 the party system has gradually fragmented, giving the eight-party system of today. In 1988 the Green Party first gained parliamentary representation; it lost representation in 1991 and regained it in 1994. In 1991 the

Christian Democrats and New Democracy first gained parliamentary representation; New Democracy, a populist right-wing party, lost its representation in 1994. In 2010 the Sweden Democrats, a radical populist right-wing party, first gained parliamentary representation. Government formation in Sweden is heavily dominated by the divide between the right-wing (*Alliansen*) and left-wing (*De rödgröna*) blocs. These two blocs have a half-century-long history but, in recent decades, the number of parties within the blocs has increased and the names of the blocs have changed (Aylott 2011: 314; Hagevi 2015b: 79). The Swedish government has generally been formed either by social-democratic prime ministers (mostly one-party minority cabinets) supported by left-wing parties or by right-wing parties (mostly multi-party coalition cabinets). Since 1991 the Social Democrats, the Green Party and the Left Party have formed the left-wing bloc, while the Moderates (belonging to the conservative parties of the European party families), the Centre Party, the Liberals and the Christian Democrats have formed the right-wing bloc. No populist right-wing parties, such as the Sweden Democrats, have formally joined either of the two political blocs. In recent decades, the major political adversaries and competitors for the post of prime minister have been the party leaders of the Social Democrats and the Moderates (Möller 2015). Table 1.1 shows parties in cabinet and distribution of seats in the Swedish Parliament, by party, since 1970.

The studies in this book are oriented mainly towards the party groups in the Riksdag, where the parties are the main actors (Hagevi 2000a: 145). Party cohesion is strong: when MPs vote in Parliament, they cast 99 per cent of their votes along party lines (Staberg 2000: 32). Public policies are formulated within parties by their MPs, who are at the centre of cartelisation. Swedish MPs report extensive interaction with the various faces of the parties – that is, the party on the ground, the party in central office and the party in public office (Hagevi 2000a) – and MPs are therefore at the centre of any possible cartelisation. The MPs are dependent on the party members in their constituencies for renomination to the ballot (Johansson 1999) and for the possibility of re-election by voters.

In parliamentary systems, a parliament can be categorised as mainly deliberative (like the British Parliament) or as a working parliament, of which the Swedish Parliament is a good example (Hagevi 2000b: 243–7). In working parliaments, the strength of parliamentary committees – the ability to influence the outputs of parliament – is important (Shaw 1979: 394). Several studies in this book recognise the importance of committees and make use of this knowledge (see Chapters 3 and 5 to 7 of this book). The absence of a single majority party or a majority coalition of parties has made minority cabinets usual in Sweden (Strøm 1986, 1990). During deliberation in committees, majority voting coalitions are sometimes formed

Table 1.1 Distribution of Seats in Swedish Parliament by Party, and Parties in Cabinet, 1970–2014

	Year of Election													
	1970	1973	1976	1979	1982	1985	1988	1991	1994	1998	2002	2006	2010	2014
Left-wing														
Left Party	17	19	17	2	20	19	21	16	22	43	30	22	19	21
Green Party	–	–	–	–	–	–	20	–	18	16	17	19	25	25
Social Democrats	163	156	152	154	166	159	156	138	161	131	144	130	112	113
Right-wing														
Centre Party	71	90	86	64	56	44	42	31	27	18	22	29	23	22
Liberals	58	34	39	38	21	51	44	33	26	17	48	28	24	19
Christian Democrats	–	–	–	–	–	–	–	26	15	42	33	24	19	16
Moderates	41	51	55	73	86	76	66	80	80	82	55	97	107	84
Populist right														
New Democracy	–	–	–	–	–	–	–	25	–	–	–	–	–	–
Sweden Democrats	–	–	–	–	–	–	–	–	–	–	–	–	20	49
Total	350	350	349	349	349	349	349	349	349	349	349	349	349	349
Parties in cabinet (party of prime minister italicised)	*S*	*S*	C, *M*, L/L[a]	C, *M*, L/C, L[a]	*S*	*S*	*S*	*M*, L, C, CD	*S*	*S*	*S*	*M*, L, C, CD	*M*, C, L, CD	*S*, G

Note: Swedish party names: Left Party (LP) – *Vänsterpartiet* (before 1990, the Communist Left Party – *Vänsterpartiet kommunisterna*), Green Party (G) – *Miljöpartiet de gröna*, Social Democrats (S) – *Socialdemokraterna*, Centre Party (C) – *Centerpartiet*, Liberals (L) – *Liberalerna* (before 2015, the Liberal People's Party – *Folkpartiet liberalerna*), Moderates (M) – *Moderaterna* (before 1969, the Right Party – *Högerpartiet*).
[a] Reconstruction of cabinet during parliamentary term of office.

by negotiations between MPs from different parties (Sannerstedt 1992; Sjölin 1993; cf. Chapters 3 and 5 of this book). It is important to note that party discipline is still effective in committees: MPs represent their parties in the committees and do not act as individuals (Sannerstedt 1992).

The Swedish Parliament has fifteen standing (permanent) committees (in Swedish, *utskott*; between 1970 and 2010 there were sixteen standing committees), each with seventeen MPs as committee members (appointed by Parliament to serve throughout the term of office).[3] Committee membership is proportional to the number of MPs from each party. All bills must be deliberated on in committee before being voted on in Parliament. It is impossible to kill a bill in committee: the committees must always, after deliberation, adopt a position in a committee report and send it to the 349 MPs for a final decision in full session. Views deviating from the committee majority are included in the committee reports as reservations. In virtually all cases, the final decision made in the parliamentary session is the same as in the committee (Hagevi 1998: 51–2). In addition to the standing committees, other committees (in Swedish, *nämnd*) have other types of roles. One of them is the European Union (EU) Affairs Committee (*EU-nämnden*). Ahead of meetings in the European Council or the EU Council of Ministers, the Prime Minister and all cabinet ministers must gain support for their policies from the majority of MPs in the EU Affairs Committee, though the government's propositions are not formalised in the same way as ordinary government bills in the standing committees and the positions of the committee are not put to parliamentary vote in full session. Because of this, the committee reports are somewhat different from the reports of standing committees (see Chapter 5 of this book).

CONTENTS OF THIS BOOK

In the rest of this book, six empirical studies of the Swedish case highlight various factors that the cartel party theory takes to be conducive to cartelisation, and discuss countervailing forces as well (Chapters 3 to 8). We explore whether party elites are becoming increasingly alike and increasingly removed from grassroots and constituents due to processes of professionalisation; whether opposition to government is waning in the wake of globalisation and Europeanisation; and whether parties are becoming more alike by adapting to general processes of mediatisation in politics. Chapters 7 and 8 investigate key factors not yet sufficiently acknowledged either by authors or critics of the cartel party theory: gender representation and party culture; we ask whether these factors act as countervailing forces to cartelisation. In the concluding Chapter 10, we discuss how the empirical results presented here might lead us to rethink accepted ideas about cartelisation, convergence and increasing similarities among parliamentary parties.

Chapter 2 provides a conceptual analysis of the cartel party type. Henrik Enroth unpacks the cartel party concept by considering the use of the term 'cartel' in cartel party theory specifically, as well as the etymology and ordinary usage of the term. Enroth argues that this concept in itself has been a carrier of confusion and ambivalence in the cartel party theory, conveying as it does a vacillation between cartelisation construed in terms of parties acting jointly, on the one hand, and in terms of their acting similarly but severally, on the other. This ambivalence, Enroth argues, is integral to cartel party theory as stated and restated by its authors and proponents, a conceptual peculiarity that makes the theory a slippery subject for empirical testing. By way of conclusion, Enroth suggests that there are normative and historical reasons for this: the cartel party concept evokes time-honoured misgivings about parties as vehicles for interest mediation and collective action, a theme also developed by Herbert Kitschelt in his Introduction.

In Chapter 3, Magnus Hagevi and Karl Loxbo focus on the core assumptions of the cartel party theory. Three main questions are scrutinised:

1. Are parties withdrawing from civil society over time, instead becoming increasingly integrated into the state (Mair 1994: 7–8, 2013: 83–9; Katz and Mair 1995, 2002)?
2. Are the policy positions of political parties converging over time (Katz and Mair 1995, 2009; cf. Kitschelt and Rehm 2014)?
3. Are the policy positions of party elites increasingly detached from the policy positions of party members and voters (Katz and Mair 2009; cf. Kitschelt and Rehm 2014)?

To study the first question, which concerns the potentially widening gap between parties and civil society, Hagevi and Loxbo analyse data on party membership size and increased public financial subsidies to parties. While there is indeed a tendency towards a widening gap between party members and voters, Hagevi and Loxbo demonstrate that voters are increasingly expressing confidence in parties. Second, to examine convergence between parties, Hagevi and Loxbo employ data from the Comparative Manifesto Project; comparisons of voters' and parliamentarians' opinions in unique time series; and voters' perceptions of policy convergence among parties. Finally, the chapter analyses possible oligarchic tendencies in parties. This section highlights the *increasing* importance of party congresses over time.

A fundamental tenet of the cartel party theory is that public financial subsidies to political parties are replacing parties' dependence on their memberships and the income derived from membership dues (Katz and Mair 1995, 2009). This is said to be changing party organisations, entailing a shift in the balance of power from the party on the ground and in central office to the party in public office (Katz and Mair 2002: 123; Wolinetz 2002: 148; Krouwel 2012). In Chapter 4, Magnus Hagevi investigates whether the social composition of Swedish party groups and the pre-parliamentary political experience of members of the Riksdag have become more homogeneous, due to the increasing professionalisation of party politics. According to the mass-party ideal, political parties are open to all members. The rise and spread of state-financed party funding enables cartel parties to employ increasing numbers of professional politicians (Borchert 2003). As a result, the norm of self-selection is increasingly being replaced by the norm of employment, that is, of being recruited, hired and paid by an employer. Compared with self-selection, it is presumably more common for a person hired to be similar to the person responsible for recruiting/hiring (Hensvik et al. 2010). However, Hagevi's findings do not support the contention that increasing party subsidies from the state are related to a more socially homogenous parliament, with recruitment of parliamentary members from the growing extra-parliamentary pool of professional politicians becoming more dominant.

Several scholars argue that globalisation and Europeanisation, by transferring political authority and power to non-partisan supranational institutions, have led to depoliticisation and party system cartelisation at the national level. As a result, opposition to national governments in the classic sense is thought to be in decline, while opposition in principle – particularly embodied by anti-system parties – is believed to be on the rise. Although this is a widely purveyed view, the main proposition of waning opposition has never been subjected to systematic empirical scrutiny. The aim of Karl Loxbo's Chapter 5 is to rectify this lacuna in previous research by exploring the degree of depoliticisation in the Swedish Riksdag between 1972 and 2013. To evaluate what is referred to as the depoliticisation thesis, Loxbo studies the existence of minority reports, drawing on approximately 5,000 committee reports to all committees in the Swedish Parliament. The results, Loxbo demonstrates, are straightforward. In contrast to the expectations of the cartel party theory, the chapter presents evidence that partisan struggles in general, and conflicts over supranational integration in particular, have intensified significantly over time. Therefore, this chapter casts doubt on the presumptions of depoliticisation and the waning of classical opposition that are central to the cartel party theory.

Mediatisation – the process by which fundamental aspects of political life become affected and in part constituted by the media (Hjarvard 2007) – has also been posited as an important reason for the cartelisation of political parties. Instead of the mass-party ideal, in which the party's membership organisation constitutes the central ideological link between the people and the government, cartel parties are presumed increasingly to use appearances in mass media for direct political communication from the party in central office to the electorate (Katz and Mair 2002). In Chapter 6, Douglas Brommesson and Ann-Marie Ekengren set out to test the argument that mediatisation is a force for cartelisation. They do this by investigating how members of parliament involved in foreign policy decision-making in Sweden and Finland think of the media's effects on party politics. The cartel party theory and its critics offer competing expectations of how politicians adapt to the media. According to the cartel party theory, mediatisation fosters a common media logic, which becomes a force for homogenisation. According to Herbert Kitschelt (2000), media logic could be expected to favour individualisation and fragmentation. In spite of similar consensual systems in the two countries, the results indicate that Finnish parliamentarians see mediatisation as a force of homogenisation while Swedish parliamentarians express a mixed view of the effects of the media.

The cartel party thesis proceeds from the purported individualisation of the relationship between voters and parties, such that attachment and identification between specific social groups and parties are held to be in general decline (Katz and Mair 2009). Therefore, instead of seeking, as the mass party did, to mobilise and represent citizens based on appealing to distinct social groups endowed with divergent interests (Duverger 1954; Lipset and Rokkan 1967), the cartel party presumes an 'increasing homogeneity of experiences and expectations of the vast majority of citizens' (Katz and Mair 2009: 758). In the parliamentary arena, moreover, cartelisation is supposed to reduce conflict while severing parties from their constituents. In Chapter 7, Helena Olofsdotter Stensöta and Anna Högmark put this assumption of diminishing conflict to the test by examining whether and how gender – a cleavage not hitherto acknowledged by either the proponents or critics of the cartel party thesis – supports or counteracts cartelisation. Stensöta and Högmark elaborate on and juxtapose the theoretical expectations of cartel party theory and gender representation theory respectively, formulating these as two contrasting hypotheses. While the cartel party theory expects political conflict in parliament to decline, research on gender representation suggests the contrary: increasing conflict between women's and men's interests. Using the same empirical data that Karl Loxbo analyses in Chapter 5, both of these hypotheses are examined. The findings suggest that increasing numbers of women in parliaments correlates with increasing levels of political conflict, contrary to the cartelisation hypothesis.

Considering another potential countervailing force to cartelisation so far unacknowledged by proponents as well as critics of the cartel party theory,

Katarina Barrling considers the impact and tenacity of party culture in relation to cartelisation in Chapter 8. The case studied is that of seven parliamentary groups in the Swedish Parliament and the research question is whether their organisational cultures have changed in the last twenty years and, if so, whether this has always been in line with the logic of cartelisation; that is, has the organisational culture of the party groups developed towards more pragmatism, professionalism and hierarchy? Again, previous research has pointed to Sweden as a country where conditions are particularly favourable for cartelisation, which is why the case can be considered a crucial one. The chapter's main conclusion is that there is no overall pattern of parties coming closer to one another: the actual, observable changes in party culture being strengthened pragmatism in the Moderates and, conversely, increasing idealism in the Greens. The change in the Moderates is in agreement with the logic of cartelisation, although the underlying reason for the change seems to be adaptation to the exigencies of holding office, rather than cartelisation. The cultural change in the Green Party is contrary to the logic of cartelisation. Rather than any transformation of party culture, Barrling concludes, these shifts are best understood as parties reverting to their entrenched structures and habits.

In Chapter 9, Mats Sjölin and Henrik Enroth discuss the normative implications of the cartel party theory. While normative concerns have played an important part in successive statements and restatements of the cartel party theory, normative treatments of cartelisation and democracy have nevertheless been conspicuous by their absence from critical commentary on and response to the theory, which have focused almost exclusively on questions of empirical support and theoretical consistency. Therefore, based on the empirical findings presented in the book, this chapter adopts a normative point of view on the conditions and consequences of cartelisation. To come to terms normatively with the cartel party theory, Enroth and Sjölin make use of two popular divergent accounts of what we ideal-typically should expect of parties in a modern democracy: the first model puts a premium on parties acting responsively in relation to their constituents, while the second emphasises parties as means of holding governors to account. Normatively, Enroth and Sjölin note, the issues raised by the cartel party theory evoke the values of accountability as well as responsiveness, thus drawing on both models. Moreover, in vital respects the cartel party theory goes beyond the concerns introduced in these models, towards a more radical critical or sceptical stance against parties as mediators between voters and policy-makers. Today, Enroth and Sjölin conclude, what emerges most forcefully from a consideration of the normative aspects of Katz and Mair's work is not so much the threat of convergence and collusion as the very opposite: the entrenchment of conflict.

The concluding chapter notes that, despite Sweden's favourable conditions for cartelisation, the cartel party theory of Katz and Mair is not supported in

Magnus Hagevi and Henrik Enroth

our study. However, the findings indicate that Swedish politics is a fertile environment for cartelisation, with the increased importance of public party subsidies paving the way for professionalisation, mediatisation of politics and the weakening of links between parties and civil society, indicated by shrinking party membership. Still, our data suggest no collaboration of the kind posited by the cartel party thesis. On the contrary, our results indicate that political conflict between the parliamentary parties is, in fact, increasing – among established as well as new parties. Also, new social cleavages other than those formed in the nineteenth century are sometimes aligning new groups of citizens with new parties. The causal mechanism proposed by the cartel party thesis – that parties are losing their connection with civil society, resulting in party collaboration as well as convergence – is therefore not supported. Again, the weakest link here is the kind of collaboration that the cartel party theory posits, a notion for which our study finds no systematic support. This underscores the conceptual ambiguities and tensions at the heart of the cartel party theory, as discussed by Enroth in Chapter 2 of this book. In general terms, our results very much call into question the core notion of the cartelisation of Western party systems. Looking ahead, we argue that researchers need to develop more accurate models of party competition. Angelo Panebianco's concept of the electoral professional party (1988) is promising in this regard, as is the critique of the cartel party theory and the alternative suggestions advanced by Herbert Kitschelt (2000, 2007a, 2007b).

NOTES

1. In Swedish: *December-överenskommelsen.*
2. The only substantial policy-related matter that the parties specified in the December Agreement was the promise of future negotiations about defence and security, retirement pensions and energy. However, defence and security is traditionally an area of agreement across left- and right-wing parties (Möller 2015) and retirement pensions have been a done deal since the 1990s (Loxbo 2007). Only a multi-party agreement across left- and right-wing parties about energy policies would be new (though no such agreement has been reached as yet).
3. The standing committees are listed in Chapter 7 of this book.

Chapter 2

On the Concept of a Cartel Party

Henrik Enroth

The first chapter discussed the hypotheses associated with the cartel party theory. Here, I focus not on those hypotheses per se but on some of the terms and concepts by way of which the cartel party theory has been shaped and conveyed. My attention is centred on the cartel concept itself. Katz and Mair flesh out their ideal type using a number of terms that differ in meaning and genealogy, some of which are metaphorically laden and freighted with ordinary usage while others are more specific to academic discourse. In the following, therefore, I consider more than what a conventional conceptual analysis would attend to, that is, what the authors of the cartel party theory do with their terms and concepts and whether those terms and concepts are ambiguous as to their meaning and vague as to their reference (cf. Sartori 1984). I also consider what those terms and concepts do to the theory into which they are introduced, especially the concept of a cartel as it has been handed down historically from a variety of sources and historical contexts (cf. Farr 1989; Skinner 2001).

This less-than-orthodox take on conceptual analysis in a discussion of an academic theory is the result of two related convictions. First, according to reigning dogma in the modern philosophy of language, terms and concepts gain their meaning and significance by being used in context (Pitkin 1973: 71–98; Farr 1989). However, they also tend to haul their semantic and connotative baggage across contexts in a manner that is never entirely up to their users in any given context (cf. Koselleck 2004: 85): concepts carry baggage that cannot simply be wished or stipulated away. No matter how much we may – or may not, as the case may be – strive for conceptual clarity in our theories, the terms and concepts we use have history. And, *pace* Humpty Dumpty in Lewis Carroll's *Through the Looking-Glass*, their past usage means that our current usage is never simply at our discretion (Carroll 2001: 297).

Second, metaphor matters in academic theory no less than in other systems of thought or genres of text (cf. Ricoeur 1978; Lakoff and Johnson 1980; Derrida 1982). If a theory has been built around compelling metaphors, as is undeniably the case with the cartel party theory, then the usefulness – and indeed the very meaning – of the theory will turn largely on what we make of the metaphors in question. I suggest that understanding the words and metaphors enlisted, albeit not always explicated, by the authors of the cartel theory is essential to understanding the theory itself. If we wish to come to terms with the cartel theory – say, concerning the dearth of clearly stated causal mechanisms (e.g. Kitschelt 2000) – a good place to start is the authors' less-than-straightforward way of using words, especially with the cartel concept itself. Incidentally, this concept is conspicuously absent from most commentary and critique of Katz and Mair's work, perhaps in part due to the persistent prejudice against metaphor among many social scientists. The cartel concept-metaphor is the elephant in the room, as it were, in the existing literature on the cartel party theory.[1]

My point is not to reiterate the common complaint that metaphor leads us astray: that it is incidental to whatever is deemed essential in any nominally serious discourse, an improper vehicle of thought, a mere matter of style that in no way affects – or should be allowed to affect – the supposed substance (cf. Derrida 1982). On the contrary, as we shall see, the point is rather that the cartel party theory may be altogether dependent on metaphor in a more pro-found sense. As I hope will become clear, the very theoretical statements to be conveyed vacillate between the metaphorical and the literal: it ultimately seems to be a matter of interpretation whether evidence of a cartelised party system is evidence that the system in question *is* a cartel, or evidence that it is *like* a cartel. As I shall argue, this usage of 'cartel' is not altogether easy to make good theoretical sense of and the authors of the cartel party theory are less than forthcoming on the matter.

In the next section, I delve briefly into the etymology and ordinary usage of 'cartel' and 'collusion', attending as well to their use in the cartel party theory. As I hope will become clear, the etymological and lexical excursions that follow are not trivia for their own antiquarian sake but provide important clues to theoretical concepts that remain to be clarified in the cartel party theory. The second section then turns to some of those concepts, especially co-operation, convergence and depoliticisation. These are all, I argue, marked by the same tension or ambivalence between cartelisation construed in terms of parties acting jointly, on the one hand, and in terms of their acting similarly but severally, on the other. The third section considers the efforts of Katz and Blyth to elaborate on the cartel concept with reference to economic theory, a move that has, arguably, done little to lessen the impression of conceptual ambiguity. The fourth section, finally, is devoted to conclusions drawn from the perspectives of conceptual analysis and conceptual history, respectively. Whereas these two approaches run parallel as well as intersect in the course of the chapter, I end giving the upper hand to conceptual history. At that point I hope my reasons for doing so will have become clear.

CARTELISATION AND COLLUSION

We should start, then, with the word 'cartel'. To be etymologically and tropologically correct, 'cartel' is not a metaphor but a metonym (cf. Burke 1941; Ricoeur 1978: 55–8). The medieval Latin *cartellus* means paper or letter, of the same origin as *charta*, while 'cartel' in the European vernacular came to refer not to the piece of paper itself but to what was declared in print on it, namely, 'an agreement or association' (*OED*). In our latter-day usage, which dates back to the end of the nineteenth century and originally to Germany, the agreement or association in question is typically one 'between two or more business houses for regulating output, fixing prices, etc.; also, the businesses thus combined; a trust or syndicate' (*OED*).

Prior to this modern usage, the term 'cartel' had also been used for other kinds of agreement, relating, for instance, to the exchange or ransom of prisoners or, in medieval Europe, to the rules of engagement between the combatants in a joust (*OED*; Grimm and Grimm 1860; Littré 1956). From the medieval to the modern usage, the reference of the term extends metonymically, step by step, from the paper on which the agreement was originally printed to the printed agreement itself to its empirical indices, that is, to the kind of activity or behaviour sanctioned by the agreement. And, from the medieval to the modern usage, a cartel minimally presupposes some kind of agreement and co-operation, albeit in the modern usage not necessarily a piece of paper on which the agreement has been drawn up.

The first time the term occurs in a political context can be dated with some precision. In 1887 the National Liberal and the Conservative parties in imperial Germany formed a coalition to support each other's candidates, to further Bismarck's policies. Maurice Duverger refers to this coalition as a 'cartel' in his classic *Parties politiques* (1954: 325–6), and the *Oxford English Dictionary* cites in this connection the *Annual Register* of 1888, which follows the German usage of the day in referring to 'the German Unionists, or "Cartell party"' (*OED*). So, the term 'cartel party' is not Katz and Mair's invention, nor are party cartels per se the product of the latter-day conditions that they describe and theorise (cf. Koole 1996). As Duverger's many examples show, parties have formed cartels – known and named as such – intermittently throughout the history of modern parliamentarism (Duverger 1954: 85, 231, 325–6, 330, 334–5, 340, 343, 348).

But we should not leap too hastily from term to concept. As Duverger points out, the German cartel of 1887 was a case of the Chancellor availing himself of an agreement between the parties to further his own political interests (Duverger 1954: 325), not a case of parties availing themselves of the resources of the state to further *their* interests, which is what Katz and Mair have in mind with the cartel party ideal type. In the latter case, regarded from the intra-party perspective, 'as the party in public office gains ascendancy within the party as a whole, its particular interests will be treated as being the interests of the party writ large' (Katz and Mair 2009: 756) and, from the inter-party perspective, 'interests are now much more shared', which 'facilitates cooperation' (Katz and Mair 2009: 757). Most notably, 'a very important part of their shared interest is to contain the costs of losing, and in this sense to find an equilibrium that suits all of their "private" interests' (Katz and Mair 2009: 757).

But as Ruud Koole has remarked, this latter case is not historically unique to the current era (1996: 515–6). In the present context, the question is not so much what is new about a cartel of parties and whether a new ideal type is actually called for in party research (Koole 1996: 515); what matters is what is implied by the cartel concept in this context. *Pace* Katz and Mair, let it be noted that the modern cartel concept in itself says nothing about the interests that may or may not be served by a cartel. In Germany, in 1887, the agreement clearly served the interests of the Chancellor and was presumably 'brought about by Bismarck' (Duverger 1954: 325); in the contemporary situation that Katz and Mair want to cover with their ideal type, the parties themselves are supposedly the beneficiaries of the agreement. So, if it indeed 'makes sense for us to expect that parties will cooperate with one another' (Katz and Mair 2009: 756), such co-operation can be said to constitute a cartel regardless of whose interests may be served. The cartel concept suggests only that an agreement has been made to co-operate in a way that limits the competition between the parties to the agreement.

The notion of interests – especially 'private' or 'particular' – insinuates itself even more forcefully into Katz and Mair's cartel concept with the next item on our list. As they have suggested, 'it is clearly a small step from consideration of cooperation and agreement to consideration of collusion' (2009: 756). Collusion, we are told, is 'obviously an important element in the cartel argument' (2009: 754). Etymologically, 'collusion' simply means 'playing together', from the Latin *colludere*. The Latin word itself implies nothing about the nature of the playing; lexically, however, the term suggests conspiracy and foul play. In its entry, the *Oxford English Dictionary* gives us 'secret agreement or understanding for purposes of trickery or fraud; underhand scheming or working with another'.

Insofar as collusion is taken to be an 'important element' in cartelisation, this would seem to suggest that the cartel concept includes not only co-operation but also co-operation that is covert, underhand and pursued 'for purposes of trickery or fraud'. Although it is supposedly but a small step from 'co-operation and agreement' to 'collusion', this is still a step that Katz and Mair have ultimately, and understandably, been reluctant to take: connotations of conspiracy are more than they have been prepared to acknowledge. As they pointed out in their 2009 restatement of the theory, 'the term [cartel] was not intended to imply or depend on an actual conspiracy and it is particularly in this respect that the choice of denomination may have been less than perfect' (757). As they went on to explain, 'it is possible to produce the *effects* of collusion without any illicit communication or covert coordination' (2009: 757, italics in original).

It is far from clear what is being disowned here. We can bracket with relative ease the connotations of shady back-room deals associated with the term 'collusion' in ordinary usage. Indeed, in Katz and Mair's texts 'collusion' often seems to be used more or less synonymously with, or as a qualifier of, 'co-operation', as when 'inter-party collusion' is used of a situation in which 'the goals of politics become self-referential, professional, and technocratic, and what substantive interparty competition remains becomes focused on the efficient and effective management of the polity' (2009: 755). Here 'collusion' seems to designate a specific kind of co-operation, one that revolves around the parties' shared self-interest in professional survival and in reducing the costs associated with losing office.

Hence the problem: if we can indeed use 'collusion' as synonymous with or as a qualifier of 'co-operation', and if, at the same time, Katz and Mair are at pains to distance themselves from the sense of conspiracy associated with the term, then we need to know just what is being claimed and what is being rejected with regard to this notion. Two possible interpretations suggest themselves. Reading the lines I just cited, we have no way of saying whether what is intended here is a situation in which ostensible *effects* of collusion can be 'produced' without there being *actual* collusion – that is, self-interested co-operation of the kind suggested above – or whether what is intended is instead a situation in which we may have self-interested co-operation without conspiracy. Both interpretations involve our moving more or less imaginatively from what Katz and Mair literally write to what they may or may not have intended to say.

The crucial question about the term 'collusion' in the cartel party theory is, arguably, not whether Katz and Mair believe that cartelisation necessarily entails 'illicit' communication or 'covert' co-ordination but whether it necessarily entails *any* form of co-ordination or agreement to act. If Katz and Mair are relatively clear on the former point, they are, as we shall see next, curiously evasive on the latter. While we can lose the connotations of conspiracy associated with 'collusion' without an ensuing loss of meaning in the cartel concept, we cannot as readily shed the notions of co-operation and agreement that come with the term 'cartel'.

CO-OPERATION, CONVERGENCE AND DEPOLITICISATION

Having thus put our metaphors in order, we must now take a look at some of the less fanciful – if no less intriguing – terms by means of which the cartel party concept is fleshed out, beginning with 'cooperation'. To add insult to injury, Katz and Mair not only claim that what they refer to as the effects of collusion can be had without 'covert coordination' but also suggest, all in the course of two paragraphs, that 'cooperation [between parties in a cartel] need not be overt or conscious' (2009: 757).

Without haggling excessively over words, if co-ordination or co-operation need be neither covert nor overt nor conscious for us to infer the existence of a cartel of parties, this certainly raises the question of what we should make of the relationship between cartelisation and inter-party co-operation. We need not delve deeply into the philosophy of action to see the difficulties in the idea of unconscious co-operation.[2] Arguably, this awkward idea is the result of a certain sliding or slippage in the cartel party theory from the notion of con-certed action – which Katz and Mair, in keeping with etymology and ordinary usage, allow is essential to the cartel concept: 'the idea of a cartel implies concerted action' (2009: 757) – to the notion of similar behaviour, which does not in itself suggest the existence of a cartel. Consider, for instance, the following sentence, which is worth quoting in its entirety:

> That is, even if parties might be disinclined to rely heavily on overt deals with one another, their mutual awareness of shared interests, and their sense of all being in the same boat and relying on the same sorts of resources, means that we can conclude by hypothesizing collusion (or its functional equivalent) and cartel-like behaviour. (Katz and Mair 2009: 757)

It is unclear whether 'cartel-like behaviour' is tantamount to actual co-operation – that is, concerted action between parties – or whether mere like behaviour will do. Nor is it clear what a functional equivalent of col-lusion would be. Suggesting that something is functionally equivalent to concerted action reasonably means either that it serves the same systemic function as concerted action in a given context or, more loosely, that it has the same effects as concerted action. Katz and Mair's claim that we can have the effects of collusion without illicit communication or covert co-ordination suggests the latter, but this is guesswork. Going with that guess, the quotation could be construed as saying that parties acting severally on shared interests can be expected to produce effects that are tantamount to those that would result from their acting jointly in an actual cartel: like behaviour among parties that share the same interests would then be functionally equivalent to concerted action, in the sense that both would presumably yield the same empirical effects.

Note that this would be to say – contrary to ordinary usage and etymology – that we are justified in speaking, however loosely, of cartels even without concerted action, as long as we can point to shared interests among 'governing' or 'mainstream' parties (Katz 2002; Katz and Mair 2009: 756–61). Or, sliding in the other direction, if we add to this Katz and Mair's presumption that 'a very important part of their shared interest is to contain the costs of losing, and in this sense to find an equilibrium that suits all of their "private" interests', then we are led back again to the notion of concerted action, since this, as Katz and Mair point out, 'also means cooperation'. As we saw above, we are then immediately ushered in the opposite direction again with the qualifier 'even if this co-operation need not be overt or conscious' (2009: 757).

Lest I be accused of splitting hairs or playing with words, I should emphasise that I take this equivocality to be indicative of an unresolved tension in the conceptual foundations of the cartel party theory, a tension that resonates throughout the structure of terms and concepts built on those foundations. Take 'convergence'. Insofar as this term is used to designate increasing similarities between different units, the concept is clearly central to the cartel theory: the idea of increasing similarities between parties is supposedly the hard core of the theory. Still, the term is tricky, as Kitschelt et al. (1999: 438) have noted in another context. We think we know what we mean when we speak of convergence, but the concept covers – often indiscriminately – different ways in which units might become more alike. One vexed question concerns what we might call the *dynamics* of convergence: does convergence mean that the units in question become more alike by endogenously moulding themselves into a similar form, as it were, or does it rather mean that they become more alike under the influence of exogenous factors, or both (cf. Kitschelt et al. 1999: 438)?

Consider also convergence's next of kin – depoliticisation – for illustration. The thrust of this concept is clear enough: it has to do with removing actually or potentially contentious issues or policies from overt contestation or competition. Katz and Mair speak in this connection of 'participation in a cartel-like pattern of constrained competition with other parties' (2009: 757). Let it be noted that depoliticisation thus understood does not necessarily imply cartelisation in the sense of actual co-operation or collusion. While talk of contentious issues being removed from an agenda or arena poses questions about how those issues are being removed, we need not postulate concerted, let alone convoluted, action among parties in a cartel as the only way such removal might happen.

Indeed, Katz and Mair themselves point to a number of exogenous factors that they suggest have been conducive to depoliticisation in this sense, such as the fall of the Berlin Wall, the signing of the Maastricht Treaty and the establishment of the World Trade Organization. 'The principal effect of these developments', Katz and Mair claim, 'was substantially to undermine the stakes of traditional electoral competition' (2009: 754). Nonetheless, when Mair discussed the depoliticisation of the European Union, he argued not only that 'the EU is largely depoliticized' but also 'that this is part of a more or less deliberate policy by mainstream political elites who are reluctant to have their hands tied by the constraints of popular democracy' (Mair 2007: 8). Also, to the same effect: there 'may well be a potential for conflict over Europe – over its reach, its form, and its sheer size – but, at least as yet, the parties that contest elections, particularly at national level, seem to want to push this to the shadows' (Mair 2007: 12; cf. Bartolini 2005: 246–7).

Yet, illustrating the problem at hand, it is never specified whether this deliberate strategy – whether the parties pursuing what they 'seem to want' – in fact involves co-operation or collusion, or whether this is rather a matter of the parties acting similarly but severally, on the same cues and with the same script, if you will. In short, even if we wish to attribute depoliticisation at least in part to identifiable doers and their deeds rather than solely to transformative events and processes in the EU and beyond, it is still unclear whether the action – or inaction – involved should be construed as like behaviour or concerted action, or indeed both.

THE POLITICAL ECONOMY OF THE CARTEL PARTY

The same ambiguity in the cartel concept is also palpable in Blyth and Katz's turn to economic theory to flesh out the cartel concept. Citing George Stigler on different forms of collusion in oligopolistic markets, they refer to the cartel as 'a joint sales agency', the point of which is 'to maximise joint profits of oligopolistic firms through the restriction of competition'. Price decisions made through a cartel are 'strategically interdependent', in that 'market price *can* be set by the firms themselves rather than being dictated by competition, so long as they co-operate' (Blyth and Katz 2005: 39, italics in original).[3] As Stigler himself explains, whether in cartels or in other forms of collusion, oligopolistic firms in this scenario 'must agree upon the price structure appropriate to the transaction classes which they are prepared to recognize' (Stigler 1964: 45). Let it be noted that co-operation is a presupposition here; Stigler, for one, is concerned with the enforcement of agreement, not with its existence or non-existence.

As Blyth and Katz also note, 'therein lies the rub', in that 'such collusion has the character of a multi-person prisoner's dilemma', that is, a situation in which 'it may be objectively rational to co-operate' whereas 'the dominant strategy in such a situation is to defect and go for market share at the other firms' expense' (2005: 39). With the problem thus cast in game-theoretic terms, Blyth and Katz suggest that it contains its own solution, on the assumption that oligopolistic markets 'typically create Cournot-Nash rather than competitive equilibria'. While this situation does not in itself 'create a cartel', it presumably 'opens up cartelistic possibilities', promising a solution to the problem of defection. In such a situation, 'one firm can act as price leader and "signal" to the others their own revised demand schedules', at which point 'other firms can join in, thus limiting their own outputs and achieving higher profits than would be achieved by unilateral defection'. The resulting situation, Blyth and Katz explain, 'is a Nash equilibrium', a situation in which no firm 'has an incentive to defect given the others' choices' (2005: 39). Let it be noted that the presupposition here is the reverse of Stigler's: the Nash equilibrium was devised for non-cooperative rather than co-operative games. As Nash himself put it, the kind of equilibrium that bears his name 'is based on the *absence* of coalitions, in that it is assumed that each participant acts independently, without collaboration or communication with any of the others' (Nash 1951: 286, italics in original).[4]

This is certainly not the place – nor am I the person – to discuss the interpretation and usefulness of the Nash equilibrium for understanding oligopolistic markets and the formation of cartels. I simply wish to highlight the obvious difference – and the tension – between conceiving of cartels in terms of co-operation and interdependence, on the one hand, and conceiving of them in terms of actor-independence and the absence of co-operation, on the other. Applying these notions to the cartel party, Blyth and Katz argue that in the 1980s and 1990s, party elites embraced 'new ideas about the economy as a way of ratcheting down constituent expectations', which is to say – in 'cartel terms' – that 'they were signalling other players' (Blyth and Katz 2005: 43). This very step – the translation into 'cartel terms' of what party elites were in fact doing when expressing new ideas about the economy – is precisely the problem: for how do we know that publicly expressing those ideas is tantamount to 'signalling other players', even granted that this *is* tantamount to lowering expectations among constituents? What does such 'signalling' entail?

The problem is illustrated by an example that recurs in the theory. On more than one occasion, the airline industry is mentioned as a case of de facto cartelisation that would not require us to search for 'the smoking gun of covert conspiracy' (Katz and Mair 2009: 761):

> Airlines do not price their seats according to market demand. Rather, they release a certain quantity of seats at a given price, with that price being set by the quantity released by the other players. This can of course result in instabilities and fare wars, but if one carrier emerges as the price leader then a stable market equilibrium quite often results. (Blyth and Katz 2005: 56)

'Think of all the times one logs on to the Web to look for a fare and finds so little difference in price differences [*sic*] between carriers', Blyth and Katz continue, and they conclude by asking, rhetorically, 'Is this really because the cost structures of these firms are so similar?' (2005: 56). The force of this example derives, of course, from what we think we know from experience. However compelling – and morally satisfying – we may find examples of dubious business practices drawn from the world of commercial aviation, to this we must nevertheless reply: 'Probably not, but is this really because these firms are in fact colluding or co-ordinating their prices?' *Pace* Katz and Mair, the airline example is neither self-explanatory nor beyond questioning. A primer in the field cautiously notes that

> there is a distinct problem when analyzing cartel and collusion issues in the airline industry, namely the fact that the prevalence of information in the industry makes it fairly simple for airlines to match the prices and output of competitors. Therefore, the fact that two airlines have price fluctuations that match exactly does not mean that they are in collusion, but more likely that they are competing fiercely. (Vasigh, Fleming and Tucker 2008: 224)

In fact, it is far from clear what this empirical example suggests about party competition or the lack of it, popular misgivings about the airline industry aside. What is illustrated by the airline example may well be a situation in which there is mutual adaptation rather than all-out competition, but it need not be a situation in which there is actual co-ordination. For another thing, and more importantly in the present context, even if 'careful content analysis of public statements' by mainstream parties did indeed reveal 'patterns analogous to the signalling of price changes typical of the airline industry' (Katz and Mair 2009: 761), this would not settle the analytical question of what, if anything, can be read from such patterns concerning the existence and nature of inter-party co-operation, nor would it settle the vexed conceptual question of whether we even have to look for co-operation in order to establish the existence of a cartel.

THE CARTEL CONCEPT REVISITED: CONCEPTUAL
ANALYSIS *VERSUS* CONCEPTUAL HISTORY

I mentioned in the introduction an ambition to combine two approaches in my exploration of the cartel concept: combining the attention to conceptual ambiguity and vagueness in conventional varieties of conceptual analysis with a sensitivity to the force of metaphor, etymology and ordinary usage that is more indebted to conceptual history and related methods. These distinct – if arguably complementary – approaches to the analysis of concepts each suggest different conclusions.

Donning first the mask of a conceptual analyst of the Sartorian ilk, we should note that the cartel concept appears both excessive and underdetermined in the cartel party theory. As historically bequeathed to us, the cartel concept does not necessarily entail reference to whatever interests we may suspect are served by a cartel, although the presumption in the modern usage certainly tends to be that the parties to the agreement also benefit from it. As we saw in the case of the German cartel parties of 1887, this may best be treated as an empirical matter having to do with the manner in which a cartel is formed and maintained. As long as we can point to an agreement to co-operate in such a way as to constrain competition between the parties to the agreement, such co-operation can be said to constitute a cartel, quite regardless of whose interests may or may not be served. Including references to interests in the cartel concept seems a case of conceptual drift, of excess semantic baggage for which there is no real use.

At the same time, and more problematically, Katz and Mair's usage tends to leave behind some of the things that we *do* need the cartel concept to haul across the contexts in which it is used. In the absence of actual co-operation or an agreement to co-operate, to speak of cartels and cartelisation seems an open-and-shut case of conceptual stretching, of the kind famously and forcefully condemned by Sartori (1970), still assuming, that is, that we take our cue from ordinary usage and etymology. To clarify: saying this is not to deny that we may well have good reasons – empirically as well as normatively – to pay heed to various forms of convergence and depoliticisation in which the smoking gun of conspiracy cannot be found, and in which it would probably be a mistake to look for it; those phenomena, however, may be better named by other labels.

Also, it is not as if we are reduced to bloating the cartel concept to cover those phenomena. As we saw in the previous section, the economics discourse offers cognate categories that could well prove useful here. Stigler's generic usage of 'collusion', with 'cartel' as one of three species subsumed under it, is but one option. From this point of view, the mistake is not so much wanting to attend to other phenomena than conspiracy in the analysis

of convergence and depoliticisation. Katz and Mair's mistake – if it is one – is
to stretch the cartel concept to cover those other phenomena as well, dulling
whatever analytical edge this concept might have (cf. Sartori 1970, 1984).
The mistake, as it were, is to evoke the smoking gun of conspiracy where one
is not really prepared to look for it.

Mutatis mutandis, we can say of Katz and Mair's treatment of the cartel
concept what the inimitable Martin Hollis once said in a different context of
Quentin Skinner's reluctance to speak of motives in the understanding of historical texts: the party researcher 'can spin his yarn, knit the actor a cap and,
if a critic doubts whether the actor was actually wearing the cap, retort that we
need not ask' (Hollis 1988: 140). The validity of Hollis's objection to Skinner
aside, in this case we do need to ask. Our modern concept of a cartel seems
to require not only that the cap fit – not only that the observable behaviour *be
consistent with* co-operation, or, more generally, concerted action – but also
that the parties in the purported cartel indeed be wearing the cap: that what
they engage in *is* in fact concerted action as implied by the cartel concept (cf.
Katz and Mair 2009: 761). Phrases like 'cartel-like behaviour' and references
to collusion's 'functional equivalent' in effect make it impossible to decide
whether the cartel concept should be construed literally or metaphorically in
the cartel party theory: again, is evidence of cartelisation evidence that the
system in question *is* a cartel, or evidence that it is *like* a cartel?

Still in keeping with the ambitions of conventional conceptual analysis, we
should also consider the analytical consequences that follow from this usage.
As Katz and Mair have pointed out, many of the empirical findings on the
basis of which the cartel party theory has been worked out are now largely
unquestioned, such as declining party membership and increasing reliance
on state funding, as well as increasing detachment among parties from established collective identities in the citizenry (2009: 755–6). If all this is true,
then the analytical and critical thrust of the theory must reasonably lie in the
causal mechanisms it suggests by way of explanation of those findings. The
problem here is not only, as Herbert Kitschelt has remarked, that 'maybe it
is not cartelisation after all that drives whatever tendencies toward convergence are detectable in established democracies' (2000: 169), but also that
the cartel concept makes it less than clear just which causal mechanisms we
may expect to find under the label 'cartelisation', and whether the parties in a
purported cartel are best seen as actors, agents, or patients (cf. Hollis 1988).
If these fundamentals are unclear, does this mean that we perhaps would be
better off abandoning the cartel concept altogether, in the name of habitually
hailed theoretical virtues such as parsimony and consistency? In the empirical chapters that follow, we avoid prematurely jumping to this conclusion,
preferring instead to work with, and around, the ambiguities and tensions in
the cartel concept.

If nothing else, this seems a prudent strategy, as I can readily imagine a number of different responses to these questions, some of which would disregard the conceptual issues raised here and go straight to whatever is taken to be empirical and theoretical bedrock while others might revise the conceptualisations suggested by the authors of the cartel party theory. Perhaps luckily, this is not the end of the story even within the narrow confines of my contribution in this chapter, though these questions and the suggested conclusion point to the limits of conventional forms of conceptual analysis in this case. What if we instead approach the cartel concept from the vantage point of conceptual history? From this perspective, the point of analysing the strained usage of theoretical terms and concepts is not to score points or swiftly and categorically dismiss concepts and theories found wanting in clarity and consistency, but rather to ask why and whence came the demonstrable tensions and ambiguities in the cartel concept, and what are their implications (cf. Pitkin 1973, 1998; Hacking 1999: 5).

To my mind, this latter question is best answered by reference to the normative rather than empirical-theoretical aspects of the cartel party theory. This is a subject that I have discussed at some length elsewhere and this is not the place to revisit that discussion (see Enroth 2017). In Chapter 9 of this book, we offer a more sustained normative consideration of the cartel theory in the light of the findings in this book. For now, we need only recall that the cartel party theory was originally articulated with a strong normative accent. As Katz and Mair made clear in their original statement of the theory, 'the rise of the cartel-party model as an empirical phenomenon is also associated with a revision of the normative model of democracy', that is, that 'electoral democracy may be seen as a means by which the rulers control the ruled, rather than the other way around' (Katz and Mair 1995: 21–2; cf. Katz 2005; Katz and Mair 2009).

Acknowledging the normative dimension in the cartel party theory might help us explain or understand – rather than merely dismiss – Katz and Mair evoking the smoking gun of conspiracy while simultaneously declining to look for it, or, to employ Hollis's sartorial metaphor, their knitting a cap to fit the cartel party type while avoiding – or evading – asking whether anyone will actually wear the cap. Seen in this light, terms such as 'cartel' and 'collusion' are not only analytical concepts more or less clearly defined and consistently used in the cartel theory; in the course of their modern usage, especially in the political context, these terms have also acquired considerable evaluative force. They have become words of disapprobation, used in the cartel theory, as elsewhere, to establish the phenomena to which they refer as legitimate objects of criticism and, hopefully, reform (cf. Farr 1989; Skinner 2001).

It should be noted that the connotations of agreement and co-operation that are integral to the cartel concept evoke the normative prehistory of our

modern concept of the political party – both the misgivings historically associated with faction and the way in which those misgivings were first made
manageable in early-modern political discourse in the name of 'party'. As
Terence Ball has argued, this latter development has much to do with the
Whiggish notion that what we now know as parties are best seen as parties
to a contract – a covenant of rulers and ruled (1989: 165–7). The normative
problem with the cartel party from such a contractualist point of view is that
it is, in effect, party to two contracts: one a public and presumably legitimate
agreement between rulers and ruled, resting on popular consent; the other a
private and illegitimate agreement between some or all of the parties that are
party to the former contract, the effect of which is to alter or even nullify the
terms of that first and prima facie legitimate agreement. In other words, the
terms of the agreement between the parties in a cartel are such that the parties,
qua parties to a supposedly legitimate agreement between rulers and ruled, no
longer speak and act as such, that is, as parties to a contract between political
representatives and their constituents.

John Locke put this objection in the idiom of his day in the *Second Treatise*, when he pointed out that what 'makes an inroad upon Government'
is not least the tendency 'to set up one part, or Party, with a distinction
from, and an unequal subjection of the rest' (1993: 197, §158). As Ball has
remarked, for Locke any 'part, or Party' attempting such a move immediately
'ceases to be a proper party to the contract and becomes a "rebel". The rebel,
in effect, makes his part or party into a faction inimical in its operation to a
previously agreed upon conception of the common good' (Ball 1989: 167).
Such early-modern suspicions of faction and of private interests masquerad-
ing as public or general interests reverberate in modern party theory, from
Michels to Duverger to Sartori (Duverger 1954; Michels 1962; Sartori 1976;
cf. Rosenblum 2008). They re-echo in Katz and Mair's criticism of the cartel
party for failing to represent its constituents, while presumably pursuing the
private interests of its own professional elite (Katz and Mair 1995; Mair 2009,
2013; cf. Kitschelt 2000; Enroth 2017).

Seen in this light and in this historical perspective, the cartel party denomination highlights time-honoured normative concerns about particular and
private *versus* public and general interests that 'party' could once be used to
contain, albeit not put to rest, in political discourse. More generally, the modern suspicion of cartels – whether in the economic or in the political context –
arguably has much to do with deep-seated intuitions about the conditions and
consequences of collective action; these are intuitions handed down from,
among other sources, this contractualist strand in modern thought, however
remote this might all seem from latter-day lamentations of the sad state of
party politics and representative democracy.

From this point of view, the ambiguities and tensions in the cartel concept
should be seen not simply or solely as the result of sloppy usage or poor

conceptualisation. Rather, these ambiguities and tensions are the result of different conceptual and rhetorical possibilities that come with the evaluative and the analytical dimensions, respectively, in the usage of terms such as 'cartel' and 'collusion', and that precariously co-exist in the cartel party theory. In these conceptual and rhetorical resources, the prehistory of the modern party form still reverberates. If there are grounds for criticism here, it must be that the cartel concept is enlisted to do quite a bit of work by the authors of the cartel theory, analytically as well as normatively, without its users' fully acknowledging, or even realising, the work it is in fact doing. This brings us back, inevitably, to Humpty Dumpty by way of conclusion: "'When I make a word do a lot of work like that", said Humpty Dumpty, "I always pay it extra'" (Carroll 2001: 298). Taking the strained usage discussed here as grounds for categorically rejecting the cartel concept – or even the cartel theory – would be not only an over-reaction but also a failure to heed the nature and conditions of concept-formation in the social sciences.

NOTES

1. For 'concept-metaphor', see Spivak (1998: 157).

2. Should we nonetheless choose to go there, a plethora of philosophical puzzles awaits in the general concept of collective action. For two helpful discussions of relevance in the present context, see Segerberg (2005) and Stoutland (1997).

3. Stigler does not, in fact, say that the cartel *is* a joint sales agency. He says that 'the cartel with a joint sales agency' is one of three forms of collusion between firms, the other two being 'outright merger', which is 'the most comprehensive', and 'joint determination of outputs and prices by ostensibly independent firms', which is the least comprehensive (Stigler 1964: 45). Fortuitously or not, Blyth and Katz elide Stigler's distinction between the latter and the cartel form. Arguably, a good deal hangs here on our construal of 'ostensibly independent' and 'strategically interdependent'. However, it should also be noted that in Stigler's typology all three forms involve 'agreement' on 'a price structure' (Stigler 1964: 46).

4. The cartel theorists' turn to game theory, and indeed the 2005 Blyth and Katz piece in its entirety, can be seen as an implicit response to Herbert Kitschelt's (2000) criticism of Katz and Mair's original (1995) statement of the cartel theory for not convincingly addressing the endemic problem of cartel defection and enforcement. In any cartel, Kitschelt reminds us, '*each* participant has an incentive to defect from the cooperative arrangement *all* participants wish to maintain' (2000: 168, italics in original). Blyth and Katz's response to this classic prisoner's dilemma in a sense evades rather than addresses the problem, in that the kind of equilibria they introduce into their argument do not presuppose any co-operative arrangement in the first place. The upshot of this move is a further removal of the cartel concept from the conventional understanding outlined above.

Chapter 3

Are the Predictions of the Cartel Party Thesis Supported in the Swedish Case?

Magnus Hagevi and Karl Loxbo

In this chapter, we set out to scrutinise the two core hypotheses of the cartel party theory in the Swedish case. As stated in previous chapters, the evolution towards cartelisation implies that party organisations, and the nature of inter-party competition, are being fundamentally transformed over time. What is more, according to Katz and Mair (2009: 760), a disturbing consequence of this hypothesised transformation is that the legitimacy and representative role of parties are gradually being eroded (Katz and Mair 2009: 762; Mair 2013: 76). A key – indeed the most crucial – prediction of the theory, therefore, is that representative democracy as such is gradually becoming hollowed out (Katz and Mair 2009: 762; Mair 2013: 76). Recalling Robert Michels's traditional 'iron law of oligarchy' (Michels 1962), the first core hypothesis of the cartel party theory (Katz and Mair 1995: 15–21, 2009: 754–5, 761) is that party elites will abandon traditional ideological quests and instead develop common interests in securing their own professional careers (see Chapter 4 of this book). In this process, the elites of established parties strike covert deals across the left–right divide (see Chapters 2 and 5 of this book) to replace their dependence on membership fees with generous public financing. As a result, established parties develop increasingly oligarchic membership organisations, which enable elites to cut themselves off from civil society. Instead of functioning as representative links between civil society and the state, professionalised party organisations are integrated into the state bureaucracy.

The second key hypothesis, which was thoroughly elaborated on by the architects of the cartel party thesis in the mid 2000s (Blyth and Katz 2005; Katz and Mair 2009), is specifically concerned with the changed nature of inter-party competition. This hypothesis argues that established parties have, more or less deliberately, changed from 'maximising competitors into risk averse colluders' (Blyth and Katz 2005: 40). The main theoretical prediction, in other words, is that policy-making becomes increasingly depoliticised as established parties collude with one another in order to downsize voters' expectations (see Chapter 5 of this book). The postulated transformation of European party systems has profoundly disrupted the functions of representative democracy. In the wake of policy convergence, Katz and Mair suggest that established parties on the left and right will eventually turn out to be 'indistinguishable from one another in terms of their main policy proposals' (Katz and Mair 2009: 760).

Our aim in this chapter is to evaluate whether or not these far-reaching predictions of democratic decline are warranted. More precisely, drawing on rich and diverse data sources, we set out to test whether the main hypotheses of the cartel party theory are consistent with reality when tested on central aspects of parties and party system development in Sweden.

The remainder of this chapter is structured as follows. In the next section, we operationalise the two main hypotheses outlined above by presenting four testable sub-hypotheses. Thereafter, we present our data and test these four hypotheses. In the last section of the chapter, we draw conclusions and discuss the implications of our findings for the validity of the cartel party thesis.

IF THE CARTEL PARTY THESIS IS CORRECT, WHAT IS TO BE EXPECTED?

When Katz and Mair first launched the cartel party thesis in the mid 1990s, elite collusion on state subsidies to finance party organisations was described as the key indicator of cartelisation (Katz and Mair 2009: 754–7; see also Mair 1994: 7–8). Like other scholars at the time, Katz and Mair noted a decline in party loyalty among citizens, which prompted party elites to turn to the state in search of alternative, and ever-increasing, sources of party financing (Katz and Mair 1995: 15, 2009: 756–8). However, drawing on such observations, Katz and Mair saw more profound democratic implications than other scholars did. They forcefully argued that public financing – which party elites, by the way, grant to themselves – explains why the top echelon in parties was able to distance themselves from the influence of civil society, while still ensuring that their organisations survived, and even thrived. An essential theoretical prediction of the cartel party thesis is that party elites' abandonment of civil society, which is manifested by a sharp decline in the number of party members, is made possible by an ever-increasing supply of public funds to support party activity. If this fundamental aspect of the cartel party thesis is consistent with reality, we argue that the following hypothesis should hold true in the Swedish case:

Hypothesis 1: Over time, public financing of political parties should increase while the proportion of party members among citizens should decrease.

While Hypothesis 1 highlights a gradual transformation of the relationship between parties and the state, a central assumption of the cartel party thesis concerns the changed nature of the inner life of individual party organisations (Katz and Mair 2009: 262). More precisely, to free themselves from ideologically motivated policy demands that are articulated in civil society, party elites, according to proponents of the cartel party thesis, need to disempower activists in the party on the ground. In fact, Katz and Mair (2009: 759) explicitly argue that the objective of party elites is to establish oligarchic control over party organisations (cf. Katz and Mair 1995: 22; Blyth and Katz 2005: 34, 45, 55). The fate of intra-party democracy is believed to be extremely gloomy in the age of the cartel party (Loxbo 2013), leading to the second hypothesis:

Hypothesis 2: Over time, party members and party activists should lose influence over intra-party decision-making procedures while party elites should become increasingly autonomous.

In later publications on the cartel party theory, starting in the mid 2000s, the main theoretical focus shifted to elite strategies for policy-making. Adding to the central elements of collusion on party finances and the evolution of party oligarchies, the proponents of the cartel party theory now began to focus on external economic constraints – globalisation and European integration – which supposedly cripple the policy competition that defined the traditional left–right divide. Along these lines, Blyth and Katz (2005: 44) argue that the externalisation of policy-making 'curtails the supply curve of policy, thus cartelizing the party system'. Similarly, Katz and Mair (2009: 754) argue that elite collusion on policy effectively undermines 'the perceived importance of the left–right ideological divide'. In this chapter, we review these claims of ideological convergence by studying parties' competition in the electoral arena, on the one hand, and their degree of conflict or co-operation in the parliamentary arena, on the other. If political developments in Sweden are consistent with the predictions arising from a cartelised policy repertoire, we argue that the following hypothesis should hold:

Hypothesis 3: Over time, the major partisan alternatives should converge to similar ideological positions on the left–right ideological divide, while conflicts over actual policy-making should progressively disappear.

The above three hypotheses all concern the structural transformation of parties and party systems. A crucial assumption of the cartel party thesis – indeed, the *most* crucial assumption – concerns the ideal of representative democracy. In fact, an assumption of all publications on the theory is that the representative role of parties has been hollowed out in the wake of cartelisation (Katz and Mair 2009: 760). For example, the chief architect of the cartel party thesis, Mair, argues that

> the relevance of linkages which are based on trust, accountability, and above all, representation tends to become eroded, both inside and outside the parties. … In terms of their representational role, parties appear to be less relevant and to be losing some of their key functions. (Mair 1997: 153)

What is more, Mair, along with other proponents of the cartel party theory (Blyth and Katz 2005), relates the demise of the representative ideal to deliberate strategies 'by mainstream political elites who are reluctant to have their hands tied by the constraints of popular democracy' (Mair 2007: 8, see also 2013: 132–7). The consequence of this transformation in elite behaviour is not only that the representative ideal has become hollowed out but also that public trust in politicians is in a drastic spiral of decline (Mair 1997; Katz and Mair 2009). In line with these predictions of democratic decline, our last hypothesis concerns the relationship between parties and voters, as follows:

> *Hypothesis 4: Over time, political parties should become less representative of their voters, while public trust in party elites should decline.*

By testing the four hypotheses above, we argue that this chapter breaks new ground, providing the first comprehensive empirical test of the main assumptions of the cartel party theory. Given the nature of the data we have at our disposal, we cannot systematically trace the mostly implicit mechanisms of intentional elite collusion at the heart of the cartel party theory (but see Chapter 5 of this book). Even so, we contend that the data presented in this chapter give unique insights into four empirical phenomena that are crucial for evaluating all the key predictions of the cartel party theory.

TESTING THE FOUR HYPOTHESES

Hypothesis 1: Public Financing of Parties and Party Members

Hypothesis 1 highlights two of the most basic assumptions of the cartel party thesis. In the age of the cartel party, increasing public funds and rapidly declining membership figures are believed to be two sides of the same coin. More precisely, proponents of the cartel party thesis suggest that a primary reason why parties began to distance themselves from civil society in the first place was that the costs of professionalised election campaigns exceeded what party elites believed that their members were willing to pay (Katz and Mair 1995: 15–16, 20–1; 2002: 122–9; 2009: 754–8).[1] In this vein, Katz and Mair (1995: 15, 2009: 756–8) note that the individualisation of society has led to a decline in voter loyalty to political parties, prompting the parties to turn to the state in search of party financing. Katz and Mair (2002), moreover, argue that this ongoing shift towards the state can be seen as a direct cause of declining party membership among citizens. In any case, the hypothesised outcome is that political parties no longer function as representatives of civil society but, rather, have coalesced with and become part of the public sector, making them representatives of the state rather than of citizens (Katz and Mair 1995: 16, 2009: 756–7; see Mair 1994: 7–8).

Whereas some scholars contest the assumptions of the cartel party theory,[2] several studies have found that the number of party members as a share of the population has decreased rapidly throughout Europe (Widfeldt 1997: 101–9; Bonander 2009: 167–9; Biezen, Mair and Pogunkte 2012; Krouwel 2012: 230–4) and that public financing largely appears to have supplanted membership fees as the main source of party financing (Bonander 2009: 167–9; Krouwel 2012: 235–43). For example, in consonance with the cartel party thesis, Michael Koß (2011: 32–3) argues that comprehensive public financing is established when it enables consensus in political decision-making as well as in political systems in which parties prioritise holding office.[3]

Sweden has a long history of publicly financing political parties. In 1965 the Swedish Parliament passed legislation on public party financing, which was first paid out in 1966. Additionally, since 1969, counties and regional governments have had the authority to grant support to parties represented in municipal and regional councils (Gidlund 1983: 11). Moreover, in line with the cartel party theory, Gidlund argues that public financing was introduced because parties believed that membership financing was showing signs of crisis at a time when parties' expenses for increasingly professionalised election campaigns were rising (Gidlund 1983: 343–4; cf. Casas-Zamora 2005: 39; Nassmacher 2009: 265–9).

Figure 3.1 presents the overall increase in Swedish party funding from state, regional and municipal governments between 1966 and 2011. The data on funding are presented in SEK millions at fixed 2011 prices. Moreover, in Figure 3.1 the development of Swedish public party support is compared with timelines showing the proportion of party members in the Swedish population according to two surveys covering the 1968–2011 and 1986–2012 periods. The proportion of members over the shorter time period can also be compared with that of active party members (members who attend at least one party meeting over a one-year period) from 1986 to 2012.

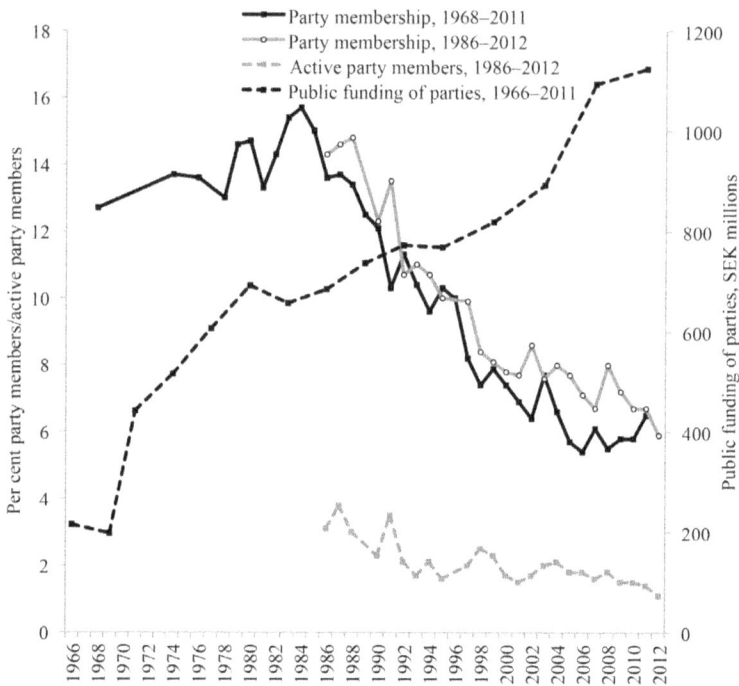

Figure 3.1 Proportion of party members among Swedish citizens, 1968–2011 and 1986–2012 (%, left-hand y-axis); Swedish public party funding, 1966–2011 (SEK millions, fixed 2011 prices, right-hand y-axis). *Sources*: Data on public party funding from Riksdagens utredningstjänst (2003: 3–7), Riksdagens årsbok (2007: 91, 2013: 97) and Rådet för främjande av kommunala analyser (2012). Data on party members 1968–2011 from Statistics Sweden (SCB 2013a) for the period 1976–2011 and from Swedish Level of Living Survey (Vuksanovic 1979: 312; Vuksanovic and Vuksanovic 1992: 281) for 1968 and 1974. Data on party members/active party members in 1986–2012 from the SOM Institute, University of Gothenburg (2014).

According to the results presented in Figure 3.1, Swedish public party funding has increased steadily over the last four decades. Since 1966 public party funding in Sweden has increased five-fold, and total public funding from the national, regional and local levels was approximately SEK 1.1 billion (approximately 120 million euros) in 2011. The development shown in Figure 3.1 implies that Swedish party funding has increased by an average of SEK 15.5 million per year over the last forty years (since the establishment of local party funding in 1969). Even if salaries for those already employed have increased more than inflation, while some of the funds have been used to purchase goods and services, the magnitude of this increase means that parties in Sweden have had favourable conditions for transforming politics into a full-time profession (see Chapter 4 of this book). The annual increase in public subsidies equals the average annual cost of about twenty-five salaried employees (SCB 2013b).

On the other hand, the proportion of party members in the Swedish population was relatively stable at 12–15 per cent until 1985, after which the proportion dropped to 5–6 per cent, remaining at this level during the mid 2000s. Although active party members have never constituted a large proportion of the population, this proportion has declined, from 3–4 per cent in the mid 1980s to approximately 1 per cent in 2012. While this change is modest – from 4 per cent to 1 per cent of the population – it is important to note that two-thirds of all active party members have abandoned their parties over the course of twenty-five years, mirroring the reduction in total party memberships as proportions of the population.

In all, the results in Figure 3.1 support the two central predictions of the cartel party theory laid out in Hypothesis 1. First, the timeline showing the diachronic development of public party funding indicates that parties, by increasingly turning to the state as a primary source of financial support, are indeed gradually being integrated into the state bureaucracy. Second, the sharp decline in party membership among citizens suggests that parties, whether intentionally or not, appear to be distancing themselves from civil society. More specifically, in line with the cartel party thesis, these results could be interpreted as indicating that the development of public party support has given parties incentives to stop mobilising citizens as party members: first, public party subsidies increase, then, when the parties' economic need for membership fees declines, the proportion of party members in the population decreases.

Hypothesis 2: Has Intra-party Democracy Deteriorated Over Time?

As stated in Hypothesis 2, the cartel party thesis argues that intra-party democracy has been in a spiral of decline over time. However, not only proponents of cartel party theory make this claim: but also most prominent party scholars have come to a similar conclusion. First, in line with Roberto Michels's (1962) 'iron law of oligarchy', most modern classics on the inner life of parties assume that elites gradually establish control over party organisations at the expense of members and activists (see, for example, Duverger 1954: 133–5; McKenzie 1982; Kirscheimer 1966; Janda 1983; Panebianco 1988). Second, in consonance with the cartel party theory, this idea appears to be particularly pronounced in contemporary party research (cf. Loxbo 2013). Third, turning to research on Swedish politics, the hypothesis that intra-party democracy is on the wane is hardly ever called into question. For example, in a government report on the current state of democracy in Sweden in the mid 1990s, Gilljam and Möller (1996: 155) conclude: 'Obviously, power has shifted from party members to party leaders'. However, when reviewing previous research, a striking feature is that systematic evidence – including comparisons over time – is mostly absent.

Still, the analyses of four different sources in this section cast serious doubts on the dominant view of deteriorating intra-party democracy in Sweden. First, while formal party statutes may be perceived as paying only lip service to the ideal of intra-party democracy (Michels 1962: 308); Hagevi and Loxbo (2015) demonstrate that formal opportunities for member influence, as articulated in the formal statutes of party organisations, have in fact improved over time in most Swedish parties. The analysis demonstrates that four out of eight parties represented in the Swedish Parliament – the Social Democrats, the Left Party, the Greens and the Centre Party – all with roots in extra-parliamentary mass parties, have recently introduced rules that allow membership referendums on party policy (cf. Bolin 2015). Although such formal opportunities for membership influence did not exist at all during the supposedly democratic era of the mass party in the 1950s, it is, of course, possible that leaders are becoming increasingly autonomous despite the introduction of formally democratic rules. However, the second piece of research we review here concerns actual intra-party decision-making and also points in a direction that directly contests Hypothesis 2.

In an article in *Party Politics*, Loxbo (2013) compares two internal policy-making processes in the largest Swedish party, the Social Democrats. The first one took place in the golden era of the mass party in the 1950s and concerned a major expansion of pension benefits. The second occurred in the (supposed) era of the cartel party in the 1990s, and concerned very unpopular retrenchments of the same pension scheme. If intra-party democracy is in a general spiral of decline, Loxbo argues that the comparison between these two decision-making procedures should *most likely* confirm this tendency. More precisely, while intra-party democracy is believed to be on the wane in all parties, Loxbo argues that the pressures for welfare cutbacks in the wake of globalisation in the 1990s should have presented Social Democratic party leaders with particularly strong incentives to obstruct activist influence and leave the legacy of the mass party behind. Yet the article concludes that Social Democratic party leaders exercised considerably less control, while activists were much more influential, in the 'age of the cartel party' in the 1990s than in the glory days of mass-party mobilisation in the 1950s. In the 1950s the Social Democratic position on the pension scheme was not even approved by the party congress, even though its final design was controversial in the party. By contrast, the widely criticised pension reform in the 1990s – which was a result of negotiations with the four right-wing parties in the Swedish Parliament – constituted the main political issue at no less than three party congresses. Additionally, three internal party consultations and one broad membership consultation were held in order to gain the final support of party members. In the end, members at the party congress forced Social Democratic leaders into difficult renegotiations with the four right-wing parties. Although the results of this case study obviously cannot be generalised to other parties, the detailed historical comparison highlights a very different development to the one hypothesised by proponents of the cartel party theory. Moreover, when turning to our third data source, we argue that the predictions of declining intra-party democracy become even less convincing.

Previous research on intra-party democracy in Sweden demonstrates that, in the era of the mass party, party leaders could generally dominate policy decision-making at party congresses (Loxbo 2013; Thomassen and van Ham 2015; Hagevi and Loxbo 2015), including any internal opposition to the leader's favoured policies, by managing the decision-making process behind closed doors. However, in an era of mass communication, the opportunities to establish dominance in secret over unruly activists have become seriously constrained. The primary reason is that the relationship between party organisations and the media has changed dramatically over time. Figure 3.2 presents a media analysis that illustrates the magnitude of this change. More precisely, for the years preceding general elections in Sweden, when all parliamentary parties scheduled party congresses, the timeline in Figure 3.2 shows the frequency with which the Swedish print media write about the status of intra-party democracy at these party congresses.

In Figure 3.2 the dotted line between 1981 and 1990 shows the number of articles in all Swedish newspapers, whereas the solid black line between 1993 and 2013 shows only the articles in six of the leading Swedish newspapers. The results indicate a dramatic increase in media coverage of the state of intra-party democracy at the congresses of Swedish parties. While increasing media coverage obviously does not say anything about the actual democratic qualities of Swedish party organisations, we argue that the timeline in Figure 3.2 has at least two implications for the hypothesis of declining

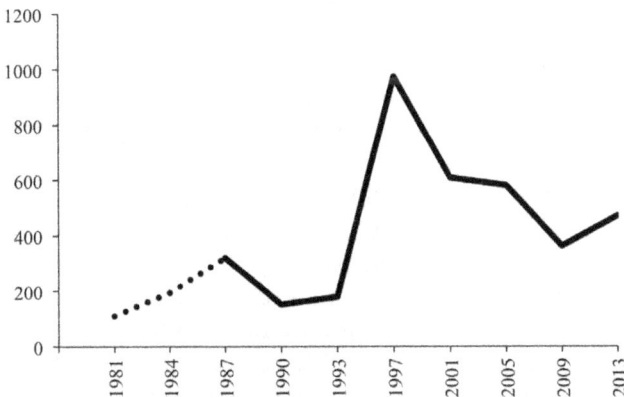

Figure 3.2 Status of intra-party democracy at congresses of parties represented in Swedish Parliament, 1981–2013, in years preceding general elections (number of newspaper articles). *Source*: Data obtained using search engine Retriever.

intra-party democracy. First, even if party elites are actually striving to dominate members and activists, the massive increase in media coverage has likely
made it more difficult for party elites to behave openly as oligarchs by forcing
their will upon party members. More precisely, whereas bargaining between
party elites and activists was largely an internal, and sometimes even secret,
matter in the past, such proceedings are today more open to the public, while
internal controversies increasingly attract media interest. In fact, a stark difference over time is that controversial intra-party proceedings are today often
directly broadcast on TV and online.

Second, increased media coverage arguably makes it easier for members
who contest the official party line to voice their concerns with the party
line in public. If party leaders still want to appear 'democratic' – and it is
reasonable to expect that most of them do when communicating with the
wider public – they likely have greater incentives than in the past to compromise with members who dispute their political and ideological approach
in public.

Lastly, to assess whether the predictions of Hypothesis 2 are consistent
with reality, we turn to unique survey material, from two random samples in
1999 and 2013, exploring how Swedish citizens view the opportunities for
party members to influence party policy. While an obvious objection to this
kind of data is that general public perceptions are more or less irrelevant to
evaluating how parties actually function internally, we argue that it is plausible to expect that citizens who claim to be enlisted members of parties have
first-hand experience of the inner life of parties. We therefore distinguish
between all respondents of the survey and those who claim to be registered
party members.

We argue that the following two conclusions can be drawn when reviewing the comparison between the two surveys presented in Table 3.1. First,
while most Swedish citizens in both 1999 and 2013 believed that party
members have poor prospects of influencing party policy, the share of
positive responses increased by 5 percentage points between 1999 and
2013. Correspondingly, the share of citizens responding that members have
poor prospects of exerting influence had decreased by 16 percentage points.
Second, and more importantly, this positive shift in opinion is much more
evident among party members, who, arguably, have first-hand experience of
intra-party decision-making. More precisely, whereas the proportion of party
members responding that prospects for exerting influence were poor clearly
outweighed the proportion that responded that prospects were good in 1999,
the relationship was the reverse in 2013. Consequently, while the cartel party
thesis expects intra-party democracy to be in a spiral of deep decline over
time, Swedish party members themselves report that they are experiencing
exactly the opposite development.

Table 3.1 Perceptions of Party-Member Influence over Intra-Party Policy-Making, 1999 and 2013 (%)

	Good Prospects	Poor Prospects	Don't Know	Sum, %	n	Difference (Good–Poor)
All respondents						
1999	13	57	30	100	1528	−44
2013	18	41	41	100	1535	−23
Difference (2013–1999)	*+5*	*−16*	*+11*			
All party members						
1999	31	58	11	100	131	−27
2013	42	37	21	100	110	+5
Difference (2013–1999)	*+11*	*−21*	*+10*			

Sources: Petersson et al. 2000; Erlingsson and Persson 2014; Erlingsson, Hagevi and Loxbo 2015; all of which use data from the SOM Institute, University of Gothenburg.
Note: The survey question reads as follows: 'How well do you think the parties function?' in terms of 'giving party members influence over party policy'. Respondents were given the following response options: 'very good', 'fairly good' (merged into 'good prospects' in Table 3.1), 'fairly poor' and 'very poor' (merged into 'poor prospects' in Table 3.1), and 'don't know'.

Although comprehensive and systematic evidence on the evolution of intra-party democracy is still lacking, our test of Hypothesis 2 in this section highlights a very different development from the one hypothesised by proponents of the cartel party theory. Considering that the basic predictions about internal cartelisation are based on loosely formulated hypotheses rather than concrete empirical findings, we maintain that a more – or at least equally – plausible hypothesis is that party leaders are losing, instead of gaining, control over intra-party policy-making over time. If this reversed hypothesis – that intra-party democracy is improving, rather than declining – is correct (Teorell 1998), then the few remaining party members exercise more influence over party policy than did members of mass organisations in the past, while party leaders face greater difficulties satisfying their principals than their predecessors ever did (cf. Kitschelt 2000: 175). In any case, considering that empirical evidence on the fate of intra-party democracy is scarce, and in some publications non-existent, we argue that proponents of the cartel party thesis have idealised the democratic qualities of the mass party (e.g. Thomassen and van Ham 2015: 403), while seriously overestimating the control exercised by present-day party leaders.

Hypothesis 3: Convergence and the End of Ideological Controversies

When turning to Hypothesis 3 – which expects ideological and political convergence between parties – it is important to note that the idea that traditional ideological conflicts are gradually declining over time is one of the more established notions among researchers on European party systems. By suggesting that convergence has its roots in intentional collusion between party elites (Blyth and Katz 2005; Katz and Mair 2009), proponents of the cartel party theory take this hypothesis a step further. While cartelisation implies a far-reaching convergence between the ideological positions of parties in the electoral arena (see, for example, Mair 1997: 133), it is also – as stated in Hypothesis 3 – expected to curtail controversies over policy-making in the parliamentary arena (e.g. Katz and Mair 1995: 22, 2009: 754; see also Chapter 2 of this book). To evaluate these interrelated claims of party system cartelisation, we rely on three data sources. First, when reviewing and evaluating the widely purveyed assumption that the programmatic positions of the main partisan alternatives are converging in the electoral arena, we draw on data from the Comparative Manifesto Project (CMP). Second, we review the assumption of convergence between left and right among party elites themselves, drawing on eight surveys of MPs from all Swedish parties. Third, to assess the controversial, and arguably most crucial, claim that cartelisation also reduces the stakes in policy-making, blurring the distinction between government and opposition (e.g. Katz and Mair 1995: 22), we build on a unique database of parliamentary decision-making. This database consists of content analysis of 4657 coded reports on government bills from all standing committees in the Swedish Parliament between 1970 and 2014 (see Chapter 5 of this book).

The results in Figure 3.3 are based on the widely accepted operationalisation of the left–right ideological continuum in the CMP (see Budge 2013). The bars in Figure 3.3 show the positions on the left–right scale of the five traditional parties in the Swedish party system in three time periods between 1944 and 2014.

Although the CMP definition of the left–right scale has been criticised – it does not, for example, account for country-specific differences or other contextual variations (cf. Dinas and Gemenis 2010) – the results in Figure 3.3 give general insights into the main trend of ideological convergence/divergence over time in the Swedish party system. The main results clearly indicate programmatic convergence between the parties. When comparing the 'golden age' of the mass party, 1948–70, with the suggested age of the cartel party, 1991–2014, the main partisan alternatives in Swedish politics, the Social Democrats and the Moderates, have both closed in on the ideological centre. Despite signs of convergence, the main finding, when considering the whole seventy-year period, is that the ideological distance between the main contestants in the Swedish party system has in fact remained remarkably stable over time. It appears as though the widely purveyed hypothesis of far-reaching programmatic convergence between the main partisan alternatives gains only weak support from the Swedish case. Second, when reviewing how Swedish MPs position themselves on the left–right scale over time, the

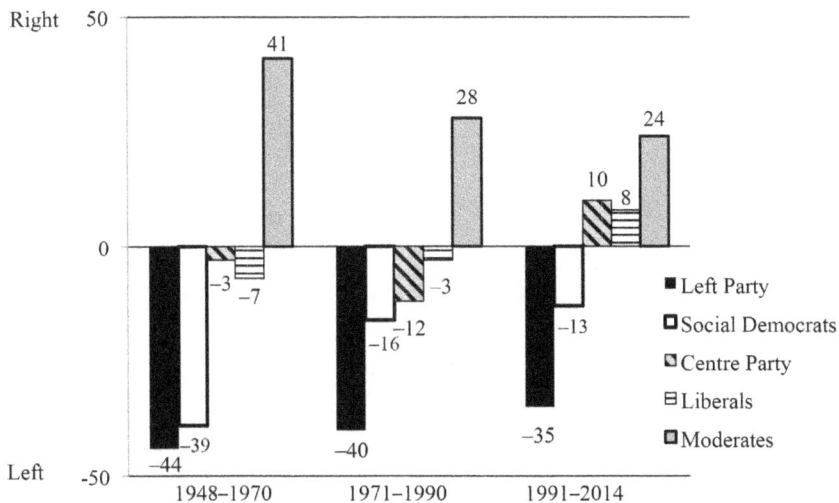

Figure 3.3 Left–right programmatic convergence/divergence between five tradition-ally dominant parties in Swedish party system, 1944–2014 (index points). *Source:* The Comparative Manifesto Project (CMP) database (Volkens et al. 2016).

conclusion of stable ideological divisions, rather than far-reaching conver-gence, gains further support.

Figure 3.4 shows the mean position of the MPs in each parliamentary party group between 1985 and 2014. Similarly to the analysis of the manifestos, the results indicate that the positions of the main partisan alternatives in Sweden – the Social Democrats and the Moderates – both display a tendency to gravitate slowly towards the ideological centre over time. However, yet again, the most striking result is not a shift towards ideological convergence; instead, ideological divisions have remained fairly stable over time. When considering this measure of ideological divisions in the parliamentary arena – independent of the manifestos, analysed above – the hypothesis of ideological convergence once again fails to gain strong support.

Still, a pertinent objection to the above analyses of parties' ideological positions is that all measures are abstract indicators of ideological rhetoric, or even of subjective ideological views, far from the real world of political decision-making. It could be that parties strive to retain the ideological dis-tance between one another on a strictly rhetorical level, while still converging to the same policy positions when engaging in parliamentary decision-mak-ing. Along these lines, a central prediction of the cartel party theory is that the development of convergence in policy-making blurs the 'the distinction between parties in office and those out of office' (Katz and Mair 1995: 22). However, our third, and most critical, test of Hypothesis 3 explicitly concerns the evolution of conflicts in parliamentary policy-making.

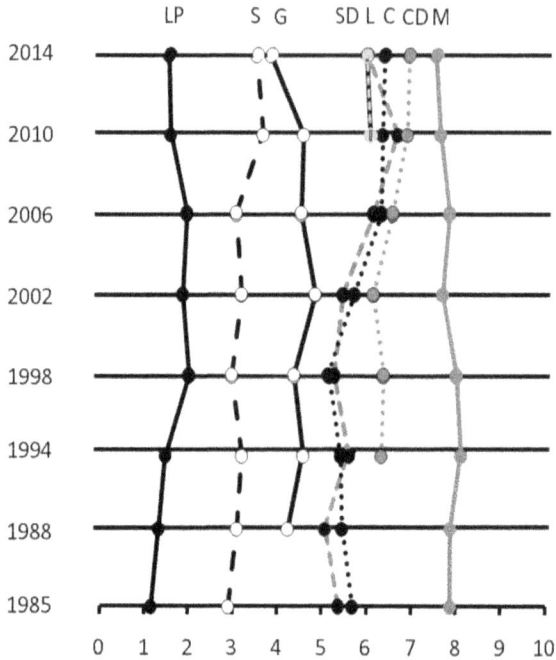

Figure 3.4 Subjective left–right positions of Swedish MPs, 1985–2014 (mean, by parliamentary party group). *Source: Swedish Parliamentary Survey*, 1985–2010 (Wängnerud et al. 2012); *Swedish Parliamentary Survey*, 2014 (Karlsson and Nordin 2015).

The bars in Figure 3.5 show the proportion of committee reports in the Swedish Parliament, for all governments between 1970 and 2014, where opposition parties rejected the entire policy bill proposed by the government. Government parties are defined as the formal members of the cabinet, whereas the opposition parties are those outside government. Moreover, due to the Swedish two-bloc system (see Chapter 1 of this book), we make the following distinctions between parties in opposition: the largest opposition party is called the 'main opposition party',[4] whereas smaller parties that do not participate in government, but are in the same bloc as the main opposition party, are labelled 'opposition parties' in the plural (see Chapter 5 of this book).

The results in Figure 3.5 run strongly counter to the predictions of policy convergence in the cartel party theory. In sharp contrast to Hypothesis 3, intense controversy over policy-making – that is, when the opposition rejects government bills outright – has risen markedly over time. Additionally, the overall trend towards increased policy contestation is equally or even more obvious when only policy areas of strong relevance to the left–right divide are considered. Although conflicts declined sharply between 2010 and 2014, because the right-wing government controlled only a

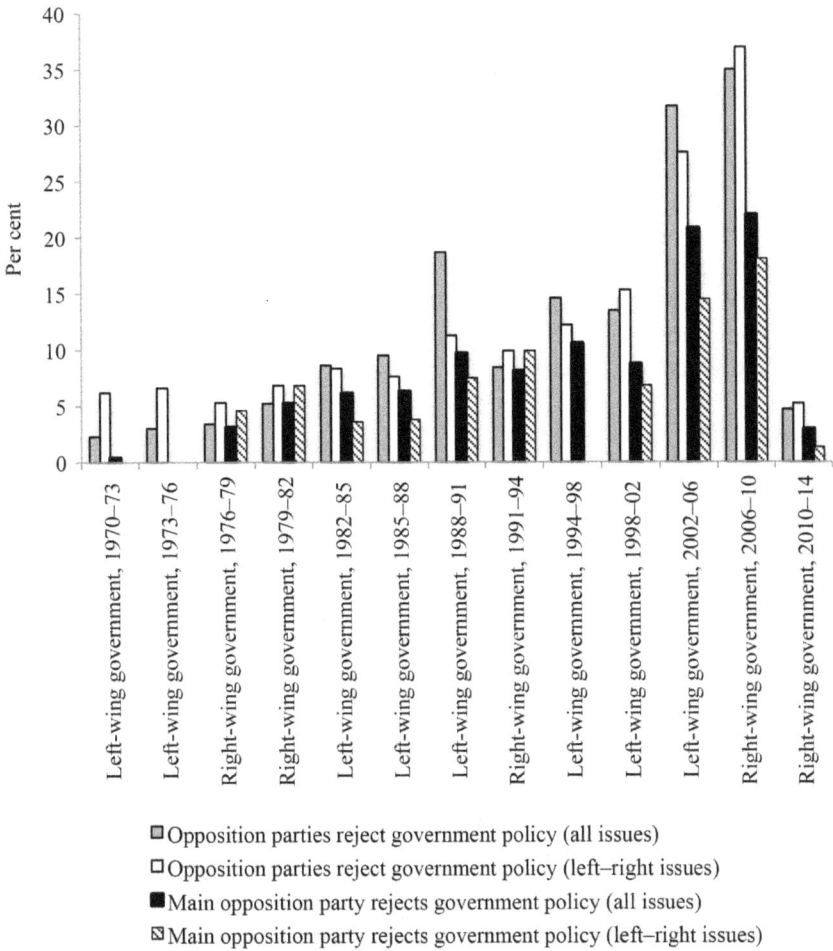

Figure 3.5 Proportion of committee reports where main opposition party and other parties in opposing bloc reject proposed government bills of thirteen governments, in all policy areas and left–right policy areas, 1970–2014 (%). *Source*: Content analysis of 4,657 committee reports of the Swedish Parliament, 1970–2014.

minority of seats in parliament,[5] the overall trend is unmistakable: since the mid 2000s, mainstream parties in opposition have clearly become more confrontational. Overall, this finding highlights a general development in the relations between left-wing and right-wing parties that points in the opposite direction to the transformation suggested by the cartel party theory.

In sum, our two indicators of ideological convergence only weakly support Hypothesis 3. The analysis of parliamentary policy-making, on the other hand, casts serious doubt on crucial assumptions of the cartel party theory.

Hypothesis 4: Reduced Representation and Trust?

As previously stated, a crucial element of Katz and Mair's claims is that representational links between voters and their elected politicians, as well as political trust in general, are withering away with the emergence of the cartel party (Katz and Mair 1995, 2009: 760; Mair and Katz 1997: 103–5, 109–11, 115–16).

We made these assumptions explicit in Hypothesis 4 and we set out to test them using unique data from surveys of the Swedish population and of Swedish MPs. With this aim in mind, we first study political representation as issue congruence between MPs and voters and, second, we review the evolution of political trust among voters.

Representation

As pointed out by Herbert Kitschelt (2000: 154), the claim that account-ability and representation have become hollowed out over time implies that party leaders are increasingly acting according to different political preference schedules from those endorsed by their voters. Kitschelt (2000: 165–6), however, criticises Katz and Mair for not accounting for empirical research indicating how well elected politicians represent voters. In several studies of Swedish political representation, Sören Holmberg (1974, 1989, 1997, 2000, 2004, 2011, 2014a; Holmberg and Esaiasson 1988; Esaiasson and Holmberg 1996) also states that issue congruence – that is, the degree to which voters and elected politicians have similar preferences regarding these issues – is important for implementing the will of the people and is therefore a central indicator of a well-functioning representative democracy (see also Wester-ståhl and Johansson 1981).

Based on empirical results on the actual state of political representation, researchers have tended to adopt a sceptical view of the claims of the cartel party theory (Thomassen and van Ham 2015: 189). As Kitschelt and Rehm (2015) conclude in their study of policy congruence between voters and can-didates for the European Parliament:

> If dealignment and cartelization theories were right, we would expect that in the countries with the longest and most durable democratic experience and with the greatest affluence and postindustrialization, cartelization, or at least the unrav-eling of representation on ideological dimensions of policy making, has gone furthest. The evidence shows just the opposite. (Kitschelt and Rehm 2015: 188)

Here, we will test whether the implications of the cartel party thesis for the representation of voters by elected politicians are supported when it comes to this kind of issue congruence. We will pay special, but not exclusive, attention to the left–right dimension in Swedish politics. The left–right scale has been called a 'super issue which summarises the programmes of opposing groups' (Inglehart and Klingeman 1976: 244). The left–right dimension has long been the dominant issue dimension in Swedish politics (Oscarsson and Holmberg 2013: 224–7), even more so than in many other party systems (Bengtsson et al. 2014: 159, 176–7). Because of the dominance of the left–right dimension, issues related to it are well established among voters, parties and MPs. Therefore, issue congruence with regard to left–right issues is probably greater than it is for other issues. Furthermore, in the Swedish context, the left–right dimension displays the strongest correlation with issues concerning the role of the state in the economy and the need for economic equality (Hagevi 2015a: 68, 150–1). According to Katz and Mair (2009: 754, 760), it is particularly issues of importance to the left–right ideological divide that are depoliticised by party leaders and parties, who tend to collaborate with each other and cause their policies to converge in such a way that policy representation of voters by elected politicians is called into question. Moreover, as already demonstrated in this chapter, MPs from Sweden's two largest parties have tended to converge somewhat on the left–right dimension.

First, we will study representation in relation to the subjective left–right position when individuals indicate their own position. Voters tend to use their subjective left–right position as a shortcut when investigating the bundle of important issues tied to the left–right dimension (Hagevi 2015a: 62–8). The importance of this position for representation is related to its role as a cognitive heuristic, as it 'provides a general orientation toward a society's political leaders, ideologies and parties' (Inglehart and Sidjanski 1976: 225) that simplifies the complex reality when voters choose between a set of parties in elections. To study voters' subjective left–right positions, and their perceptions of their preferred party's left–right position, we used data from Survey 2014, conducted by Surveyinstitutet (Hagevi 2015c). To measure MPs' self-placement on the left–right scale, we use the *Swedish Parliamentary Survey*, 2014 (Karlsson and Nordin 2015). Figure 3.6 shows the results.

If the implications of cartel party theory (weakening representational ties between voters and parties, especially concerning the left–right dialectic) are borne out, we argue that two transformations should be evident in the left–right positions of voters and elected politicians. First, if parties fail to represent their voters, we suggest that voters' own positions on the left–right scale are unlikely to correspond to their perception of the position of their preferred party, or of that party's MPs, on the left–right scale. However, as Figure 3.6 shows, voters' self-placement on the left–right scale corresponds closely to their perception of where their preferred party and its MPs are situated on that scale.[6] Actually, the congruence between MPs and voters seems to have increased compared to the findings in older studies (Holmberg 2014a).

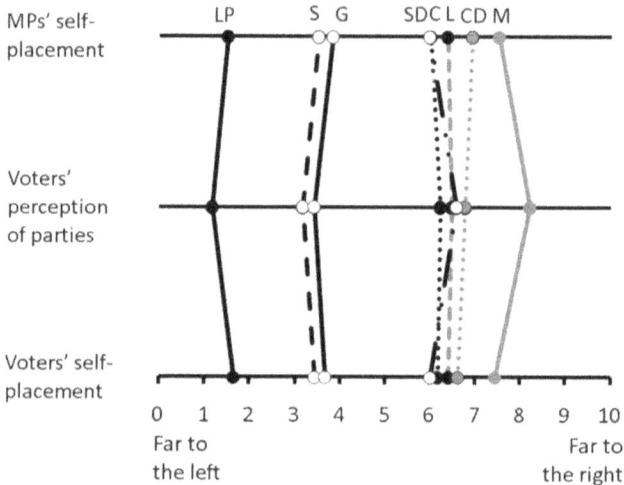

Figure 3.6 **Left–right self-placement of voters and MPs, by party, and perceived left–right position of voters' preferred party, 2014 (mean).** *Sources*: Data on voters are from Survey 2014, Surveyinstitutet, Linnaeus University (Hagevi 2015c). Data on MPs are from the *Swedish Parliamentary Survey*, 2014 (Karlsson and Nordin 2015).

Therefore, the elite convergence already discussed in this chapter could have increased the congruence between MPs and voters.

Second, if the positions of voters correspond to MPs' and parties' positions on the left–right scale, the cartel party theory would imply that parties and MPs, as part of the party elite (Katz 2002), are likely to converge towards the centre of the left–right scale, while voters are likely to display more polarised opinions (Kitschelt and Rehm 2014, 2015: 180, 184–93). Differently put, this transformation should, as stated by Katz and Mair (2009: 760), indicate that mainstream parties 'are largely indistinguishable from one another' and that 'the representative roles' of parties have been eroded. However, as Figure 3.6 shows, on the left–right scale, MPs and voters are equally polarised. Therefore, concerning representation of the subjective left–right scale, the general postulates of cartel party theory are not supported.

What about the risk that the above result is purely random, that perhaps other surveys will produce different results? In Sweden, the congruence of subjective left–right positions between voters and MPs has been measured since 1985 and among voters since 1973.[7] Although, during this period, the differences between voters and MPs have been small, this does not change the main conclusion that the cartel party theory is not supported by the evidence from Sweden.

Subjective thoughts and feelings may not convey substantial information about congruence in concrete issues pertaining to the ideological left–right divide, concerning, for example, public healthcare, taxes, education and environmental concerns. However, in several studies, Holmberg demonstrates that congruence between voters and MPs in Sweden also applies to specific issues (1974, 1997, 2000, 2004, 2011, 2014a; Holmberg and Esaiasson 1988; Esaiasson and Holmberg 1996). More precisely, Holmberg has recurrently created left–right indices for voters and MPs since the mid 1980s based on typical left–right issues (Oscarsson and Holmberg 2013: 222–35; Hagevi 2015a: 150–1). Within each time period, voters and MPs were asked the same survey questions but the questions themselves have changed over time. Using the left–right indices constructed by Holmberg, we therefore argue that it is possible to test the implications of the cartel party theory by drawing on left–right issue congruence between voters and MPs. Figure 3.7 shows the main results of Holmberg's (2014a) study of left–right issue congruence between voters and MPs in 2010. The five-point indices range from 1 (left) to 5 (right).

We argue that two conclusions can be drawn from the analysis of Holmberg's left–right indices. First, to indicate misrepresentation, the MPs' left–right positions should not correspond to their voters' positions. According to Figure 3.7, however, MPs and their voters are aligned in the same order, from left to right according to party, with small discrepancies only for the Centre Party. Second, MPs ought to converge to the centre of the left–right dimension while voters should tend to be more polarised (Kitschelt and Rehm 2014, 2015: 180, 184–93). However, as Figure 3.7 shows, the opposite occurs: voters converge around the centre of the left–right dimension while parties and MPs are more polarised than voters. The analysis, in other words, refutes some of the basic assumptions of the cartel party theory. Actually, at all measurement points between 1985 and 2010, Holmberg discerns a polarised model 'with greater ideological antagonism between parties in parliament

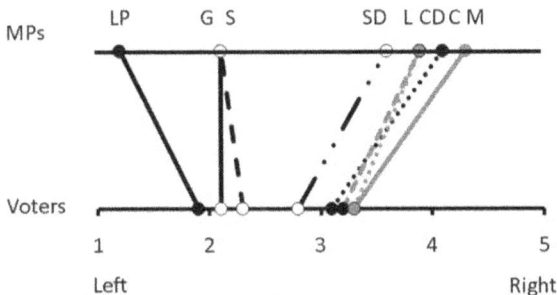

**Figure 3.7 Left–right issue congruence between voters and MPs, 2010 (mean, by MPs'
party affiliation and voters' party choice during election).** *Sources*: Data for the indices
are reported by Holmberg (2014a: 104). Data on the voters are from a study of the 2010
Swedish National Election Study (Oscarsson and Holmberg 2013) and on MPs from the
Swedish Parliamentary Survey (Wängnerud et al. 2012).

than among voters' (Holmberg 2014a: 105, our translation; see also Esaias-son and Holmberg 1996: 92–7).

In addition, using the left–right indices constructed by Holmberg (2014a: 104, 115), we have also calculated the absolute differences of means between MPs with the same party affiliation and their voters at each measurement point from 1985 to 2010 (the maximum value is 4 and the minimum value is 0). The voter–MP relationship for each party is represented by a dot in Figure 3.8. If representation has eroded over time, as expected in the cartel party theory (Katz and Mair 2009: 760), we should expect lower issue congruence between voters and MPs. To test whether or not this alleged trend is consistent with reality, we calculated the regression line between measurement time (year) and left–right issue congruence between voters and MPs by party. Decreased congruence would mean a positive slope, as the issue disagreement between voters and MPs increases; conversely, a negative slope indicates increased congruence as the issue disagreement becomes smaller.

As shown in Figure 3.8, the overall congruence between MPs and their voters is high and has remained fairly stable over time, although a slightly positive regression slope indicates a very weak tendency towards lower congruence over time. This change over time, however, explains only 1.4 per cent

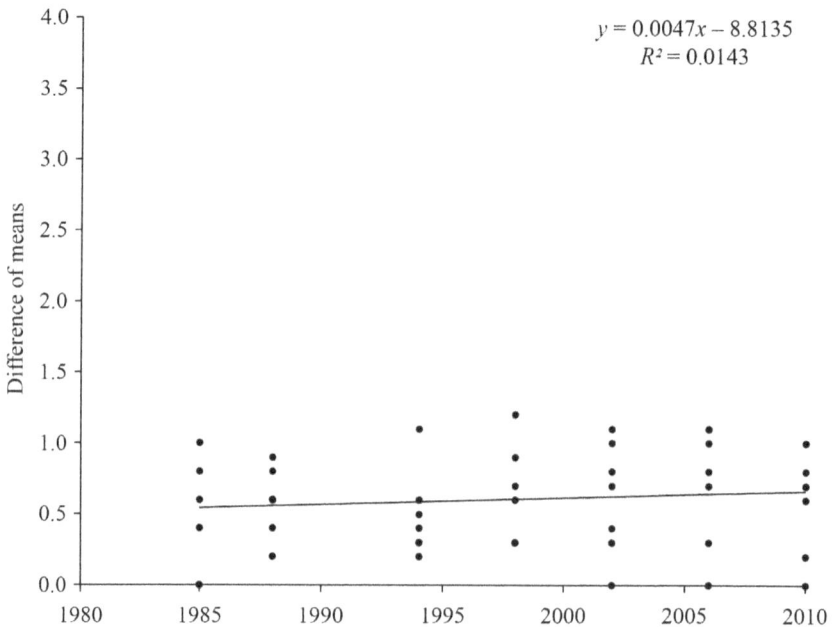

Figure 3.8 Left–right issue congruence between MPs and voters, by party, 1985–2010 (absolute differences of means and OLS regression). *Source*: Data from Holmberg 2014a: 104, 115.

of the variation in congruence between MPs and voters indicating that the overall degree of congruence in left–right issues is remarkably stable. Accordingly, when it comes to the important left–right issues incorporated into the indices, we find no support for the claimed implications of cartel party theory for political representation.

Although the left–right dimension remains vital for voting, and for how well MPs represent their voters, the significance of the libertarian–authoritarian value dimension has increased in recent decades in Sweden (Hagevi 2015a: 66–76), as in many other political systems (Kitschelt 1994; Flanagan and Lee 2003; Häusermann and Kriesi 2015: 228). In addition, although the left–right dimension has long been dominant in Swedish politics, there have always been issues with hardly any connection to it. Therefore, it is also important to look at issue congruence between MPs and voters on all issues, not only those that are relevant to the left–right divide. To this end, Holmberg (2014a: 114) has also calculated the issue congruence for central issues in Swedish politics, including left–right issues and other issues, from 1985 to 2010.

By calculating the absolute difference between the mean of MPs' and voters' positions on each issue when the response options are coded 1–5, and from this calculating the mean of these differences across issues by party, Holmberg (2014a: 114) obtained the average difference of means between voters and MPs, with a smaller difference indicating higher congruence. In Figure 3.9, we first plotted the average difference of means by party; we then calculated the regression line that extends over time. Decreased congruence would result in a positive slope as the issue disagreement between voters and MPs increases, whereas a negative slope indicates increased congruence as the issue disagreement becomes smaller (note that the index includes non-left–right issues as well as the left–right issues reported in Figure 3.8).

When reviewing the results in Figure 3.9, we find only small differences in policy views between voters and MPs. Once again, the overall congruence between MPs and their voters is high and rather stable over time, though the regression slope is positive and indicates a tendency towards reduced congruence over time (Holmberg 2014a: 100–1). This change over time explains 15.2 per cent of the variation in congruence between MPs and voters. When comparing this result with the analysis of left–right issues (see Figure 3.8), we find a greater reduction in congruence between MPs and voters in the former case. As the substantial difference between these two analyses is from the consideration of non-left–right issues, we conclude that the primary source of the reduced congruence between MPs and voters is issues of low relevance to the left–right divide. More precisely, in line with previous research, we find that MPs' greatest divergence from voters pertains to issues linked to the libertarian–authoritarian dimension, such as tougher penalties for criminals,

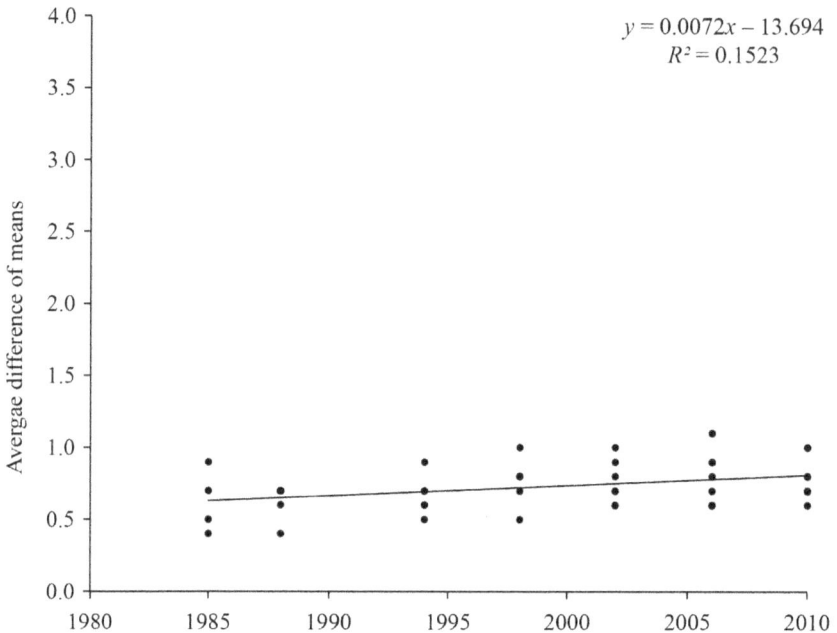

$$y = 0.0072x - 13.694$$
$$R^2 = 0.1523$$

Figure 3.9 **Issue congruence between MPs and voters, by party, 1985–2010 (average difference of means and OLS regression).** *Source*: Holmberg 2014a: 114.

banning pornography and reducing immigration of refugees (Loxbo 2011; Hagevi 2015a). In most Swedish parties, MPs do not want to implement tougher penalties for criminals, ban pornography or reduce immigration of refugees as much as their voters do (Holmberg 2014a: 96–7).

In all, our findings indicate that the representational link between elected politicians and voters has not weakened in such a way that an erosion of representation is at hand. When it comes to the important left–right dimension, we find no support for the implications that the cartel party theory would claim for political representation, whereas there is a weak tendency towards reduced issue congruence between MPs and voters concerning other issues. However, this tendency does not justify a warning about the erosion of representative democracy as in cartel party theory. There is simply no support in our data for such a warning, at least not yet.

Trust in Politicians and Parties

According to the cartel party theory, the erosion of representational links also implies that 'parties risk losing their legitimacy' (Katz and Mair 2009: 760; see also Mair 1997: 153).[8] To measure political trust, we used two items from the Swedish National Election Study, which has traced this attitude among

Swedish voters since 1968. In these surveys, voters responded to two cynical statements about politicians and parties: 'Those people who are in parliament and run things don't pay much attention to what ordinary people think' and 'Parties are only interested in people's votes, not in their opinions'. For both items, the response options were 'totally agree', 'broadly agree', 'broadly disagree' and 'totally disagree'. As a measurement of political trust, Figure 3.10 shows the share of Swedish voters, 1968–2010, who responded 'broadly disagree' and 'totally disagree'.

As seen in Figure 3.10, the level of political trust among Swedish voters has made a U-turn, as indicated by changed responses to the two cynical statements about parties and politicians. Over the course of the thirty years from 1968 to 1998, the level of trust among voters declined from around 50 per cent disagreeing with the cynical statements about parties and politicians to around 25 per cent. Since 1998, however, the overall level of political trust in Sweden has increased, with about 44 per cent of voters disagreeing with both cynical statements in 2010 – a level of trust similar to that of the early 1970s. As we have not detected any great amount of policy elite convergence or loss in the representative roles of parties or elected politicians, this comes as no surprise.

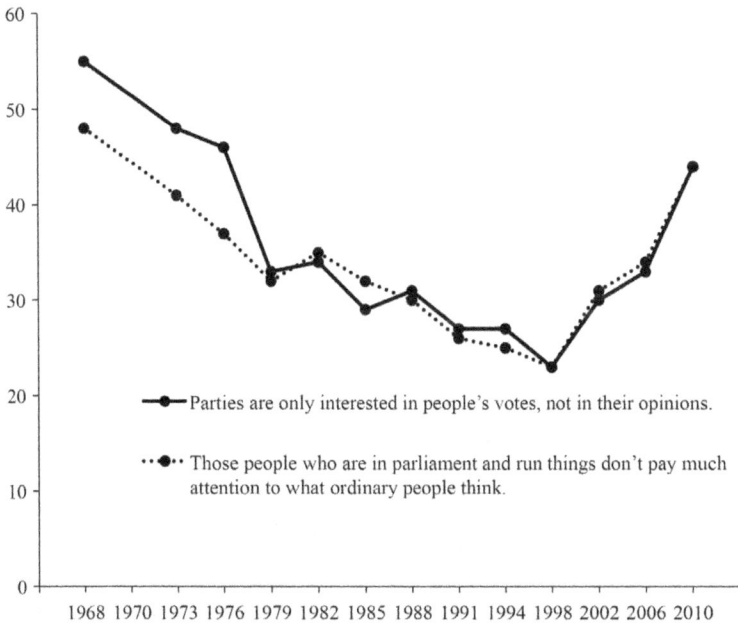

Figure 3.10   Political trust, 1968–2010 (% choosing responses 'broadly disagree' and 'totally disagree'). *Source*: Oscarsson and Holmberg 2013: 349. Data from Swedish National Election Studies, 1968–2010.

In contrast to the cartel party theory's prediction of a drastic decrease in the legitimacy of political parties (Mair 1997: 153; Katz and Mair 2009: 760), political trust seems to be relatively high among Swedish voters.[9]

Accordingly, as we found no major erosion of political representation or trust – but rather stability or the opposite tendency – our results do not support Hypothesis 4. Over time, erosion of the representational function of political parties has been minor and does not involve the important left–right issues. Moreover, contrary to cartel party theory, our findings suggest that political trust has increased in recent decades in Sweden.

CONCLUSION

In this chapter, we have scrutinised the core assumptions of cartel party theory in the Swedish case. At the heart of this theory is the deterioration of representative democracy caused by the supposed erosion of political parties' democratic and representative functions (Katz and Mair 1995, 2009). Indeed, this presumed decline could not be studied without comparisons over time. Therefore, drawing on extensive longitudinal data and several complementary sources, we have contributed to the literature by testing four sub-hypotheses, all of which are derived from the two general hypotheses of the cartel party theory (Katz and Mair 2009: 755).

As posited in Hypothesis 1, the public funding of political parties has increased over time, while the share of party members in the Swedish population has decreased. As it turns out, when reviewing extensive data on party funding and membership figures, our results lend clear support to these basic assumptions of the cartel party theory. In line with this theory, our results could imply that parties are moving away from civil society and instead are becoming integrated into the state.

However, regarding Hypothesis 2 – which predicts that party elites will have established oligarchic control over party organisations – we found no empirical evidence that intra-party democracy is locked in a spiral of decline over time. Instead, our findings suggest that proponents of the cartel party thesis idealise the democratic qualities of the mass party, while seriously overestimating the control exercised by present-day party leaders.

Scrutinising the data related to Hypothesis 3 – which suggests that the main partisan alternatives will converge to similar ideological positions – we found some support for the existence of programmatic convergence between parties in the electoral arena and, to a lesser extent, among MPs in the parliamentary arena. However, while mainstream parties have indeed converged to increasingly similar positions, we found no evidence of cartel-like elite collaboration that undermines ideological conflict between parties in the parliamentary arena. Instead, our analyses of parliamentary decision-making over time indicate exactly the opposite tendency: rather than withering away, policy conflict between the major parties has increased over time, also with regard to left–right issues.

Turning to Hypothesis 4 – which holds that representation and trust are locked in a spiral of decline – we find that it is not, with some minor exceptions, supported. More precisely, we detected no major erosion of the representational link between parties and voters concerning the important left–right dimension. In addition, relative to voters' views, we found no elite convergence but rather a polarisation of MPs' political views (Holmberg 2014a). Still, when it comes to issues of low relevance to the ideological left–right divide, the degree of congruence between MPs and their voters has declined somewhat. We suggest that this indication of reduced representation may be partly attributable to the growing importance of issues related to the libertarian–authoritarian dimension. When we measured the levels of politi-cal trust, however, we found a significant upturn among Swedish citizens after the turn of the century. The level of political trust has now returned to the level of the early 1970s, so this finding contradicts the prediction of hollowed-out trust made by cartel party theory.

However, even those parts of our study that support the claims of the cartel party theory leave room for doubt. Specifically, as made clear in Chapter 2 of this book, it is far from obvious how to interpret the testable indicators of cartel party theory (Enroth 2015). It is important to note that there are other plausible theoretical explanations other than the notion of cartelisation for the development of increased public party financing, declining party membership among citizens and convergence between established parties. Individualisa-tion, for example, may be seen as an alternative cause, independent of the cartel party thesis, of declining party membership in the population (Koole 1996: 513; cf. Katz and Mair 2009: 757–8). In addition, increased public funding of parties may be interpreted as a by-product of the expansion of the welfare state (Pierre, Svåsand and Widfeldt 2000), while convergence between political parties could be seen simply as a consequence of parties' intensified struggles to compete for the median voter in order to maximise their support (Downs 1957; Kitschelt 2000). Second, the explanations put forward for the observed changes that appear to be in line with the cartel party theory are not indisputable. It is not obvious that the professionalisa-tion of parties – a transformation that is indeed taking place in the Swedish case (Hagevi 2014b) – has had the effects that the cartel party theory claims (see Chapter 4 of this book). Conversely, as demonstrated in this chapter, the decline in party membership as a share of the population is not paralleled by a corresponding decline in the functions of intra-party democracy (Loxbo 2009, 2013; Hagevi and Loxbo 2015). What is more, in this chapter, we also found that convergence at the elite level may actually lead to improved political representation. In addition, in other cases, our analysis demonstrates that elite polarisation may result in a decline in issue congruence between voters and MPs (Holmberg 2014a). The proponents of cartel party theory did not foresee any of these developments.

Finally, we arrive at the cartel party theory's gloomy predictions of democratic decline. Although one may conclude that representative democracy and the representational role of political parties are in dire need of revival, this is not – however apparent the need for improvement may be – evidence of a change for the worse since the 'golden age' of party democracy in the 1960s (Thomassen and van Ham 2015: 403; cf. Mair 2008: 218). Accordingly, in the absence of either historical comparisons or empirical evidence in the first place, we maintain that proponents of the cartel party thesis sometimes appear to base their conclusions of demo-cratic decline on idealised, and unsubstantiated, views of the democratic qualities of the past.

Indeed, some assumptions of cartel party theory are not easy to examine empirically because their outlines are rather vague and abstract, making it difficult to present concrete and testable indicators (Enroth 2014; see also Chapter 2 of this book). Moreover, with the exception of some ad hoc sug-gestions (see, for example, Katz and Mair 2009: 790), the initiators of the cartel party thesis have not explicitly or systematically delineated all the testable assumptions of their theory. Instead, much of the possible testing is based on implicit interpretations of concepts and relationships mentioned in the literature on the cartel party theory. For example, empirical studies of collaboration and collusion often take the assumptions of cartel party theory for granted at the outset. Likewise, some of the indicators we propose and find suitable may be open to criticism. In addition, even though our study presents hard data about political parties in fields in which other scholars only make assumptions, we must admit that we still lack data in large areas relating to the central claims of cartel party theory. Above all, the internal development of democracy within political parties remains a neglected area of research. It is difficult to design empirical studies of collusion. Recalling Roberto Michels's traditional theory of the evolution of party oligarchy, Katz and Mair (2002: 133) assert that inter-party collaboration is a function of the changed intentions, motives and preferences of party leaders. In line with Kitschelt (2000: 156–7), this type of change could be interpreted as a psychological process playing out among party leaders as a group. How-ever, when analysing mass data, it is not possible to gain insights into such phenomena (see Chapter 5 of this book). At its core, the concept of inter-party collusion involves secrecy between party leaders (see Chapter 2 of this book), and it goes without saying that studying secret deals is difficult if it is even feasible.

NOTES

1. As indicators of parties' shift towards the state, Katz and Mair (1995: 20, 2009: 755–6) also mention (in addition to public financing) public regulation of what political parties may and may not do; government experience; access to public sector resources (e.g. political office and investigatory resources); and privileged access to state-regulated TV and radio.

2. In a comprehensive comparative study of twenty-five party systems, Karl-Heinz Nassmacher (2009) finds no support for the view that increased election campaign costs have led to the establishment of public party financing; rather, public financing seems to have enabled campaign costs to rise. Likewise, Pierre et al. (2000: 16–18) and Nassmacher (2009: Chapter 5) find no uniform support for the view that public financing arose to replace declining membership, nor that the establishment of party financing led to membership decline.

3. However, in contrast to the cartel party theory, Koß (2011: 205–6) argues that public party financing is introduced as parties strive to realise their political pro-grammes (see also Scarrow 2004).

4. In Sweden, either the Moderates or the Social Democrats have occupied the position of main opposition party since 1979. Between 1970 and 1976, the Centre Party occupied this position.

5. In many cases, when the right-wing government lacked parliamentary support, it refrained from introducing bills to Parliament (Möller 2015: 301). This caused fewer overt conflicts in parliamentary committees between 2010 and 2014.

6. Regarding how voters perceive the left–right positions of parties, we can add Holmberg's (2014a: 111) finding that MPs perceive a small difference between them-selves and their voters on the left–right scale.

7. Over this period scholars have reported a shift from left to right among both voters and MPs (Oscarsson and Holmberg 2013: 222–4; Holmberg 2014a: 109–11), the shift being more pronounced among MPs than among voters. In the mid 1980s MPs tended to position themselves to the left of the citizens who voted for their par-ties (Esaiasson and Holmberg 1996: 102–3), but, since 2006, most MPs have tended to position themselves to the right of people who voted for their parties (Holmberg 2014a: 110–1).

8. Contrary to Katz and Mair, Holmberg argues that increased elite polarisation risks reducing the issue congruence between voters and MPs. Holmberg (1999: 121) claims that politics has 'become more polarized at the elite level, arguably provid-ing less representation and a larger gap between the performance of parties and the expectations of the people'.

9. However, the opposite assumption of Holmberg (1999: 121), that is, that increased elite polarisation and reduced issue congruence between voters and MPs will lead to greater political distrust, is not supported either. Our assessment of the relatively modest elite convergence of MPs on the subjective left–right scale is that this policy change is insufficient to explain the sharp increase in political trust occur-ring since the turn of the century. This increase in political trust among Swedish vot-ers remains a puzzle to be solved.

Chapter 4

Professional Politicians as Representatives

Magnus Hagevi

Parties are partnerships of professionals, not associations of, or for, the citizens. (Katz and Mair 1995: 22)

With this statement, the founders of cartel party theory, Richard Katz and Peter Mair, clearly declare how they view the tensions between professional politicians and citizens' democratic participation. They clarify their doubts that professional politicians can truly represent citizens: 'Recognition of party politics as a full-time career entails acceptance, and even encouragement, of a number of tendencies that earlier conceptions of democracy regarded as undesirable' (Katz and Mair 1995: 22; see also Best and Cotta 2000b). According to Katz, professional politicians become more similar to each other and develop more differences from other, non-professional politicians. Likewise, Katz (2001: 288) references Pippa Norris and claims that professional politicians come to 'share certain characteristics in terms of similar educational backgrounds, common standards for regulating, qualifying, and restricting members for entry, and recognised hierarchical pathways for career promotion' (Norris 1999: 87).

According to Katz and Mair (see also May 1973; Katz and Mair 2002, 2009), the professionalisation of politics has consequences for the establishment of cartel parties:

Most importantly, politicians feel a need to lower the costs of electoral defeat. ... One result of this is the toning down of competition. Furthermore, as politicians pursue long-term careers, they come to regard their political opponents as fellow professionals, who are driven by the same desire for job security, who confront the same kinds of pressures as themselves, and with whom business will have to be carried on over the long term. (Katz and Mair 1995: 22–3)

Actually, Katz and Mair (2009: 761) go so far as to claim that 'the party-political career path … is one of the potential causes of systemic cartelization' and that the increase in the number of professional politicians 'would also be an indicator of individual party approximation of the cartel party type' (see also Katz and Mair 1995, 2002).

Is the route via professional politics an increasingly important pathway for gaining entrance to parliament at the national level? And does that mean that professional politicians as a group are more socially homogeneous than MPs with no professional pre-parliamentary experience of politics?

In this chapter, I argue that, over the 1985–2010 period, the professionalisation of politics has changed the recruitment to parliamentary party groups and the social composition of MPs in the Swedish Parliament. I will demonstrate that the career path to becoming an MP of a parliamentary party group has changed and that pre-parliamentary professional experience of politics has become more important for legislative recruitment. As I will explore here, professional politicians are individuals whose occupation is linked, in some way, to working in politics.

However, I will refrain from calling the increase in the number of professional politicians a sign of cartelisation or, as Katz and Mair (2009) put it, of an approximation of the cartel party type. Relating the existence of professional politicians to that of the cartel party, I claim that 'politics becoming a profession' (Katz and Mair 1995: 19) is a *potential cause* of cartelisation as well as a *necessity* for its development (Borchert 2003: 7). This means that it is difficult, probably impossible, to develop cartel parties without the increased professionalisation of party politics. However, an increase in the number of professional politicians does not automatically mean that cartel parties have emerged. To distinguish cartelisation and the traits of the cartel party, I believe it is necessary to consider whether internal democracy is withering away in increasingly top-down-controlled parties and whether these parties are colluding and converging (see Chapters 3, 5 and 7 in this book). This is, however, beyond the scope of this chapter.

In the vein of cartel party theory (Katz and Mair 2009: 759; Scarrow and Gezgor 2010: 5–6), I assume that the incentives for parties to mobilise citizens as members as well as the incentives for citizens to join parties are more selective in the era of professional politics than in the earlier era of political amateurs. As Maurizio Cotta and Heinrich Best (2000: 495) put it, 'while democratization refers to an opening of the channels for political participation and legislative recruitment to more social groups, professionalization refers to the process whereby those recruited tend to … restrict access to the parliamentary arena'. The assumption of the cartel party is that parties and citizens' reasons for becoming party members during the mass party era were more general and ideological than in the era of professionalised parties (Katz and Mair 1995, 2009). In this chapter, I argue that party members receiving economic compensation for political engagement is more common in the twenty-first century than in the last decades of the twentieth century.

Furthermore, I will investigate whether the increasingly common professional political career path also means that MPs, whatever party they represent, are becoming more similar to each other (Cotta and Best 2000) in terms of the personal characteristics associated with great political resources (Verba et al. 1995). If so, as the number of MPs with extra-parliamentary professional political experience (I will define such experience below) increases in the Swedish Parliament, the composition of MPs may become more homogenous.

In the domain of cartel party research, little is known of the actual empirical effects of legislative recruitment in the proclaimed era of the cartel party (however, see Best and Cotta 2000a; Borchert and Ziess 2003). This is unfortunate because, according to the cartel party thesis, parties are allocating more of their resources to parliamentary party groups (Katz and Mair 1995, 2002); parties are being steered top-down by core party leaders in parliament (Katz and Mair 2009); and parliamentary party groups, not party members on the ground, are the main reference group for the core leaders. Also, in a cartel party, the parliamentary party groups are the main recruitment pool from which core leaders are drawn (Katz 2002). If so, this means that the composition of parliamentary party groups – as well as the characteristics of the party group members – has become more important.

Extant research into professional politicians demonstrates that, especially in proportional representation systems, the professionalisation of politics is rooted in party politics (Borchert 2003: 1; cf. Jun 2003). A growing proportion of those elected, and of those appointed by elected assemblies, is comprised of professional politicians. In many political systems, the professionalisation of politics accelerated in the 1960s and 1970s (Eliassen and Pedersen 1978; Svåsand 1991: 127; Cotta and Best 2000; Borchert and Zeiss 2003; Koß 2011). Political campaigning is often portrayed as a driving force of the professionalisation of politics (Mancini 1999; Katz and Mair 1995: 15, 2009: 758; Plasser and Plasser 2002). In addition, Swedish parties tend to be increasing the professionalisation of their political campaigns (Nord 2013), with higher costs and increased public party subsidies as a result (Gidlund 1983; Koß 2011). Political professionalisation, marked by the hiring of more party staff, is also a way to compensate for the loss of party members (Hagevi 2014b). A research group investigating unelected professional politicians at the national level in Sweden (Garsten, Rothstein and Svallfors 2015) found them to constitute a growing proportion of professional politicians in Sweden, being fairly young, highly educated and evenly distributed between the sexes. They often changed jobs and their salaries were good, but not overly so.

The researchers found that these politicians' chief motivation was to exert influence and make policy, but that they were not ambitious in seeking election.

In Sweden, as Petersson et al. (1997: 110) noted, the proportion of professional politicians increased from the local, via the regional, to the national level. The journalist Isaksson found examples in the Swedish political class of children of active politicians who had obtained prominent political appointments (Isaksson 2006). Although his information was extensive, it was gathered unsystematically and consisted largely of anecdotes. Formal scholars are doubtful whether all the signs of a political class are visible, even though Swedish MPs were more likely to be recruited from social groups of higher status by the late twentieth century than in the mid twentieth century (Hagevi 2003). However, scholars consider the social representativeness of Swedish MPs – that is, how the MPs mirror important social characteristics of voters – to be fairly good, at least by international comparison (Esaiasson and Holmberg 1996; Petersson et al. 1997; Wängnerud 1998).

Some researchers have reported an increase in the number of professional politicians among first-time MPs (Esaiasson and Holmberg 1996: 27; Hagevi 2003: 361; Öhberg 2011: 63). MPs with extra-parliamentary experience of professional politics tend to be rather ambitious about their careers and are often re-elected, resulting in advancement in their parliamentary careers (Öhberg 2011). These reports identify a constantly increasing share of professional politicians from 1906 to 1996, when a third of all MPs were already professional politicians when first elected to the Swedish Parliament. No reports on professional politicians among newly elected MPs are available for the period after 1996.

In the next section, I specify the concept of the professional politician, develop the hypotheses and preview the expected results. This is followed by a description of the data. Thereafter, I present the empirical results concerning changes in the extra-parliamentary pool of professional politicians and in the pool of party members. This is followed by presentation of the empirical data on recruitment from the pool of professional politicians to the Swedish Parliament and by my analysis of the social homogeneity of Swedish MPs. Finally, I summarise the findings and discuss their implications.

CONCEPT AND HYPOTHESES

In *Politics as a Vocation*, originally a lecture given in 1919, Max Weber articulates his famous description of professional politicians. The traditional politicians who lived only 'for politics' were being replaced by party politicians – functionaries, ombudsmen and holders of public office – who lived 'off politics'.

The distinction hence refers to a much more substantial aspect of the matter, namely, to the economic. He who strives to make politics a permanent *source of income* lives 'off' politics as a vocation, whereas he who does not do this lives 'for' politics. (Weber 2008: 162)

In this distinction, Weber made the point that professional politicians may also, in some way, still live 'for politics', but only under the economic condition of being paid a salary for political work – the decisive difference from political amateurs.

Despite such classic sociological studies, the shrinking core of party members relative to the increased governmental financing of parties has long been the main scholarly interest when studying the effects of political professionalisation (Katz and Mair 1995, 2009; Pierre, Svåsand and Widfeldt 2000; Scarrow 2000; Bonander 2009: 167–9; Biezen, Mair and Pogunkte 2012; Krouwel 2012: 230–43; Biezen and Poguntke 2014; Hagevi 2014b; Hagevi and Loxbo 2015; see Chapter 3 of this book). However, as Jens Borchert states:

Careers start much earlier than with the entry into the national parliament. Usually, they involve local politics, often they include regional or state politics. Recruitment into political office is followed by recruitment into professional political office. This is a very important step indeed, as professionalism breeds careerism. It is with professionalization that things like a guaranteed and regular income, the chance to maintain a political office, and the chance to rise within the hierarchy of offices become major considerations for political actors. (Borchert 2003: 3)

In agreement with Weber's (2008) notion of professional politicians, and with the cartel party description of professional politics as a lifelong career (Katz and Mair 1995, 2002, 2009), Borchert (2003: 7–8) asserts that professional politicians emerge when four preconditions are met:

1. A reliable source of income in politics;
2. A realistic chance of maintaining a job in politics or moving on to something more attractive;
3. Chances of career advancement either within or between political institutions; and
4. An increasing number of people making politics their profession under the requirements mentioned in points 1–3 above.

This definition of professional politicians highlights economic remuneration and the possibility of advancement in politics as a career. According to this definition, politics becomes more professional if elected politicians are employed as MPs or as *extra-parliamentary professional politicians*. In view of this definition, several independent academic scholars (Petersson et al. 1997; Hagevi 2003; Öhberg 2011) and journalists (Isaksson 2006) have reported on the professionalisation of Swedish politics. The general assumption is that MPs are fully professional politicians. However, there are various types of extra-parliamentary professional politicians in Sweden (Esaiasson and Holmberg 1996). Some of them hold public office at different governmental levels (local and regional) in Sweden but not all politicians are elected or appointed by elected assemblies. To politicians with public appointments, we can add the staff of MPs within party organisations, parliamentary party groups and government ministries. However, as in most advanced democracies, a growing political sector exists in Sweden outside political parties, in interest organisations, lobby groups, PR firms and other organisations with agendas that are at least partly political. The growth of extra-parliamentary professional politicians in Sweden is attributable to the spread of political positions offering full- or part-time employment and to the state-financed party funding that increasingly enables parties to employ professional politicians or to purchase political services (Hagevi 2000a, 2003; Garsten, Rothstein and Svallfors 2015; Hagevi and Loxbo 2015).

Borchert (2003: 3–4) further distinguishes between professional politicians and a political class using two concepts from Karl Marx, 'class in itself' and 'class for itself', the former being objectively defined while the latter constituted by actors identifying themselves as a class with common interests (Byeme 1996). According to Borchert (2003: 5), the concept of 'political class' highlights the same process of collusion and control from the core party leadership as does the cartel party theory. Therefore, to constitute 'a class for itself', professional politicians must also possess common interests, forming a cartel. In line with the cartel party thesis, such common interests would be evident if the professionalisation of politics caused the core leaders of different parties to co-operate and converge ideologically (Katz and Mair 1995, 2002, 2009; Katz 2002). According to Katz and Mair (1995, 2002, 2009), this would result from the common interest of professional politicians: job security. Facing possible electoral defeat and the loss of political appointments, professional politicians, according to the cartel party thesis, face higher stakes than do political amateurs with non-political careers to fall back on. To ensure job security, professional politicians may have a common interest in forming a cartel between parties.

In this chapter, I limit my examination to how the emergence of professional politicians, not of a political class, has changed the composition of the Swedish Parliament. Indeed, professional politicians are a *potential cause* of cartelisation as well as a *necessity* for the development of the cartel party/political class. However, I will not investigate whether professional politicians also give rise to cartel parties or a political class (on this, see Chapters 3 and 5 of this book). Following the distinction between professional politicians and political class made by Borchert, my study identifies important preconditions for the emergence of cartel parties in Sweden.

The basic recruitment pool for MPs is the members of political parties. Cartel party theory assumes that as the material incentive to respond to the interests of party grassroots declines among the party elite, citizens tend to see less value in party membership and activity (Katz and Mair 1995, 2002; Katz 2001; Blyth and Katz 2005). Based on these ideas of stronger selective incentives, I assume that the recruitment of MPs is affected by the growing importance of economic remuneration and professional politicians in local and regional politics.

Hypothesis 1: The pool of extra-parliamentary professional politicians should grow over time.

Hypothesis 1 gains support if the number of professional politicians serving at the local and regional levels is increasing over time. Hypothesis 1 is also supported if the share of party members who hold or have held political office (compensated with economic remuneration) at the municipal, regional and national levels became higher after parties' general membership rates began to decline than before this decline started.

According to cartel party theory (Katz and Mair 1995, 2002; Mair 1997; Katz 2001; Blyth and Katz 2005; cf. Panebianco 1988: 220–35; Mair 1994; Pierre and Widfeldt 1994), parties have evolved from being mass parties based in civil society to being separate, and increasingly exclusive, groups of professional politicians with membership reduced by rationalisation (see Chapter 1 of this book). As political amateurs become marginalised by the party elite, they leave the parties, resulting in lower levels of party membership (Katz and Mair 1995, 2009; Mair 2013; see Chapter 3 of this book). It seems plausible that this increasing gap between parties and civil society (Mair 2013: 43–4) should also change the social composition of party membership. I argue that this recruitment pool has changed since party membership has dropped and public party finance has increased. Susan Scarrow and Burcu Gezgor (2010: 5–6) acknowledge two reasons for such a change in party membership. First, the incentives to become a member may change when party membership shrinks, collective incentives being replaced with more selective incentives (see Hypothesis 1). Collective incentives for party membership as an act of group solidarity or a part of civic culture have declined in importance. Instead, selective incentives such as the possibility of gaining influence and economic compensation for time spent in party politics have become more important (Kirchheimer 1957; Scarrow, Webb and Farrell 2000; Lundqvist 2011). Second, the threshold for joining a party increases as the number of party members decreases. For instance, with fewer party members, it is more unusual for citizens to come across political grass-roots activists trying to recruit new members (Strömblad 2003). To pass the threshold and join a party, an individual's political resources must be stronger than when party membership was more common among citizens. According to the thorough research conducted by Verba et al. (1995; see also Hagevi and Loxbo 2015), strong political resources are usually related to male gender, middle age, higher education, middle-class occupation and ties to civil society, such as church activity.

If the use of economic incentives in exchange for political engagement is more common, and if the threshold for joining parties is higher, this may change the social composition of party membership, making it more socially exclusive. Accordingly, I will test whether the recruitment of MPs has changed due to a similar change in the composition of party membership. As selective incentives become more important, they may increase the proportion of party members with experience of public office, because such positions are economically remunerated (Hagevi 1999). Because scholars assume that the threshold for engaging in partisan politics is higher than before, the social characteristics scholars usually associate with strong political resources may become more common among party members.

Hypothesis 2: The social composition of party membership should have changed and become more exclusive with the drop in party membership rates and the increase in the number of professional politicians.

In accordance with Verba et al. (1995; cf. Öhberg 2011) and their conclusions concerning strong political resources, Hypothesis 2 gains support if the proportion of party members who are male, middle-aged, religiously active (indicating strong ties to civil society),[1] highly educated and employed in non-blue-collar jobs increases and if this change is not explained by general changes in the same social characteristics in society.

The professionalisation of politics expands the number of extra-parliamentary professional politicians. I argue that this expansion, in turn, creates an important segment interested in career advancement in political parties: professional politicians who can devote considerable time to politics and, directly or indirectly, promote their own political careers. The opportunities to form and take part in political networks, gain political knowledge, learn the political game and become an expert in an issue area – all things that enhance the competiveness of a person ambitious for a political career – tend to be far better for employed politicians than for grassroots activists who participate during their spare time. Employment as an extra-parliamentary politician is clearly beneficial in the competition for political appointments. I therefore argue that extra-parliamentary professional politicians are more often elected to parliament than are other party members. The prior employment of politicians when they are first elected to parliament provides an indication of this. Over time, it will therefore be more common for Swedish MPs already to be working as professional politicians when they are first elected to parliament.

Hypothesis 3: The proportion of MPs who are already professional politicians when they are first elected to parliament should increase as the pool of extra-parliamentary professional politicians expands.

Hypothesis 3 is supported if employment as extra-parliamentary professional politicians among first-time elected MPs increases over time. If no such change is observed, Hypothesis 3 is not confirmed.

In politics, as in all organisational recruitment, homosociality and similar norms may have an effect. I will therefore investigate whether the professionalisation of party politics increases the importance of homosociality and similar norms in the recruitment process. Homosociality originally described social (non-sexual) bonds between people of the same sex (Lipman-Blumen 1976). Accordingly, when recruiting, men tend to recruit men and women tend to recruit women (Holgersson 2003). However, similar norms may be at work concerning social class, education and family relations (cf. Hensvik et al. 2010). This means that a tendency to include similar people and reject dissimilar people may be at work, so that recruiters tend to recruit people of the same gender, educational background, occupational class and so on as themselves.

According to the mass-party ideal, political-party membership is open to all citizens, in a sort of self-recruitment process. However, the professional politician sector is not open in the same way as party membership. Although, for instance, homosociality is operative in political organisations (Niklasson 2005; Bjarnegård 2013), the process of employment changes the career prospects of party members. The expansion of the professional political sector means that the norm of self-selection is increasingly being replaced with the norm of employment, that is, of being recruited, hired and paid by an employer. In such circumstances, the employer may feel that more is at stake, at least when it comes to the economic costs of hiring. In professional politics, hiring and employment constitute an extra space for the potential influence of homosociality and other norms with similar effects to operate. Compared with open recruitment based on ideological incentives, hiring may result in the engagement of personnel with characteristics similar to those of the people responsible for recruitment (Holgersson 2003; Hensvik et al. 2010). If so, as the recruitment of MPs from the extra-parliamentary pool of professional politicians becomes more dominant, MPs will become increasingly homogenous in social characteristics over time.

An alternative explanation to homosociality and similar norms is the recruitment of relatives and friends. If so, the proportion of MPs with politically active family members ought to increase with the growth in the number of professional politicians. The increase in family connections within party politics will hereinafter be considered a kind of homogenisation of MPs' social composition.

Hypothesis 4: The social composition of MPs should become more homogenous over time as their recruitment from the growing extra-parliamentary pool of professional politicians becomes more frequent.

I measure the degree of homogeneity using the normalised Herfindahl index (H). Hypothesis 4 gains support if the normalised Herfindahl index for gender, age, churchgoing, education, occupation and family ties, respectively, indicates greater homogeneity among Swedish MPs. The more social characteristics that display greater homogeneity, the stronger the support for Hypothesis 4; the fewer social characteristics that display greater homogeneity, the weaker the support. This hypothesis also gains support if MPs with extra-parliamentary professional experience are more homogenous than other MPs.

DATA

Besides MPs, I consider as professional politicians all those employed in political posts by authorities at the local (municipal), regional and governmental (government ministry) levels, or employed by parties and interest organisations (Esaiasson and Holmberg 1996: 25). However, due to problems of data collection, even though they certainly could be regarded as professional politicians, this measure does not include persons employed in PR firms and similar enterprises working on political issues as professional politicians.

I test Hypotheses 3 and 4 using data compiled in the *Swedish Parliamentary Survey* (Wängnerud et al. 2012). These data have two sources. First, the survey collected biographical data on the age, occupation and education level of Swedish MPs from the biographical book series *Fakta om folkvalda* (*Facts about the Popularly Elected*) (1986, 1989, 1992, 1995, 1999, 2003, 2007, 2011), edited and published by the Riksdagens förvaltningskontor (the Swedish Parliament Administration). In this section, those data are supplemented with data from a study by Peter Esaiasson and Sören Holmberg about social representation in the Swedish Parliament, 1906–1961 (Esaiasson and Holmberg 1996), based on secondary data originally compiled by Lars Sköld and Arne Halvardsson (1966). Second, the *Swedish Parliamentary Survey* collected data, including questions on Swedish MPs' churchgoing and their parents' political activity, by sending mail questionnaires to MPs in the first year of their term of office, that is, in 1985 (response rate 97 per cent), 1988 (96 per cent), 1994 (97 per cent), 1998 (94 per cent), 2002 (94 per cent), 2006 (94 per cent) and 2010 (89 per cent) (Wängnerud et al. 2012: 4).[2] To test Hypothesis 1, I used data on extra-parliamentary professional politicians in Swedish municipalities and regions compiled by the Sveriges kommuner och landsting (Swedish Association of Local Authorities and Regions) (Hagevi 1999) and Statistiska Centralbyrån, SCB (Statistics Sweden), the Swedish government bureau of statistics (Järnbert and Olofsson 2012). Data on the gender, age, church-attendance, level of education and occupation of party members and the Swedish population, 1986–2012, was collected by the SOM Institute, University of Gothenburg, by annual mail questionnaires (SOM Institute 2014; Vernersdotter 2014) sent to a sample representative of the Swedish population aged 16–85 years (response rates 52–67 per cent). I used this data to test Hypothesis 2.

THE EXTRA-PARLIAMENTARY POOL OF PROFESSIONAL POLITICIANS

Most Swedish politicians are not professionals. They are citizens with 'ordinary' jobs who reserve some of their spare time for political duties. To enable political participation, there are numerous non-professional public offices at the local and regional levels. These offices however, are becoming fewer. Before a municipal reform in 1971, the number of local public offices had exceeded 187,000, including more than 125,000 local politicians; after the reform only 75,000 public offices, including 50,000 local politicians, remained. By 2011 the number of public offices had declined to about 62,600 at the local level and about 7,000 at the regional level, and the total number of politicians had declined to about 38,000 at the local level and about 4,600 at the regional level (Järnbert and Olofsson 2012: 11–19).

In 1954 only fifteen municipalities employed at least one full-time politician, whereas in 1974 about 200 of 284 municipalities employed at least one full-time politician. This increase coincided with the expansion of the welfare state, a project managed by local and regional authorities (Strömberg and Westerståhl 1984). In 2014 almost all municipalities had at least one full-time politician. In addition to this is the growth in numbers of part-time politicians. Figure 4.1 shows the number of part-time (at least

40 per cent of full time) and full-time politicians at the local and regional levels.

It appears as though Swedish local and regional politicians have become more professional than ever before. This development is correlated with decline in the numbers of both party members (see Chapter 3 of this book) and of non-professional politicians at the local and regional levels. In addition, the remuneration levels in municipalities have increased significantly and expenditure on municipalities' own political activities has increased sharply, despite significant decline in the numbers of municipal public offices and local politicians since the 1980s (Hagevi 2014b). This implies that the emphasis on so-called selective incentives – in this case, incentives directed towards individual politicians in the form of financial compensation (Panebianco 1988) – is a key strategy by which parties have sustained political commitment within their organisations (Kirchheimer 1957; Katz and Mair 2009: 759). It can be concluded that, in addition to the increased government subsidies to parties that enable them to hire more staff, raising economic remuneration for party members holding public office has become an important way to sustain political commitment within parties.

The increased focus on selective incentives corresponds to changes in the composition of party membership. While passive party members without public office have decreased, an increasing number of the remaining party members hold public office at the local, regional and national levels. In 1987, 24 per cent of party members held or had held public office in municipalities,

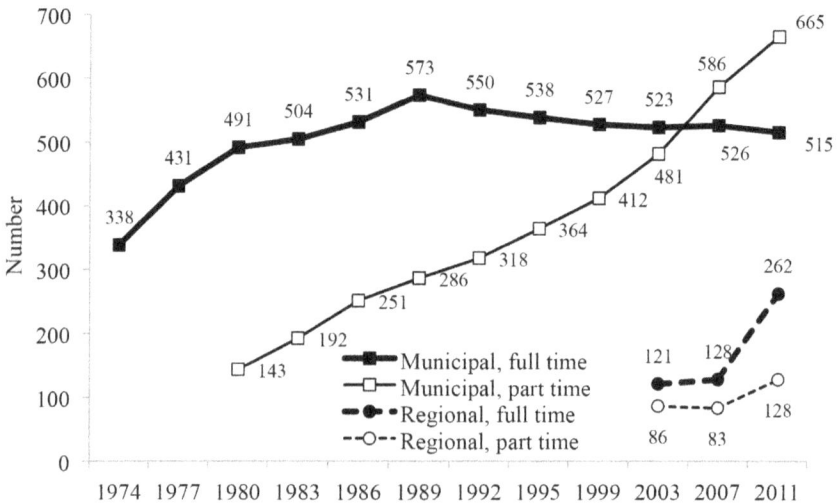

Figure 4.1   Number of full- and part-time politicians in Swedish municipalities and regions, 1974–2011. *Sources*: Hagevi (1999: 46), Järnbert and Olofsson (2012: 61, 64).

regions or the Swedish Parliament (Petersson et al. 2000: 112); by 2009, this share had reached 40 per cent (Hagevi 2010). As the level of economic remuneration in local politics has increased significantly (Hagevi 2014b), the growing number of party members with experience of service in public office indicates the increased importance of selective economic rewards for party activity. This indicates that the emphasis on selective incentives – in this case, incentives directed towards individual politicians in the form of financial compensation (Panebianco 1988) – is a key strategy by which parties sustain political commitment within their organisations. This strategy has also changed the composition of party membership, making it more common for party members to hold public office and receive economic remuneration for their political activity. This result supports Hypothesis 1.

The increase in party subsidies means that more people now have politics as their profession without being elected or without being appointed by an elected assembly. In addition, the political staffs of parliament and government offices have increased in size (Ivarsson Westerberg and Nilsson 2009; Hagevi 2014b). According to an estimate in 2000, full-time professional politicians active in political parties at the national, regional and local levels totalled about 1500 people (Hagevi 2003: 359); nothing suggests that the professionalisation of party activities has decreased since then (Kölln 2014). Also considered to be extra-parliamentary professional politicians are politically active people recruited by interest organisations, lobbyists, PR firms and companies. These people and their organisations may be hired by political parties or by any organisation with an interest in politics. A 2014 national study estimated this type of political professional as totalling about 1,500–2,500 people (Garsten, Rothstein and Svallfors 2015).[3]

Based on the empirical data and literature cited in this section, it is clear that the pool of extra-parliamentary professional politicians is a growing and important factor when examining the recruitment of MPs. Adding to this, selective incentives are becoming a more important factor in sustaining activity among party members. By this token, Hypothesis 1 – that the pool of extra-parliamentary professional politicians is growing over time – gains support.

THE POOL OF PARTY MEMBERS

According to Hypothesis 2, the social composition of party membership has changed, becoming more exclusive, since the drop in party membership rates. According to extensive research, the Swedish decline in party membership started in the mid 1980s and levelled out in the mid 2000s (Widfeldt 1997; Hagevi and Loxbo 2015; Karlsson and Lundberg 2015; see Chapter 3 of this book). If this fall in party membership means that the threshold for entering partisan politics is higher than before, the social characteristics that Verba et al. (1995) associated with strong political resources – being male, middle-aged, religiously active (indicating civil society resources), highly educated and with middle-class employment – may become more common among party members. Tables 4.1 through 4.5 compare these characteristics among Swedish MPs, party members and other citizens, 1986–2012, across time intervals corresponding to parliamentary terms. The time series starts when the general party membership decline began in the mid 1980s. Tables 4.1, 4.3 and 4.4 indicate strong political resources in terms of the percentage of males, regular churchgoers and university education. Table 4.2 compares mean ages; a high mean age, also indicating strong political resources (Verba et al. 1995).[4] Table 4.5 presents the percentage who are blue-collar workers, indicating weak political resources.

I will comment on party members first, returning to Swedish MPs later. From the first period to the last, the proportion of university-educated members and their mean age has increased while the proportion of regular church-goers and blue-collar workers has decreased. The ratio of men to women is now at the same level as before the membership decline (although the percentage of men increased at the beginning of the decline, it returned to its original level in the last period).

Some of these changes mirror similar changes in society at large, as can be seen if we compare the differences in percentages between MPs and the general population over time. Smaller differences indicate that party members better mirror the population; larger differences that they do not mirror the population so well. If the differences in percentages increase over time, this indicates a more exclusive membership body (except for the share of blue-collar workers, where the opposite is the case). The differences in percentages become smaller for blue-collar workers as well as for the mean age of members. For the percentages of males and the university-educated, the differences become larger; the difference in percentage of churchgoers does not significantly change. Concerning the proportion of males, however, the measured change in the difference in percentages is partly due to a decline in the numbers of men in the population, from 50 per cent in the first period (1986–1987) to 47 per cent in the last period (2010–2012). Official government records, however, indicate no such trend in the proportion of males in the general population (SCB 2015). To draw a valid conclusion, we must consider that the percentage difference in the proportion of men among party members and the remaining population may be somewhat exaggerated. In all, this means that the increased proportion of university-educated members and the decreased proportion of blue-collar workers indicate a more exclusive body of party members; the changes in the proportions of males and churchgoers and in the mean age do not indicate any such increased

Table 4.1 Males Among Swedish MPs, Party Members and Remaining Population, 1986–2012 (%, N/n in parentheses)

	MPs	Party Members	Population	Difference, MPs–Population	Difference, Party Members–Population
1986–7	68 (349)	51 (405)	50 (2,789)	+18*	+1
1988–90	62 (349)	52 (395)	49 (2,548)	+13*	+3
1991–3	67 (349)	60 (602)	50 (4,567)	+17*	+10*
1994–7	59 (349)	59 (514)	49 (4,517)	+10*	+10*
1998–2001	57 (349)	57 (1,101)	49 (12,667)	+8*	+8*
2002–5	55 (349)	55 (1,111)	47 (12,794)	+8*	+8*
2006–9	53 (349)	56 (1,054)	47 (13,532)	+6*	+9*
2010–12	54 (349)	52 (993)	47 (14,535)	+7*	+5*

Source: Data are from the SOM Institute (2014) and the *Swedish Parliamentary Survey* (Wängnerud et al. 2012); *$p < 0.05$.

Table 4.2 Ages of Swedish MPs, Party Members and Remaining Population, 1986–2012 (Mean, N/n in Parentheses)

	MPs	Party Members	Population	Difference, MPs–Population	Difference, Party Members–Population
1986–7	50 (349)	48 (405)	41 (2,384)	+9*	+7*
1988–90	50 (348)	49 (385)	42 (2,502)	+8*	+6*
1991–3		50 (591)	43 (4,504)		+7*
1994–7	48 (349)	52 (511)	44 (4,494)	+4*	+8*
1998–2001	49 (349)	54 (1,101)	46 (12,654)	+3*	+8*
2002–5	48 (347)	54 (1,110)	7 (12,779)	+1	+7*
2006–9	48 (346)	54 (1,050)	49 (13,508)	–1*	+5*
2010–12	47 (349)	55 (991)	50 (14,519)	–3*	+5*

Source: Data are from the SOM Institute (2014) and the *Swedish Parliamentary Survey* (Wängnerud et al. 2012); * $p < 0.05$.

Table 4.3 Regular Churchgoers Among Swedish MPs, Party Members and Remaining Population, 1986–2012 (%, N/n in Parentheses)

	MPs	Party Members	Population	Difference, MPs–Population	Difference, Party Members–Population
1986–7	16 (335)				
1988–90	12 (333)	21 (385)	10 (2,494)	+2	+11*
1991–3		21 (595)	9 (4,495)		+12*
1994–7	14 (333)	22 (508)	9 (4,431)	+5*	+13*
1998–2001	18 (325)	22 (1,065)	9 (12,277)	+9*	+13*
2002–5	17 (323)	18 (656)	8 (7,900)	+9*	+10*
2006–9	12 (324)	18 (807)	7 (10,457)	+5*	+11*
2010–12	10 (307)	16 (603)	7 (8,520)	+3	+9*

Note: 'Regular' means at least once a month.
Source: Data are from the SOM Institute (2014) and the *Swedish Parliamentary Survey* (Wängnerud et al. 2012); *$p < 0.05$.

Table 4.4 University Education Among Swedish MPs, Party Members and Remaining Population, 1986–2012 (%, N/n in Parentheses)

	MPs	Party Members	Population	Difference, MPs–Population	Difference, Party Members–Population
1986–7	46 (322)	11 (186)	16 (1,138)	+30*	−5
1988–90	48 (333)	19 (395)	19 (2,504)	+29*	0
1991–3	55 (321)	21 (588)	19 (4,471)	+36*	+2
1994–7	62 (320)	25 (498)	24 (4,384)	+38*	+1
1998–2001	67 (316)	30 (1,084)	28 (12,430)	+39*	+2
2002–5	67 (316)	29 (1,090)	30 (12,630)	+37*	−1
2006–9	72 (323)	33 (1,037)	33 (13,355)	+39*	0
2010–12	75 (310)	41 (961)	36 (14,171)	+39*	+5*

Source: Data are from the SOM Institute (2014) and the *Swedish Parliamentary Survey* (Wängnerud et al. 2012); *p < 0.05.

Table 4.5 Blue-Collar Workers Among Swedish MPs, Party Members and Remaining Population, 1986–2012 (%, N/n in Parentheses)

	MPs	Party Members	Population	Difference, MPs–Population	Difference, Party Members–Population
1986–7	9 (347)	45 (372)	48 (2,210)	−36*	−3
1988–90	8 (331)	34 (371)	47 (2,266)	−39*	−13*
1991–3	5 (330)	38 (556)	47 (4,093)	−42*	−9*
1994–7	6 (329)	42 (461)	45 (4,013)	−39*	−3
1998–2001	7 (344)	33 (1,027)	43 (11,527)	−36*	−10*
2002–5	7 (340)	34 (1,007)	43 (11,323)	−36*	−9*
2006–9	6 (338)	34 (970)	42 (12,210)	−36*	−8*
2010–12	6 (343)	33 (911)	42 (13,224)	−36*	−9*

Source: Data are from the SOM Institute (2014) and the *Swedish Parliamentary Survey* (Wängnerud et al. 2012); *p < 0.05.

exclusivity. However, these changes in the difference in percentages are rather small.

Among Swedish MPs, the mean age and percentages of males and church-goers have all decreased over the study period. While the proportion of blue-collar workers has been consistently low, that of university-educated MPs has increased dramatically. None of the changes in terms of age or proportions of males, churchgoers and blue-collar workers indicates a more exclusive social representation of MPs. Except for churchgoing, the changes among MPs do not follow either trends among party members or, when it comes to age and the proportion of blue-collar workers, general social trends. None of these indicators supports Hypothesis 2.

The increased percentage of university-educated MPs (+29 percentage points between the first and the last periods) mirrors the same increase among party members (+30 percentage points). The level of education has also increased among the remaining population, but to a lesser extent (+20 percentage points). Most of the increase in the share of university-educated MPs can be explained by the general social trend but some can be attributed to more exclusive recruitment of party members. In this respect, Hypothesis 2 – that the composition of party membership has changed and become more exclusive since the decline in party membership rates, implying that the recruitment of MPs has also become more exclusive – is only very weakly supported.

RECRUITMENT FROM THE POOL OF PROFESSIONAL POLITICIANS

At the national level, most elected professional politicians are found in the Swedish Parliament. It would also be possible to include the Swedish delegation to the European Parliament, though I have not done so here. The Swedish Parliament has long been a bastion of professional politicians. After the democratic breakthrough in 1918, the Swedish Parliament recognised that the enlarged franchise meant that new social classes should be able to enter parliament and so it was important that MPs were remunerated sufficiently well to enable this (Hagevi 2003). However, the extra-parliamentary build-up of professional politicians has made 'politician' a possible occupation for many non-MPs. As already argued, entering the growing, but still very exclusive, pool of extra-parliamentary professional politicians is probably an important step towards being elected as an MP. If extra-parliamentary professional politicians had an advantage in internal nominations within political parties, the share of MPs who were professional politicians before being elected to parliament would increase over time. Figure 4.2 shows the percentages of Swedish MPs who were professional politicians before being elected to parliament.

The share of MPs with pre-parliamentary professional political experience has increased over the years. This supports Hypothesis 3, that the proportion of MPs who are already professional politicians when first elected to parliament increases as the pool of extra-parliamentary professional politicians expands. Actually, in 2010, every second MP was already a politician by profession when elected to the Swedish Parliament. The significant pre-parliamentary experience of professional politics indicates that politics has become a lifetime career. Obviously, it is increasingly advantageous to be a professional politician if one wants to be a Swedish MP. Even though the pool of extra-parliamentary professional politicians is small compared with the number of party members with no such experience, when this pool expands, so also does the proportion of MPs with extra-parliamentary experience of being professional politicians.

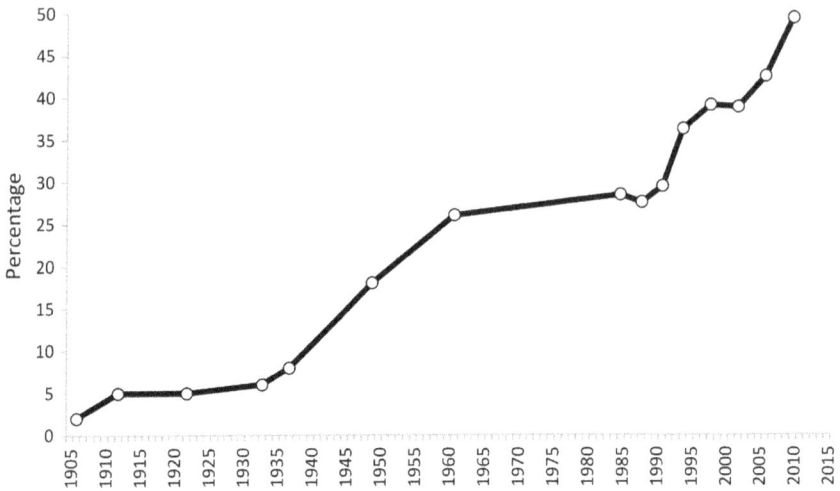

Figure 4.2 Previous occupation as professional politician when first elected as member of Swedish Parliament, 1906–2010 (%). *Source*: Data are from the *Swedish Parliamentary Survey* (Wängnerud et al. 2012).

It is also possible to link the recruitment of MPs from the pool of extra-parliamentary professional politicians to other changes. Such recruitment has expanded in two waves. The first expansion was during the emergence of the welfare state after World War II through until the 1960s. As mentioned earlier, many welfare state issues are handled by local and regional authorities in Sweden. To manage the growing administration of the welfare state, the Swedish Parliament initiated several municipal amalgamations, creating larger units that could support the rising tax burden caused by expanded public services. These larger municipalities and their expanding administrations began the increase in the numbers of professional politicians in local and regional politics (Strömberg and Westerståhl 1984). The second wave has occurred since 1990, after the general drop in party membership in Sweden (see Chapter 3 of this book). As already mentioned, parties compensated for the decline in their membership by professionalising politics. These two waves of extra-parliamentary political professionalisation seem to have affected the recruitment of MPs, with more of them already tending to be professional politicians when they first enter parliament.

A HOMOGENOUS SWEDISH PARLIAMENT?

According to Hypothesis 4, the composition of MPs will become more homogenous over time as recruitment from the growing extra-parliamentary pool of professional politicians increases. This hypothesis gains support if the normalised Herfindahl index (H) indicates greater homogeneity in terms of gender, age, churchgoing, education, occupation and family ties among Swedish MPs over time. In addition, the more of these characteristics that display greater homogeneity, the stronger the support for Hypothesis 4. Figure 4.3 shows the measured homogeneity of Swedish MPs, 1985–2010.

As time has passed, Swedish MPs have tended to become more homogenous in terms of their level of education and previous professions. Therefore, in this regard, Hypothesis 4 is supported. Concerning political heritage in the form of having at least one politically active parent, on first glance Figure 4.3 indicates that Swedish MPs seem to have become more homogenous over time. However, contrary to what is expected by Hypothesis 4, the tendency over time is not for more Swedish MPs to have at least one politically active parent but the opposite: *fewer* MPs now have a political legacy from a politically active parent. Swedish MPs have become less homogenous in terms of gender and age, while no particular tendency is evident in churchgoing. In this part of the analysis, support for Hypothesis 4 is limited to education and profession.

While an increasing number of Swedish MPs were already professional politicians before winning their first parliamentary seat, some first-time

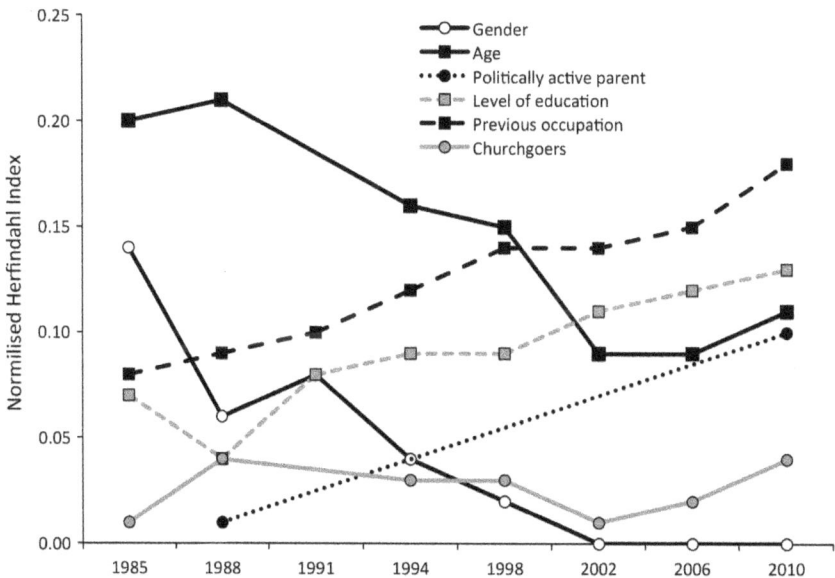

Figure 4.3   Degree of homogeneity among Swedish MPs, 1985–2010, in gender, age, political heritage, level of education, previous occupation and churchgoing (normalised Herfindahl index, H). *Source:* Data are from the *Swedish Parliamentary Survey* (Wängnerud et al. 2012); for detailed data, see Appendix 1.

Table 4.6   Degree of Homogeneity Among Swedish MPs According to Previous Occupation: Extra-Parliamentary Political Professionals (P) and Other (O) (% and Normalised Herfindahl Index, H)

	1985 P	1985 O	1988 P	1988 O	1991 P	1991 O	1994 P	1994 O	1998 P	1998 O	2002 P	2002 O	2006 P	2006 O	2010 P	2010 O
Gender																
Male	72	68	65	62	73	65	67	56	66	51	60	51	57	50	56	52
Female	28	32	35	38	27	35	33	44	34	49	40	49	43	50	44	48
Sum of per cent	100	100	100	100	100	100	100	100	100	100	100	100	100	100	100	100
N	99	248	91	240	97	233	119	210	134	210	132	208	143	194	169	174
H	0.19	0.13	0.08	0.06	0.21	0.08	0.12	0.02	0.10	0.00	0.04	0.00	0.02	0.00	0.02	0.00
Age																
Mean	48	51	48	51			47	50	48	50	47	48	46	49	44	49
18–40 years	18	8	14	9			23	14	22	17	28	25	31	22	37	21
41–50 years	44	38	51	36			40	32	32	31	31	24	33	32	30	30
51–65 years	37	52	35	54			37	53	45	48	40	50	35	42	33	45
66+ years	0	2	0	2			0	1	1	4	1	1	1	4	0	4
Sum of per cent	99	100	100	101			100	100	100	100	100	100	100	100	100	100
N	99	248	91	240			119	210	134	210	131	208	143	194	169	174
H	0.15	0.23	0.20	0.24			0.13	0.20	0.13	0.15	0.11	0.16	0.11	0.11	0.12	0.12
Churchgoing																
Regularly	12	18	10	12			9	16	12	22	14	20	9	14	8	13
Now and then	28	27	27	29			28	26	31	25	31	24	23	28	27	29
Seldom	32	32	41	32			42	35	33	37	27	35	30	31	24	32
Never	29	23	22	27			21	23	24	16	28	21	38	27	41	26
Sum of per cent	101	100	100	100			100	100	100	100	100	100	100	100	100	100
N	94	240	88	228			113	220	123	197	121	195	135	181	147	155
H	0.04	0.01	0.07	0.03			0.08	0.03	0.04	0.03	0.03	0.01	0.07	0.03	0.07	0.03

Level of education														
University degree	23	43	32	47	31	48	36	48	30	51	30	48	42	48
University studies	32	7	22	10	28	14	30	19	37	19	36	27	30	29
High school diploma	16	26	26	30	27	29	25	26	31	27	31	23	26	22
Elementary school	29	24	20	13	14	9	8	7	2	3	2	2	2	1
Sum of per cent	100	100	100	100	100	100	100	100	100	100	100	100	100	100
N	86	229	88	217	111	193	122	195	116	195	132	184	145	162
H	0.01	0.09	0.01	0.12	0.03	0.12	0.05	0.12	0.09	0.16	0.09	0.15	0.11	0.15
Political heritage														
Politically active parent	44	47											68	65
No politically active parent	56	53											32	35
Sum of per cent	100	100											100	100
N	88	226											149	156
H	0.02	0.00											0.12	0.08

Source: Data are from the *Swedish Parliamentary Survey* (Wängnerud et al. 2012); empty cells indicate unavailable data.

elected MPs had non-political prior occupations. According to Hypothesis 4, the expansion of professional politicians outside parliament should lead to more homogenous MPs. This should also mean that MPs with extra-parliamentary professional political experience should display greater homogeneity than other MPs. Table 4.6 compares the homogeneity of MPs having extra-parliamentary political experience with that of other MPs, in terms of gender, age, churchgoing, level of education and political heritage in the form of at least one politically active parent.

Based on the data presented in Table 4.6, the essential conclusion must be that there is very little support for the claim that pre-parliamentary experience of professional politics leads to a more homogenous body of MPs. Concerning age and level of education, MPs without extra-parliamentary experience of professional politics are more homogenous than MPs with such experience. When it comes to churchgoing and political heritage, MPs with extra-parliamentary experience of professional politics are somewhat more homogenous than other MPs. However, the greater homogeneity of MPs with pre-parliamentary professional political experience is based on characteristics associated with weak political resources, not strong ones. MPs with extra-parliamentary experience of professional politics are somewhat less involved in religious civil society and relatively often have parents who were not active in politics. Hypothesis 4 only gains support in terms of gender, as MPs with pre-parliamentary experience of professional politics tend to be male. However, this homosociality decreases over time and is negligible at the end of the investigation period.

CONCLUSION

Is the professional politics route an increasingly important pathway to gain entrance to parliament at the national level? Yes, according to this study, it is. Does that mean that professional politicians as a group are more socially homogeneous than MPs without professional pre-parliamentary political careers? No, not according to this study.

As previously noted in this chapter, hardly any of the devastating political changes that cartel party theory associates with the increase of professional politicians (Katz and Mair 1995, 2009) can be observed in the Swedish case, except for the growing pool of professional politicians itself. As expected by cartel party theory (Katz and Mair 1995, 2002, 2009; Katz 2002), both the number and the proportion of professional politicians have increased in modern Swedish politics. One indicator of such professionalisation is the increased share of local and regional political office-holders (receiving financial remuneration) among party members. The pool of extra-parliamentary professional politicians has grown, as has the number of Swedish MPs with pre-parliamentary experience of professional politics. These results support Hypotheses 1 and 3 of this study.

Hypothesis 2 is based on the proposition, as described by cartel party theory, that the gap between civil society and the parties will widen as professional politicians in party elites marginalise amateur party members, causing them to leave parties (Mair 1997; Katz and Mair 1995, 2002; Katz 2001; Blyth and Katz 2005; cf. Mair 1994). Hypothesis 2 expected that, since this exodus, the composition of party membership will have become more exclusive over time, in turn making the recruitment of MPs more exclusive. However, the study found mixed results for Hypothesis 2. Even though the social composition of party membership has become more exclusive according to some indicators (level of education and proportion of blue-collar workers), only the high level of education is matched by the same tendency among Swedish MPs, and then only partly. Based on this, the change in the social composition of party membership can be said to have little to do with the change in the social composition of Swedish MPs, with one exception: the increased economic incentives for party activity.

Hypothesis 4 expected that the increase in the number of professional politicians outside parliament would lead to a more homogenous social composition of MPs over time. In terms of previous occupation and level of education, Swedish MPs display greater homogeneity, which supports Hypothesis 4. Increasingly, Swedish MPs have higher education and were professional politicians before winning their first parliamentary seat. The tendency towards a higher level of education is not exclusive to Swedish MPs but can largely, though not totally, be explained by the general educational development of Swedish society. No other support could be found for Hypothesis 4. When comparing MPs with and without pre-parliamentary professional political experience, the results offer very little support for the claim that MPs with experience as extra-parliamentary professional politicians are more homogenous than other MPs.

The number of people with experience of working as extra-parliamentary professional politicians has increased in Swedish society and in the Swedish Parliament. Extra-parliamentary professional politics is a close-to-essential career path for politicians eventually wanting to win a parliamentary seat. About half of Swedish MPs were already professional politicians when they won their first parliamentary seat. This means that the previous employment of Swedish MPs has become more homogenous, because MPs are, increasingly, long-term professional politicians. However, with this exception, hardly any increased homogenisation is discernible among Swedish MPs, at least, not that can be attributed to political professionalisation. Instead, there are signs of reduced homogenisation and increased social representativeness.

Fewer current MPs, for instance, have parents who were politically active and more MPs are now women, indicating no increased gap between civil society and parliamentary party groups (cf. Katz and Mair 1995, 2009). The main conclusion of the present study is that the increase in the number of professional politicians has had few measurable effects. Therefore, the increased number of professional politicians is not necessarily a sign of the establishment of cartel parties or of the cartelisation of the party system in Swedish politics.

Is the love of money not the root of all evil? Do my conclusions mean that professional politics have not harmed parliamentary representation in any way? Such a conclusion is premature. Still, there are plenty of possible scenarios concerning the homogeneity of MPs and the risk of the parliamentary misrepresentation of citizens that scholars need to address and that I have not touched on here. I will restrict myself to mentioning two important issues for future research. The first concerns parliamentary representation of citizens' opinions (see Chapter 3 of this book). Has the professionalisation of political careers affected parliamentary representation of citizens' opinions? Second, is it possible that the prestige and career opportunities for professional politicians differ between parties? These issues need to be addressed in order to further examine the claims of cartel party theory about professional politicians.

APPENDIX

Table A 4.1 Social Characteristics of Swedish MPs, 1985–2010 (% and normalised Herfindahl index, H)

	1985	1988	1991	1994	1998	2002	2006	2010
Gender								
Male	68	62	67	59	57	45	47	46
Female	32	38	33	41	43	55	53	54
Sum of per cent	100	100	100	100	100	100	100	100
N	349	349	349	349	349	349	349	349
Herfindahl index	0.14	0.06	0.08	0.04	0.02	0.00	0.00	0.00
Age								
18–40 years	11	10		17	18	26	26	29
41–50 years	39	40		35	31	32	32	30
51–65 years	48	49		47	48	39	39	39
66+ years	2	1		1	2	1	3	2
Sum of per cent	100	100		100	100	100	100	100
N	349	348		349	349	347	346	349
Herfindahl index	0.20	0.21		0.16	0.15	0.09	0.09	0.11
Mean	*50*	*50*		*48*	*49*	*48*	*48*	*47*

	1985	1988	1991	1994	1998	2002	2006	2010
Churchgoing								
Regularly	16	12		14	18	17	12	10
Now and then	27	28		26	28	28	26	29
Seldom	32	35		37	35	31	31	27
Never	25	25		23	19	24	31	34
Sum of per cent	100	100		100	100	100	100	100
N	335	333		333	325	323	324	307
Herfindahl index	0.01	0.04		0.03	0.03	0.01	0.02	0.04
Level of education								
University degree	37	37	42	43	43	44	41	45
University studies	9	11	13	19	24	23	31	30
High school diploma	28	27	30	29	26	29	27	24
Elementary school	27	24	15	11	7	3	2	1
Sum of per cent	100	100	100	100	100	100	100	100
N	322	333	321	320	316	316	323	310
Herfindahl index	0.07	0.04	0.08	0.09	0.09	0.11	0.12	0.13
Political heritage								
Politically active parent		46						34
No politically active parent		54						66
Sum of per cent		100						100
N		330						309
Herfindahl index		0.01						0.10
Previous occupation								
Professional politician	28	27	29	36	39	39	42	49
White collar, senior management	27	26	29	24	18	19	17	16
White collar, mid and lower-level management	25	30	27	27	30	30	28	21
Blue collar	9	8	5	6	7	7	6	6
Small businessperson/ farmer	11	8	8	6	3	3	3	3
Other	0	0	0	0	2	2	4	5
Sum of per cent	100	100	100	100	100	100	100	100
N	347	331	330	329	344	340	337	343
Herfindahl index	0.08	0.09	0.10	0.12	0.14	0.14	0.15	0.18

Source: Data are from the *Swedish Parliamentary Survey* (Wängnerud et al. 2012); empty cells indicate unavailable data. Table shows normalised Herfindahl index.

NOTES

1. Verba et al. (1995) use churchgoing as an indicator of civil society involvement. In the Swedish context, churchgoing has more limited application as an indicator of individual engagement in civil society than in the United States (Hagevi 2012). However, churchgoing is a measure that has been repeatedly used in the *Swedish Parliamentary Survey* over time (Wängnerud et al. 2012) and is, even in the Swedish context, an indicator of civil society involvement.

2. Note that the *Swedish Parliamentary Survey* collected no data by questionnaire during the 1991–1994 term of office (Wängnerud et al. 2012).

3. In this estimate, persons at the regional and local levels who are employed in professional politics outside political parties and with no public office, as well as ombudspersons in parties and interest organisations at local and regional levels, remain uncounted.

4. Note that the estimates in Tables 4.1 through 4.5 concern the pool of party members, not how individual parties are socio-economically representative of their voters (Hagevi and Loxbo 2015).

Chapter 5

Cartelisation and Europeanisation?

Karl Loxbo

One of the main assumptions of the revised cartel party theory (Katz and Mair 2009) is that by transferring central political concerns to non-partisan institutions, Europeanisation[1] enables party elites to collude over an increasingly limited policy agenda (see also Blyth and Katz 2005; Mair 2007, 2013). In fact, one of the two main architects of the cartel party thesis, Peter Mair, argues that depoliticisation in the wake of European integration is not primarily a result of transformations beyond the control of policy-makers but rather of a deliberate strategy 'by political elites who are reluctant to have their hands tied by the constraints of popular democracy' (Mair 2007: 8, 2013: 115–32; cf. Bartolini 2005: 246). Still, while European integration has been widely predicted to depoliticise national policy-making (e.g. Bartolini 2005: 405; Schmidt 2006: 772; Ladrech 2002, 2007; Scharpf 2010: 239), the exact opposite expectation also holds. Specifically, in contrast to the cartel party theory, a growing body of research expects Europeanisation to become the object of increased politicisation in the national arena (e.g. Hix 1999; Kriesi et al. 2008; Hooghe and Marks 2009; Hurrelmann et al. 2013; Hutter and Grande 2014).

Whereas the cartel party theory and proponents of the 'depoliticisation hypothesis' focus on party elites, advocates of the rival 'politicisation hypothesis' instead emphasise public debates and opinion trends in the electorate (e.g. Hurrelmann et al. 2013; cf. Green-Pedersen 2012). However, while the two competing hypotheses concern diverse aspects of politics, a crucially important political arena for evaluating both of these rival claims about the fate of European democracy – arguably the most important of all – remains, somewhat surprisingly, unexplored. Although policy-making in national parliaments is obviously fundamental to the degree of politicisation in a parliamentary regime, no systematic studies have addressed the question of how Europeanisation has affected the relationship between government and opposition in the parliamentary arena over time (cf. Mair 2007; Helms 2008; Auel and Christiansen 2015).[2]

This chapter seeks to fill this gap in previous research by testing one of the main postulates of the cartel party thesis – that is, the depoliticisation hypothesis – and the rival hypothesis of politicisation, using unique data from the Swedish Parliament for a forty-four-year period between 1970 and 2014. Accordingly, rather than using indirect measures such as electoral manifestos (Toshkov 2011), media reports (Hutter and Grande 2014) or the rhetoric of politically marginalised populist right-wing parties (Kriesi et al. 2008), this chapter contributes to the literature by scrutinising direct measures of parliamentary decision-making (cf. Mair 2007, 2013). The research strategy in the chapter is threefold. First, drawing on an extensive database of parliamentary decision-making between 1970 and 2014, I compare patterns of co-operation and conflict between parties in government and the opposition in policy areas pertaining to domestic issues, on the one hand, and to Europeanised and globalised issues, on the other (cf. Loxbo and Sjölin 2016). Second, to evaluate the recurring claim that European Union affairs are virtually devoid of national opposition (Bartolini 2005: 246–7; Mair 2007: 8, 2013: 115), a separate study concerns debates in the Swedish European Union (EU) Affairs Committee between 1995 (when Sweden joined the EU) and 2012. Third, to explore the motives and preferences of policy-makers, I interviewed the group leaders of all parties in parliament, along with central actors in the EU Affairs Committee, during the 2010–14 parliamentary term.

The remainder of this chapter is structured as follows. In the next section, I discuss the concepts of politicisation and depoliticisation. Thereafter, the main assumptions of the cartel party theory are reviewed and the overall hypothesis of depoliticisation is split into two sub-hypotheses specifically concerning the relationship between the government and the opposition. Thereafter, data and empirical measures are presented. Subsequently, the hypotheses are tested and the main findings from the interviews are discussed. In the last section of the chapter, I summarise the conclusions and discuss their implications for the cartel party thesis and the rival predictions of increased or decreased politicisation.

THE CONCEPTS OF POLITICISATION/DEPOLITICISATION AND THE CARTEL PARTY THEORY

Following Elmer E. Schattschneider's (1960) widely cited definition, the degree of politicisation of a political issue can be understood to depend on the visibility, intensity and scope of the conflicts surrounding it. Whereas

Schattschneider views politics as synonymous with conflict to begin with, depoliticisation occurs when certain conflicts become progressively less visible and intense until, ultimately, their scope is so limited that they disappear from the political agenda altogether. Moreover, in Schattschneider's view, the politicisation or depoliticisation of political conflicts crucially depends on the strategies of powerful actors. As he famously put it (1960: 69), 'some issues are organised into politics, while others are organised out'.

In consonance with Schattschneider's theory, the cartel party theory – as opposed to the literature on the politicisation of Europe[3] – is completely devoted to political elites. More precisely, the degree to which conflicts are politicised, or depoliticised, does not depend on voter demand but on party strategies (cf. Kriesi et al. 2008: 10). In the following, I discuss how the cartel party theory depicts the impact of Europeanisation and, against the background of the overall depoliticisation hypothesis, I derive two sub-hypotheses to be tested in this chapter. While these hypotheses are phrased in accordance with the main assumptions of the cartel party theory, I argue that their inverted meanings are in line with the rival politicisation hypothesis.

Why Europeanisation is Hypothesised to Foster Depoliticisation

Why do proponents of the cartel party theory believe that external transformations such as globalisation and European integration result in a common desire among party elites to depoliticise national politics? The answer is threefold.

First, because Member States must adopt the *acquis*,[4] European integration is a major reason why nation-states have to converge to common policy standards. As national politics is Europeanised, proponents of the cartel party theory argue that the policy alternatives supplied by parties become increasingly limited (Katz and Mair 2009: 756–8; Mair 2013: 155). Second, as decision-making is delegated to non-partisan institutions at the supranational level, the range and repertoire of the existing policy instruments available to parties – for example, macro-economic instruments – become increasingly limited (Mair 2007: 13, 2013: 155). As a result of these two transformations, Bartolini (2005: 243) concludes that 'the theory suggesting that the nation-state has ceased to be an efficient economic manager ... applies very well to the set of European small- and medium-sized states'. Drawing on similar observations, Katz and Mair (2009: 754) argue that the importance of the left–right ideological divide has effectively been undermined as a result of European integration. Third, and most importantly, the cartel party theory presupposes that waning competition between the left and the right is, in fact, in line with the preferences of party elites in the first place (Mair 2007: 10–15, 2013: 132–7). Specifically, Mair (2013: 132) argues that the real problem facing political elites is not their limited capacity to satisfy the demands of their constituencies but that 'the mechanisms of popular democracy are increasingly incompatible with the intentions of policy-makers'. Along these lines, a fundamental assumption of the cartel party theory is that supranational institutions in Europe were intentionally constructed to be non-partisan, and non-democratic, to free European political elites from the costly demands of their national constituencies (Bartolini 2005: 246; Blyth and Katz 2005). This can also be expressed as: depoliticisation is seen as a result of conscious efforts of party elites to collude, in order to enable electorally unpopular policies and to reduce the electoral stakes when pursuing them (Blyth and Katz 2005: 47; Katz and Mair 2009: 754).

Politicisation or Depoliticisation in the Parliamentary Arena?

It is important to point out that my focus on opposition in the parliamentary arena implies a rather narrow conceptualisation of politicisation. More specifically, whereas politicisation is defined as intense and visible conflict involving a much wider range of actors than just political parties (Hutter and Grande 2014), 'parliamentary politicisation' refers specifically to constitutionally regulated conflicts between the parties represented in parliament (Sjöblom 1968: 113). While parliamentary conflicts may indeed be intense, they are not always visible to the public and their scope may be quite limited. Even so, regardless of their short-term visibility and scope, the intensity of conflicts in the parliamentary arena is eventually bound to affect the political system at large. Making a similar argument in the 1950s, Otto Kirchheimer warned that increased consensus between the government and the opposition in Western European parliaments was eventually bound to hollow out representative democracy (1957: 136, 144, 147–8, 155–6). Similarly, Robert Dahl observed a growing elite consensus – he referred to it as 'a mounting surplus of consensus' (Dahl 1966b: 397) – and argued that it would eventually bring an end to 'responsible opposition'. As seen above, virtually the same dystopian forecasts reappear in the modern-day cartel party thesis (e.g. Mair 2007; Katz and Mair 2009: 755). While this theory does not focus explicitly on the government–opposition dynamic in parliament (cf. Mair 2007), one of its key assumptions is – in line with the work of Kirchheimer and Dahl – that elite consensus is on the rise, while opposition– that is, policy competition between mainstream parties[5] – is in a state of dramatic decline (Katz and Mair 1995: 22; 2009: 756). When testing the rival hypotheses of depoliticisation *versus* politicisation in the parliamentary arena, therefore, I argue that the intensity of overall parliamentary conflict is reflected by the degree of competition and co-operation in the relations between the government and the opposition. Moreover, as seen above, the proponents of the cartel party thesis add a new twist to Kirchheimer's and Dahl's predictions of democratic decline: the demise of opposition in national parliaments is accelerated, and ultimately enabled, by Europeanisation (Mair 2007, 2013). If the overall prediction of depoliticisation in the wake of Europeanisation is correct, I argue that the following hypothesis should hold true:

Hypothesis 1: Depoliticisation of parliamentary decision-making:
Over time, we should observe an increasing rate of consensual agreement and a decreasing rate of policy conflict in parliamentary decision-making in general and in policy areas relevant to EU affairs in particular.

If Hypothesis 1 is confirmed, the basic causal logic proposed by the cartel party theory is consistent with empirical evidence on the evolution of actual policy-making. Indeed, if this proves to be the case, it would provide the first systematic support of the theory since Katz and Mair (1995) launched it in the mid 1990s. However, if the observed trend is the reverse, I argue that this would suggest that empirical evidence is more in line with the rival, politicisation hypothesis (e.g. Hutter and Grande 2014).

In addition, while Europeanisation is believed to foster depoliticisation in general, Mair (2007: 12, 2013: 115) argues that the process of European integration in and of itself is characterised by a 'remarkable depoliticisation' (cf. Bartolini 2005: 320). Indeed, collusion between elites largely defines the concept of cartelisation to begin with (Blyth and Katz 2005). The second hypothesis therefore concerns the intentions of contemporary policy-makers, as follows:

Hypothesis 2: Elite collusion on depoliticisation:
Policy-makers in government and in opposition should essentially agree on the current state of power-sharing between nation-states and the EU, whereas partisan disagreements between the left and the right on policy instruments should be non-existent.

If Hypothesis 2 is confirmed, empirical evidence would support the key argument in the cartel party thesis, which states that crippled competition between the left and the right is well in line with the preferences of party elites to begin with. The reverse result would suggest instead that conflicts relevant to European integration are increasingly politicised in national parliaments (cf. Kriesi et al. 2008: 11).

DATA AND MEASURES

The conclusions of this chapter are based on three unique data sources. First, I draw on a content analysis of reports from all standing committees in the Swedish Parliament for the years between 1970 and 2014. This extensive

database consists of a total of 4,657 coded committee reports on government bills.[6] Analyses of these data establish the basis for operationalising
and testing Hypothesis 1 (cf. Loxbo and Sjölin 2016). Second, because the
preparation of most EU policy – at least when competence is shared between
the EU and the Member States – in Sweden is largely a concern for the EU
Affairs Committee (*EU-nämnden*) (Bergman 1997), an initial basis for testing Hypothesis 2 is a separate content analysis of 1,366 debates in the committee between 1995 (when the committee was established) and 2012. Third,
to test the main assumption of the cartel party thesis laid out in Hypothesis
2, I investigated the preferences of elite politicians by interviewing the group
leaders of all parties represented in parliament, along with key representatives
of all parties in the EU Affairs Committee. In the remainder of this section,
I proceed by discussing how I operationalise the crucial concepts of government and opposition and subsequently explain how the three data sources
were used to test the two hypotheses.

Defining Government and Opposition

To distinguish between parties in government and in opposition, I followed
standard definitions in the literature (e.g. Norton 2008: 237–8). At the most
basic level, government parties are defined as the formal members of the
cabinet, whereas the opposition comprises parties outside government. I
make the following distinctions between parties in opposition. First, the largest opposition party – I refer to it as the *main opposition party* – sets the tone
(Norton 2008: 237–8). More precisely, if *the main opposition party* does not
oppose government policy, opposition is surely in a state of decline.[7] Second,
I refer to smaller parties that do not participate in government but are in the
same bloc as the main opposition party, as *opposition parties* in the plural.
Third, the two populist right-wing parties, New Democracy (represented in
parliament from 1991 to 1994) and the Sweden Democrats (which entered
parliament in 2010), in practice form a third bloc. I therefore treat opposition
from these populist-right challengers separately.

OPERATIONALISING AND TESTING THE HYPOTHESES

Content Analysis of Parliamentary Decision-making, 1970–2014

The first content analysis extends over a period of forty-four years and considers seven left-wing (Social Democratic) governments and six right-wing
(coalition) governments. While the database contains detailed information on
a great number of issues, the following information is relevant to exploring
the government–opposition dynamic under scrutiny here: (i) the content of

the government bill addressed in the committee; (ii) the content of the counterproposals[8] and reservations[9] to government bills issued by the opposition (as categorised above); and (iii) the response of the committee majority to counterproposals (cf. Sjölin 1993: 24–5). Inter-coder reliability tests were performed to ensure the reliability of the coding procedures.[10]

According to Hypothesis 1, parliamentary decision-making, particularly in policy areas pertaining to European integration, is characterised by *an increasing rate of consensual agreement on the content of policy* and *a decreasing rate of policy conflict*. Drawing on the content analysis, the following three measures have been developed to test Hypothesis 1:

1. *The degree of policy consensus*
   The cartel party thesis would expect governments to collude with the opposition over time. Therefore, the first measure used to operationalise Hypothesis 1 captures the proportion of counterproposals from the main opposition party and the remaining opposition parties, respectively, that are partly or fully accepted by a majority – that is, representatives of the government – in the committee.

2. *The degree of policy conflict*
   A movement towards increased depoliticisation would, as a corollary to the measure of consensus above, imply that the opposition is becoming increasingly accommodating to government positions. The second measure used to operationalise Hypothesis 1 captures the percentage of committee reports in which the opposition rejects the proposed government bill outright.[11] If politics is indeed characterised by inter-party collusion and convergence between policy positions, this type of intense policy conflict would obviously be rather exceptional (cf. Kirchheimer 1957: 131, 1966: 237; Dahl 1966a: xviii).

3. *Area of policy contestation*
   To test Hypothesis 1, I distinguish between three distinct arenas of policy-making. First, globalised policy concerns all government bills addressing (i) Sweden's international commercial deals and global conventions and (ii) policies that directly concern Sweden's concrete relations with international organisations (not the EC/EU), such as the OECD, the World Bank and GATT/WTO. Second, Europeanised policy concerns all government bills that directly concern Sweden's relationship with the EC/EFTA/EU. Moreover, since 1995, when Sweden became a member of the EU, government policies that are based on EU directives and EU regulations are also coded as belonging to this category. Third, all remaining policies are coded as domestic policy.

Content Analysis of Debates in the EU Affairs Committee, 1995–2014

Due to the very extensive policy agenda of the EU Affairs Committee – the committee deals with all issues on the table of the Council of EU – I have chosen to limit this part of the study. First, with regard to the evolution of controversies between 1995 and 2012, the analyses consider only two policy areas – labour market policy and policy on immigration/border control – that the literature highlights as particularly politicised by EU standards.[12] Second, to explore controversies over the reach and direction of European integration (e.g. Bartolini 2005; Mair 2007), the analyses are limited to the two right-wing governments between 2006 and 2014. According to Hypothesis 1, we should expect a dramatic decrease in controversies regarding European politics, while Hypothesis 2 predicts that disagreements over the reach and direction of Europeanisation should be non-existent. Drawing on the content analysis, the following measures have been developed to capture these aspects of the government–opposition dynamic.

1. *Rejections of EU policy*
   In the EU Affairs Committee, the opposition does not file bills or reservations but only voices its concerns, in the form of 'deviating opinions'. Although in practice a deviating opinion can imply many different standpoints, the coding highlights situations when the opposition parties – as defined above – reject the position of government outright, while also proposing an alternative standpoint (Loxbo 2014a: 130).[13] The measure used in the analyses indicates the percentage of debates in the EU Affairs Committee when the opposition rejects the position of the government outright.

2. *Contestation over European integration*
   If the opposition also expresses a view on European integration while objecting to the government position, the situation is coded to make a crucial distinction: (i) the opposition party criticises the government for lack of supranational initiatives and/or wrong priorities for the future direction of European integration; or (ii) the opposition party criticises the EU system as such and/or suggests national instead of supranational solutions. Inspired by the operationalisation of the left–right scale in the Comparative Manifesto Project (Budge et al. 2010: 22), the measure in the subsequent analyses subtracts the first from the second position, which yields a scale between +100 (only supranational alternatives) and –100 (only national/EU-critical alternatives).

Interviews as a Complementary Source

While the two content analyses provide important insights into the level of consensus and conflict in parliamentary decision-making, they are not particularly helpful when it comes to understanding the world views and preferences of policy-makers. Therefore, to test Hypothesis 2 and substantiate the findings of the content analyses, centrally placed policy-makers from all parties were interviewed. First, I interviewed the group leaders of all eight parties represented in the Swedish Parliament between 2010 and 2014. Second, for the same period, I interviewed ten representatives of the established mainstream parties and one representative of the populist Sweden Democrats in the EU Affairs Committee – including the chair and the vice chair. The main purpose of the interviews was to gain qualitative insights into how members of political elites themselves view the central assumptions of the cartel party theory.[14]

FINDINGS

Politicisation or Depoliticisation in Parliamentary Decision-making?

According to Hypothesis 1, a movement towards depoliticisation should mean that parliamentary policy-making, particularly in policy areas pertaining to European integration, is becoming increasingly characterised by consensus and less by conflict. Yet, when turning to the measures of consensus and conflict in Figures 5.1–5.3, we see exactly the opposite tendency.

First, I investigate all parliamentary committee reports 1970–2014. Figure 5.1 shows that Swedish governments on both the left and the right have become much less likely to accommodate opposition counterproposals over time.

While the proportion of committee reports with counterproposals from the opposition has risen markedly over time (see note to Figure 5.1), Figure 5.1 shows that Swedish governments have become much less inclined to accommodate opposition views when proposing bills in parliament. Moreover, the same downward trend is evident in the domestic, global (in particular) and European policy areas. Interestingly, as regards global and European policy, the share of accommodated counterproposals drops considerably *after* Sweden joined the EU in 1995. More precisely, in contrast to crucial assumptions of the cartel party thesis (Blyth and Katz 2005), the sharpest decline in consensus-seeking behaviour on the part of Swedish governments occurred *after* the supposedly most important incentives to depoliticise policy-making were introduced – that is, monetary convergence and binding externalisation of policy-making due to EU regulations (Blyth and Katz 2005). Accordingly, instead of a trend in which governments increasingly collude with the opposition (Mair 2007; Katz and Mair 2009: 762), Figure 5.1 indicates that parliamentary decision-making in Sweden has followed exactly the opposite trajectory.

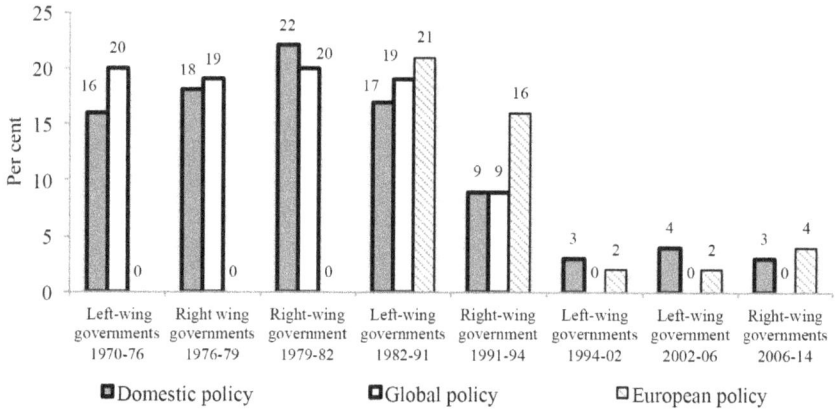

Figure 5.1 Proportion of committee reports with proposals from opposition that are partly or fully accommodated by committee majority, by domestic, global and European policy, 1970–2014 (%). *Note*: The total number of committee reports (and counterproposals for the opposition, in parentheses), for each of the successive periods of government between 1970 and 2014 in Figure 5.1, in chronological order, is as follows: domestic policy – 456 (145), 557 (270), 635 (356), 710 (446), 232 (137), 319 (225), 159 (111), and 447 (300) (committee reports, n = 3514; counterproposals, n = 1990); global policy – 98 (27), 128 (55), 135 (74), 224 (135), 67 (26), 18 (4), 22 (6), and 44 (18) (committee reports, n = 736; counterproposals, n = 345); and European policy – 3 (2), 1 (0), 2 (0), 29 (24), 82 (48), 92 (42), 60 (37), and 137 (64) (committee reports, n = 406; counterproposals, n = 217) (total committee reports, n = 4657).

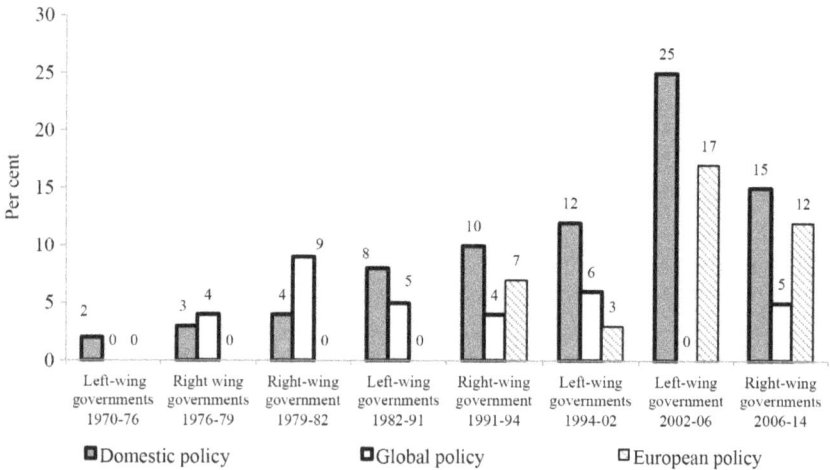

Figure 5.2 Proportion of committee reports for which main opposition party rejects proposed government bill, by domestic, global and European policy, 1970–2014 (%). *Note*: For information on the number of committee reports, 1970–2014, see *Note* to Figure 5.1.

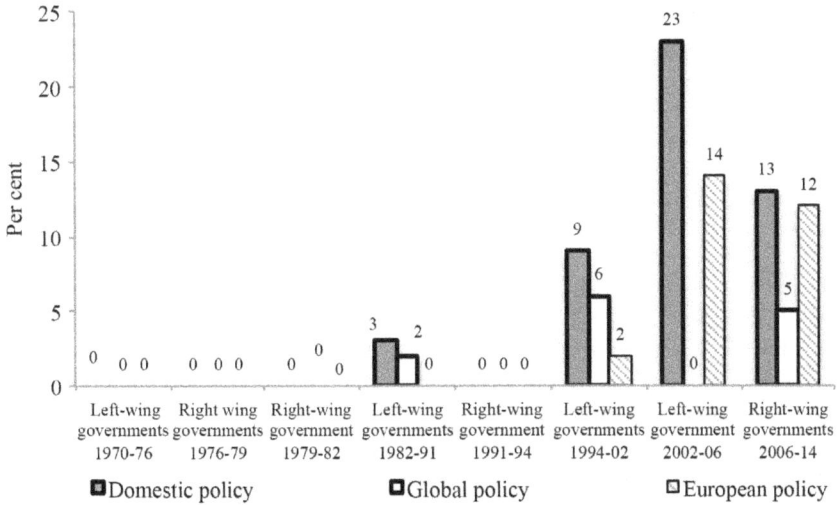

Figure 5.3 Proportion of committee reports for which main opposition party co-ordinates rejection of proposed government bills with other opposition parties, by domestic, global and European policy, 1970–2014 (%). *Note*: For information on the number of committee reports, 1970–2014, see *Note* to Figure 5.1.

Moreover, when turning to the measures of opposition in Figures 5.2 and 5.3, the trend towards intensified, as opposed to lessened, conflict in parliamentary decision-making becomes even more obvious.

Figure 5.2 shows that the degree to which the main opposition party *rejects* proposed government policies has increased substantially over time in both domestic and European affairs. While the few policies that concern strictly global policy indeed appear to have been depoliticised – that is, this area is characterised by very low levels of conflict – the overall trend is unmistakable. Therefore, in sharp contrast to the postulates of cartelisation (Katz and Mair 2009: 754), the data in Figure 5.2 indicate that conflict between the main opposition party and the party/parties in government over domestic and – more importantly – European policy have intensified significantly over time. Moreover, Figure 5.3 shows that policy rejections that are co-ordinated between the main opposition party and other opposition parties within the blocs are a rather new phenomenon. In fact, it is only after the 1990s that policy competition in all policy areas scrutinised here became polarised between the two blocs (cf. Hagevi 2015b).

In addition, when reviewing the behaviour of the two Swedish populist right-wing parties, New Democracy (1991–1994) and the Sweden Democrats (2010–2014), we find that these partisan challengers, despite their anti-establishment and Eurosceptic rhetoric (Kriesi et al. 2008), are in fact very inactive opponents of government policy.[15] I therefore conclude that the observed trend towards the increased politicisation of policy-making is a result of the changed behaviour of mainstream parties and has little to do with the emergence of populist parties on the right.

Politicisation or Depoliticisation in the Preparation of Supranational Policy-making?

Policy-making in which decision-making power is shared between the nation-state and supranational EU institutions is fundamentally different from 'normal' national politics (e.g. Schmidt 2006). Closer exploration of parliamentary decision-making in the EU Affairs Committee, which exclusively concerns such policies, should therefore provide ideal conditions for verifying the depoliticisation hypothesis.

Even so, when reviewing opposition to the government position on EU labour market policy (Figure 5.4), on the one hand, and EU policy on immigration, personal integrity and border control (Figure 5.5), on the other, the results again counter these expectations.

When reviewing the results of the content analyses presented in Figures 5.4 and 5.5, we see a staggering transformation over time. Whereas debates in the EU Affairs Committee were characterised by very low levels of conflict

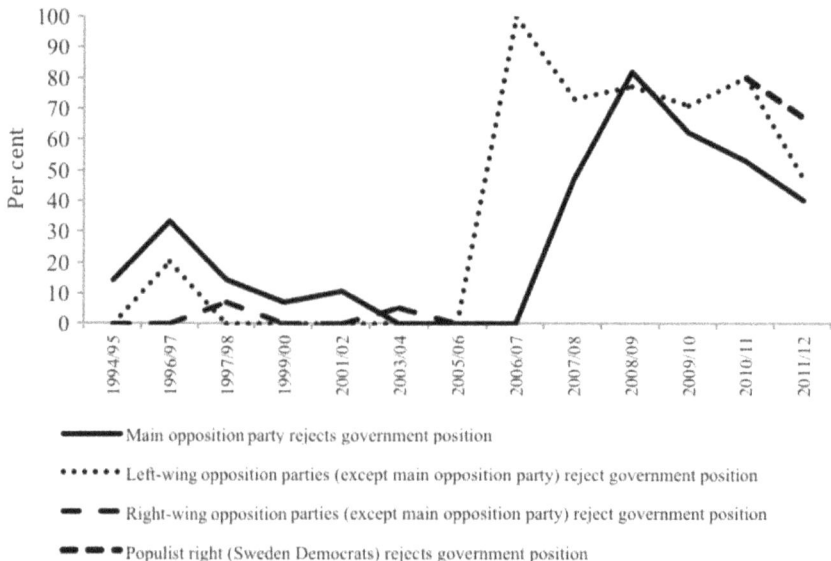

——— Main opposition party rejects government position

• • • • • • Left-wing opposition parties (except main opposition party) reject government position

— — Right-wing opposition parties (except main opposition party) reject government position

— — — Populist right (Sweden Democrats) rejects government position

Figure 5.4 Opposition to the government position on employment policy in the EU Affairs Committee, 1994/5–2011/12 (%). *Source*: Content analysis of protocols from the EU Affairs Committee.

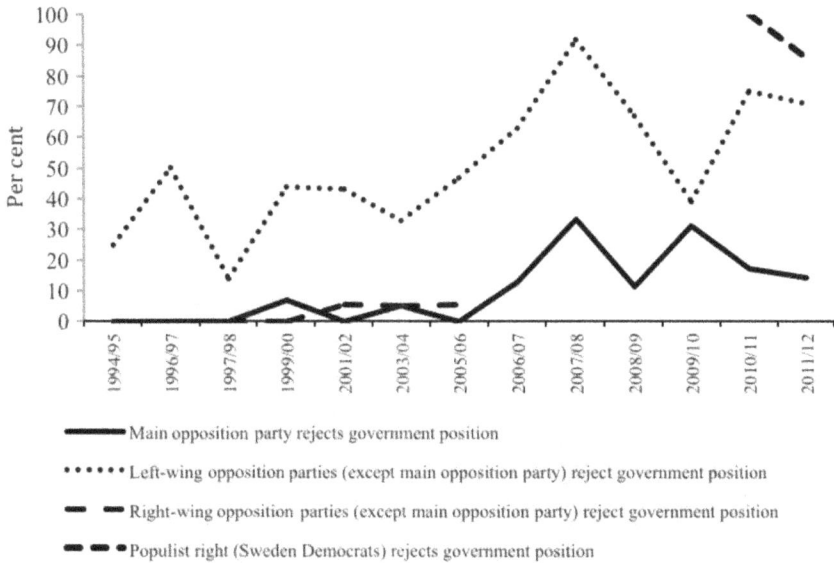

——— Main opposition party rejects government position

• • • • • Left-wing opposition parties (except main opposition party) reject government position

— — Right-wing opposition parties (except main opposition party) reject government position

■ ■ ● Populist right (Sweden Democrats) rejects government position

Figure 5.5   Opposition to the government position on immigration, personal integrity, and border control (primarily JHA) in the EU Affairs Committee, 1995/6–2011/12 (%). *Source*: Content analysis of protocols from the EU Affairs Committee.

between the government and the opposition during the Social Democratic governments in power between 1995/6 and 2005/6, the exact opposite is true during the period of right-wing governments between 2006/7 and 2011/12. While the level of contestation differs between the two policy areas under scrutiny, the trend is unmistakable: all opposition parties, including the main opposition party, have become increasingly confrontational over time.

Lastly, let us address the widely purveyed idea that the process of European integration is difficult to reconcile with national politics and, therefore, that the scope and direction of Europeanisation is becoming increasingly depoliticised (see, for example, Bartolini 2005: 347). Mair (2007: 14), for instance, maintains that opposition with regard to the EU is bound to follow a dualistic logic: either opposition is eliminated altogether, or it is directed towards the polity (the EU system) as such – what Kirchheimer (1966: 237) refers to as 'opposition in principle'. However, when reviewing the overall positioning of opposition parties on two dimensions of policy conflict in four policy arenas, evidence again contradicts the depoliticisation hypothesis.

In Figures 5.6 and 5.7, the aggregated positions of the opposition parties, 2006–2012, are presented on two overlapping dimensions. In all figures, the horizontal axis accounts for the percentage of policy rejections (0–100) – that is, occasions when the opposition party rejects the government position outright. The vertical axis, on the other hand, accounts for how the opposition

Economic regulation   Labour market policy

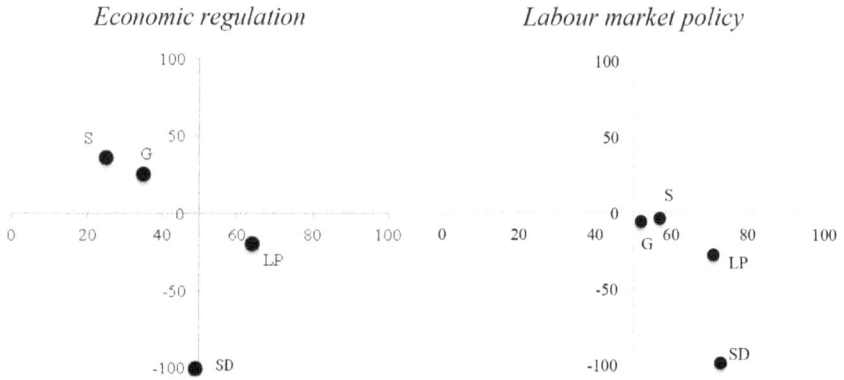

Figure 5.6 Policy rejection and positioning on Europeanisation regarding economic regulation policy [left] and labour market policy [right] of four opposition parties in the EU Affairs Committee, 2006–10 (%). *Source*: Content analysis of protocols from the EU Affairs Committee.

party, compared with the government, positions itself on European integration (with –100 indicating complete Euroscepticism, 0 a neutral stand and +100 signifying complete pro-integrationism).

First, in Figure 5.6 we can see that the degree of policy contestation, on the one hand, and opposition to the scope and direction of European integration, on the other hand, vary greatly between two policy areas of paramount importance to the left–right divide. While the main opposition party, the Social Democrats, only rejects 25 per cent of all government positions on economic regulation policies, and the Greens reject 35 per cent, both parties take more pro-integrationist stands than the government. The Left Party and the populist-right Sweden Democrats both contest a majority of the positions of the government while these parties – particularly the SD – clearly lean towards Euroscepticism. However, whereas opposition to the government position on labour market policy, shown in Figure 5.6, is characterised by significantly higher degrees of conflict than policies on economic regulation, the opposition parties, with the exception of the SD, are divided between a Eurosceptic and pro-integration stance. The data presented in Figure 5.6 thus indicate that the position on Europeanisation – at least for mainstream opposition parties – varies significantly between policy areas. This interpretation is substantiated when reviewing the corresponding patterns of opposition in two additional, non-material policy areas shown in Figure 5.7.

I argue that the analyses in Figures 5.6 and 5.7 cast yet more serious doubt on the depoliticisation hypothesis and the cartel party theory. More precisely, apart from the consistently Eurosceptic position of the populist-right party Sweden Democrats, I find no evidence supporting the proposition that

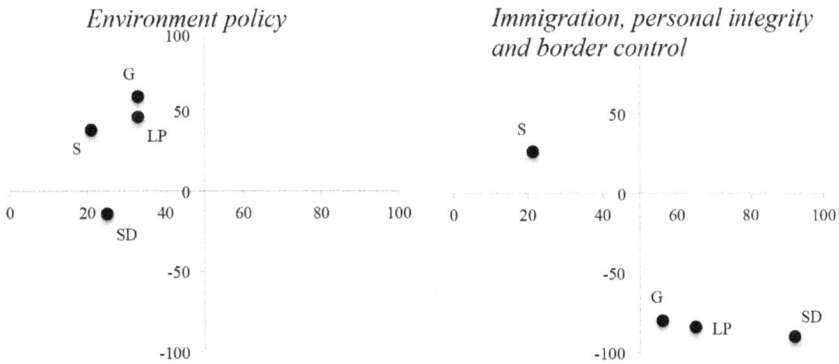

Figure 5.7   Policy rejection and positioning on Europeanisation regarding environmental policy [left] and policies pertaining to immigration, personal integrity and border control [right] of four opposition parties in the EU. *Source*: Content analysis of protocols from the EU Affairs Committee.

opposition to Europeanisation is either eliminated or directed towards the system as such (Mair 2007).

However, although the results indicate that conflicts in all policy fields, including strictly Europeanised policies, have intensified over time, the large-*n* data analysed so far cannot provide detailed insights into the mechanisms explaining this increase. A possible objection to my interpretation of the results is that the trend towards increased policy contestation in practice amounts to nothing more than 'opposition within the cartel' (Mair 2007: 14). To get more substantial insights into the motives of policy-makers, we now turn to the interviews with centrally placed politicians.

Politicisation or Depoliticisation According to Centrally Placed Policy-makers?

All eighteen members of the Swedish Parliament who were interviewed for this study agree with the basic premise of the cartel party thesis that European integration has constrained the policy space. While politicians in mainstream parties – particularly the Social Democrats and the four right-wing parties – tend to view this process of denationalisation as inevitable, the representatives of the right-wing populist newcomer in parliament, the Sweden Democrats (that entered parliament in 2010), vividly express the negative implications of this transformation:

> As a consequence of the EU, parliament has become somewhat of a charade. Although we are elected to represent the Swedish people, we really do not have much say in the decision-making process in the first place. Most decision-making takes place abroad, in Brussels. (MP Björn Söder, SD)

Although representatives of mainstream parties obviously phrased their answers differently, they nevertheless seemed to agree with the basic premise that traditional divisions between the left and right have changed as a result of globalisation and Europeanisation. Yet, while representatives of the Sweden Democrats and, to a lesser extent, the Left Party[16] basically support the main postulates of the cartel party theory and associate the hollowing out of national sovereignty with conscious elite decisions, representatives of the mainstream parties tell a different story. While all of them described the decision to join the EU in 1995 as an unavoidable consequence of external economic constraints, which forged far-reaching consensus across the blocs almost two decades ago, all representatives of mainstream parties confirmed that as a result conflict has intensified markedly over time. When analysing the interviews, this increased politicisation is explained by three central factors.

First, all interviewees, including representatives of the Left Party, explained the increased levels of conflict as a consequence of sharpened bipolarity in the party system (cf. Hagevi 2015b). As indicated by the decreasing rate of consensual decision-making and the increasing rate of conflict shown in Figures 5.1 and 5.2, the turn towards bloc politics that began in the mid 1990s has accelerated since then. Moreover, according to representatives of the left-wing parties (including Green MPs), bipolar bloc competition intensified before the 2006 election, when the four right-wing parties formed the so-called Alliance. One consequence of this shift in strategy, according to the opposition parties, was a dramatic deterioration of the co-operative climate in parliament. As stated by the group leader of the Greens, Mehmet Kaplan, 'When one bloc of parties defines itself as *the* Alliance, while publicly proclaiming that co-operation with other constellations of parties is out of the question, this naturally hollows out the will to compromise'. In addition, the interviewees also confirmed that bipolar competition has spilled over to the EU Affairs Committee. In fact, the intensification of conflict with regard to EU affairs was described by the group leader of the Social Democrats, Sven-Erik Österberg, as a result of the government's 'complete disregard for the views of the opposition'.

The second explanation, brought up in all interviews, is a process of learning whereby European affairs are increasingly treated as 'normal politics' (Hurrelmann, Gora and Wagner 2013: 3). For example, a view that appears to be typical in the Social Democratic party is that 'European integration is increasingly evaluated through the lens of traditional ideologies, which is why conflicts between left and right are resurfacing' (MP Börje Vestlund, S). Moreover, representatives of the right-wing bloc told essentially the same story. For example, the Liberal chair of the EU Affairs Committee, Carl B. Hamilton, concluded that 'European integration is increasingly forcing all parties to take stands on issues that could previously be toned down or avoided'. In addition, while the interviewees confirmed that partisan conflicts are intensifying between parties that have traditionally been pro-integrationist – the Social Democrats, the Moderates and the Liberals – representatives of parties that have a track record of Euroscepticism argue that internal disagreements over EU membership have more or less disappeared over time.[17]

Third, instead of corroborating Mair's (2007, 2013) idea of increased elite collusion over a constrained policy repertoire, all the politicians interviewed argued that it is, in fact, controversies over the future policy instruments of the EU that constitute the primary explanation for intensified politicisation. More precisely, as it has become evident that European integration is increasingly affecting domestic politics – most notably, the Swedish labour market model (Loxbo 2014a) – politicians from all parties argued that consensus on the EU between the two main rivals in Swedish politics, the Social Democrats and the Moderates, has withered away. Along these lines, all representatives of the Moderates who were interviewed – the deputy group leader along with Moderate members of the EU Affairs Committee – noted that re-emerging political conflicts with their main opponent, the Social Democratic party, concern disagreements over the future direction of welfare and labour market policy in the EU. Social Democratic MPs, on the other hand, forcefully stated that the Moderates officially support the Swedish model but unofficially pursue a neoliberal agenda. In fact, according to Sven-Erik Österberg, the group leader of the Social Democrats at the time of the interviews, the Moderates in government have used the growing constraints associated with the EU as 'an excuse to hollow out the Swedish labour market model'. Moreover, regarding the position of the Social Democratic party itself, the interviews with the four MPs of this party clearly indicate that the party's goals are firmly rooted in the vision of *eventually* 'establishing social democratic regulations within the EU as a whole' (Marks and Wilson 2000: 443). While this goal has supposedly inspired the Social Democrats ever since Sweden joined the EU in the mid-1990s,[18] the Social Democrats interviewed suggested that recent developments in the EU and, most importantly, the market-oriented turn of the right-wing government of 2006–2014 have made this goal all the more urgent.

While representatives of the right-wing parties, in particular the Moderates, claimed that opposition from the Social Democrats is inconsistent,[19] no one denied the main conclusion, namely, that conflict over EU policy instruments has intensified significantly over time.

CONCLUSION

In the revised cartel party thesis, Katz and Mair hypothesise that policy-making in the EU is deliberately delegated to non-partisan institutions by political elites who shy away from the constraints of popular democracy (Mair 2007: 8, 2013: 130; Katz and Mair 2009: 754). While this hypothesis of depoliticisation is influential in the literature (e.g. Ladrech 2002, 2007; Bartolini 2005: 405; Schmidt 2006: 772; Scharpf 2010: 239), a growing body of research instead expects European integration to result in the opposite development – more politicisation (e.g. Hix 1999; Hooghe and Marks 2009).

The aim of this chapter has been to test these rival hypotheses using extensive longitudinal data on decision-making by the Swedish Parliament. If the main postulates of the cartel party theory – including the depoliticisation hypothesis – are correct, I argue that we should see the following two transformations in the government–opposition dynamic over time. First, we should observe an increasing rate of consensual agreement and a decreasing rate of policy conflict, particularly with regard to policy-making relevant to European affairs. Second, and perhaps more at the heart of the cartel party theory, we should expect increased elite consensus on the limited policy repertoire (e.g. Blyth and Katz 2005; Mair 2007, 2013). However, the findings presented in this chapter strongly counter both expectations. Instead of finding increased consensus and decreased conflict in parliamentary decision-making and debate, the results of the content analyses point in the opposite direction. In addition, the proposition that elites are colluding on the increasingly limited policy space gains no support. On the contrary, evidence from the interviews strongly indicates that controversy over the policy repertoire available in the EU constitutes the primary explanation for intensified conflict over Europeanisation. More precisely, the results indicate a growing disagreement between left-wing parties that advocate what Fritz Scharpf (2010) refers to as *positive* integration – that is, the reconstruction of capital controls at the supranational level – and right-wing parties that are basically content with purely *negative* integration – that is, removals of barriers to free trade. Consequently, instead of corroborating the cartel party thesis and its depoliticisation hypothesis, the findings are more in line with the rival hypothesis of politicisation.

As I have studied only the government–opposition dynamic in the parliamentary arena, I do not suggest that the findings strongly support the politicisation hypothesis. While the intensity of conflict over Europeanisation has increased, it is important to bear in mind that Schattschneider's (1960) view of politicisation implies that conflicts should be visible and not occur behind the closed doors of parliamentary committees. Although closer examination of the electoral arena lies outside the scope of this chapter, the analysis of party manifestos shown in Figure 5.8 indicates that the visibility of conflicts over Europeanisation has also increased somewhat over time.

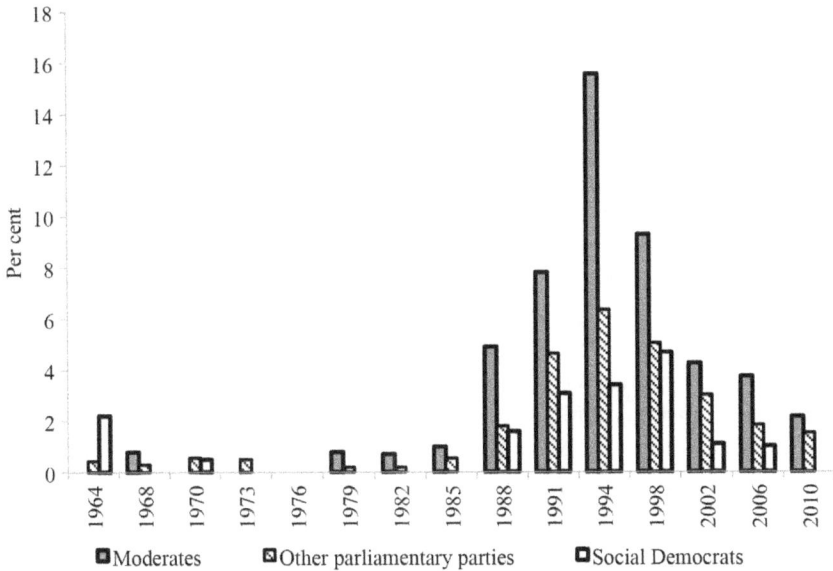

Figure 5.8　European integration addressed in electoral manifestos of Moderates, Social Democrats and all other parties, 1964–2010 (% of party manifestos for European Parliamentary elections). *Source*: Comparative Manifesto Project (CMP) database (Volkens et al. 2013).

When looking at the manifesto data shown in Figure 5.8, we see that European integration has become increasingly salient in the electoral campaigns of Swedish parties, although the issue has become less significant since Sweden joined the EU in 1995. Moreover, it is primarily the Moderates (grey bars) that have emphasised European integration, whereas their main opponents – the Social Democrats (white bars) – have largely shied away from this issue in election campaigns. While this chapter has demonstrated that the Social Democrats are increasingly competing over European policy in parliamentary committees, the findings do not provide strong support for the notion that European integration – as suggested by proponents of the politicisation hypothesis – has led to the emergence of new and politically relevant conflicts between the winners and losers of European integration (cf. Kriesi et al. 2008). Put another way, conflicts over European integration may have become increasingly visible but they certainly do not stand out as especially salient in the contest between the main opponents in the Swedish party system.

In fact, on closer examination, the increasing conflict between the government and the opposition that I have explored here mostly concerns disagreement about long-term visions rather than distinct policy alternatives. More precisely, while the Social Democrats deviate from the right-wing parties by envisioning the EU as a *future* counterweight to global capitalism (Marks and Wilson 2000), few, if any, concrete policies have been presented to realise this goal (Scharpf 2010). Therefore, it is not evident that intensified conflict over Europeanisation in Sweden is much more than amplified verbal opposition. Even so, while Katz and Mair (2009: 760) might very well be correct when concluding that 'mainstream parties … are largely indistinguishable from one another in terms of their main policy proposals', the main conclusion of this chapter is that the key assumption of the cartel party thesis is clearly mistaken in the Swedish case. More specifically, drawing on the results presented here, there is no evidence whatsoever that party elites have intentionally colluded to depoliticise politics. On the contrary, I find it much more plausible to suggest that intensified conflict in parliament reflects the desire of opposition parties, and particularly of the previously dominant Social Democratic party, to remain relevant in a world in which external constraints on policy agendas are increasingly beyond their control.

APPENDIX: INTERVIEWS WITH SWEDISH MEMBERS OF PARLIAMENT

MPs, party group leaders:

Sven-Erik Österberg (S), 9 June 2012
Margareta Pålsson (M) (deputy group leader), 8 June 2012
Johan Pehrsson (L), 23 June 2012
Anders W. Jonsson (C), 14 May 2012
Mats Odell (CD), 30 May 2012
Hans Lindhe (LP), 23 April 2012
Mehmet Kaplan (G), 16 June 2012
Björn Söder (SD), 24 October 2012

MPs in EU Affairs Committee:

Carl B. Hamilton, Chair (L), 30 June 2012
Gustav Blix (M), 31 June 2012
Susanna Haby (M), 23 June 2012
Marie Granlund (S), Vice Chair, 31 June 2012
Börje Vestlund (S), 22 June 2012
Kerstin Haglö (S), 29 June 2012
Bo Bernhardsson (S), 15 June 2012
Ulf Holm (G), 29 June 2012
Johnny Skalin (SD), 23 June 2012.

NOTES

1. Drawing on Schmidt's definition (2006: 761), I interpret Europeanisation at its most basic to mean 'the top–down impact of the European Union (EU) on its Member States'. Moreover, in relation to party organisations, Europeanisation refers to the overall response of Member States to the changes implied by European integration (Ladrech 2002: 395).

2. However, a growing body of literature deals with the formal scrutinising power of national parliaments in the wake of Europeanisation (e.g. Auel and Christiansen 2015).

3. The literature on the politicisation thesis emphasises the demand side of politics, understanding politicisation rather loosely as 'the emergence of widespread political debates which unsettle the traditional' permissive consensuses on European integration (Hurrelmann et al. 2013: 1).

4. The *acquis communautaire* is the accumulated body of European Union (EU) law and obligations from 1958 to the present day. It comprises all the EU's treaties and laws (directives, regulations, decisions), declarations and resolutions, international agreements and the judgements of the Court of Justice.

5. In the literature, the term opposition, or 'responsible opposition', refers to constitutionally regulated contestation over policy alternatives inside national parliaments (cf. Kirchheimer 1957; Dahl 1966a; Helms 2008; Norton 2008). In addition, Kirchheimer and Dahl also define another type of opposition, namely, 'opposition in principle' (Kirchheimer 1966: 237), which refers to some partisans' denunciation of the political system as such.

6. To make data collection manageable, while still allowing for comparisons over time, the mid-parliamentary-session years of the thirteen election periods between 1970 and 2014 were selected for coding. From 1970 to 1994, the election period was three years, so the second parliamentary year of the period was selected for coding, complemented with two additional years during the 1976–1979 and 1979–1982 election periods due to the change of cabinet during election periods. Since 1994, Sweden has had four-year election periods, so after this year the second and third parliamentary years were selected for analysis.

7. In Sweden, either the Moderates or the Social Democrats have occupied the position of main opposition party since 1976. Between 1970 and 1976, the Centre Party occupied this position.

8. Counterproposals from the opposition parties are those that express the official party line on an issue, that is, they are approved by the parliamentary party groups.

9. Formally, a reservation implies that a party in minority expresses a dissenting view that departs from the majority view of the committee, which, with few exceptions, supports the government bill.

10. Regarding the 1970–1990 period, see Sjölin (1993: 24); for the 1990–2014 period, 25 per cent of the material was recoded with an average coding agreement of 98 per cent. Moreover, it is important to note that the content analysis is based on basic coding of highly structured committee reports. The coding is therefore based on straightforward and transparent counts rather than on interpretations.

11. The coding scheme distinguishes between reservations in which an opposition party (i) rejects the government bill outright; (ii) objects to major parts of the policy

content without rejecting the whole bill; (iii) rejects substantial details of the bill; or (iv) objects to minor details.

12. Several scholars argue that labour market policy in the EU causes a division between parties on the centre-left and centre-right (Marks and Wilson 2000; Marks and Steenbergen 2002: 887), whereas immigration/border control relates to what is sometimes referred to as the cultural divide (Bornschier 2010). Labour market policies are handled under the Employment, Social Policy, Health and Consumer Affairs Council (EPSCO), whereas immigration/border control is handled under the Justice and Home Affairs Council (JHA).

13. In all, 255 debates between 1995 and 2013 on labour market policy and immigration/border control were coded; between 2006 and 2013, the same coding includes 640 additional debates.

14. All interviews, which were semi-structured, concentrated on the following questions: (i) How has the increasingly limited policy space affected the degree of conflict/consensus in parliament? (ii) Do major parties compete over future policy/ policy instruments in the national and supranational arenas? (iii) Have patterns of politicisation or depoliticisation changed over time and, if so, in which direction?

15. The proportion of government policies rejected by New Democracy (1991–1994) were: domestic, 1 per cent; global, 3 per cent; and European, 2 per cent. The proportion rejected by the Sweden Democrats (2010–2014) were: domestic, 6 per cent; global, 5 per cent; and European, 7 per cent.

16. The group leader of the Left Party, and a former member of the EU Affairs Committee, Hans Linde argued that policy-making pertaining to the EU tends to generate consensus between the parties that voted for membership in 1994. He stated: 'Very often, when there should be conflict, these parties agree. I am primarily thinking about the Lisbon agreement, and the Laval case, both of which should have sparked intense conflict between the Social Democrats and the bourgeoisie parties. Yet, the Social Democrats, without any conditions regarding the Swedish model whatsoever, decided to approve the Lisbon agreement'.

17. The group leader of the Centre Party argued that internal factions in his party 'have disappeared altogether' (MP Anders W. Jonsson, C), while the group leader of the Greens stated that conflicts over the EU have largely been replaced with a consensus to accept the EU but to strive for 'more precise supranational integration' (MP Mehmet Kaplan, G). Similarly, the group leader of the Left Party said that his party now agrees to 'take responsibility for membership in the EU' (MP Hans Linde, LP).

18. This claim was made by all the Social Democrats interviewed.

19. For example, as regards labour market policy, the Social Democrats sometimes advocate more European integration (via a social protocol) and sometimes the exact opposite (i.e. stricter regulation in Sweden).

Chapter 6

Homogenisation or Fragmentation?

Perceptions of Mediatisation Among Finnish and Swedish Parliamentarians

Douglas Brommesson and Ann-Marie Ekengren

In this chapter, we examine the second hypothesis of the cartel party theory, namely, that parties tend to develop more similar and more constrained policies because of a need to downsize voters' expectations and because of the 'increasing institutional externalisation' of various policy commitments (Blyth and Katz 2005: 46; see Chapter 1 of this book). The mass media exemplify the 'increasing institutional externalisation' that fosters policy similarity, that is, homogenisation, according to cartel party theory. In this chapter we consider whether the view of the mass media as a force driving increasing policy convergence can be verified.

Media developments are seen by Katz and Mair (1995: 7, 12, 15–17, 20) as changing the preconditions for political parties. Here, two trends come into play. First, according to media researchers, the media have developed into an independent actor governed by their own 'media logic' (see below). This logic has even colonised politics, making it necessary for political parties to adapt their behaviour. Second, due to fierce competition between and streamlining of media organisations, at least the traditional media have fewer resources for investigative journalism (Houston 2010: 45) than they once had. Together, these two trends make it possible for party leaders with the ability to adapt politics to media logic to control political messages (cf. Elmelund-Praestekaer et al. 2011). Once the parties in a cartel control political communication in this way, political messages across parties will become more homogenous, due to adaptation to this uniform media logic. One example of this adaptation was noted when Katz and Mair observed that cartel parties' political campaigning is increasingly 'capital-intensive, professional and centralized' (Katz and Mair 1995: 20). This leads to the use of professional media advisors, with the same kind of background, across parties, which tends to strengthen the tendency towards homogenising party messages.

To sum up thus far, according to cartel party theory, the mass media and mediatisation can be described as being among the many preconditions for cartelisation that lead to increasing policy similarity.

The concept of mediatisation as used here refers to a *process in which the media develop into an independent institution with significant power that permeates other sectors of society* (Asp 1986; Schulz 2004; Hjarvard 2008; Strömbäck 2008, 2011).

Media researchers were, of course not slow in joining Katz and Mair in noting that mediatisation has significant consequences for modern democracies (Asp 1986; Schulz 2004; Moring 2006; Krotz 2007; Hjarvard 2008; Mazzoleni 2008; Strömbäck 2008, 2011; Strömbäck and Esser 2009). Party politics is increasingly shaped with the help of the media and people outside the representative space of politics (Lievrouw and Livingstone 2009).

Mediatisation is expected to have a number of consequences for representative democracy, including individual MPs and the collective organisations they represent – the political parties. These consequences include an increase in the degree to which elected representatives communicate with citizens through the media rather than directly; the emergence of the media as an independent political actor; and the transformation of politics to meet the demands of the media – including accessibility, speed and simplification. Strömbäck and Van Aelst (2013), in one of the few attempts so far to combine party theory and mediatisation theory, argue that party organisations, as well as their communication strategies, are affected by mediatisation and media logic (see also Thesen 2013).

Media logic refers to how the media think and operate – their *modus operandi* – and it replaces political logic, which is defined as 'collective and authoritative decision making as well as the implementation of political decisions' (Strömbäck 2008: 233). Media logic entails that the media tend to simplify, polarise, identify clear and competing alternatives, and illustrate coverage with stories based on individuals.[1]

Based on competing expectations in the literature, this chapter considers whether mediatisation has had a perceived homogenising or fragmenting effect on parties, according to politicians at the parliamentary level. Current research on parties presents competing expectations as to how mediatisation will affect party politics. According to one line of argument, here represented by Blyth, Katz and Mair, mediatisation fosters a common media logic to which all parties that are part of the cartel adapt, at the expense of competing ideological logics. The parties tend to launch more similar policies and, in light of disappearing ideological differences, media logic might offer a way to retain media attention (Katz and Mair 2002, 2009; Blyth and Katz 2005). As ideological differences disappear, media logic drives every actor in the same direction, making it a force for homogenisation. According to another line of argument, however, here represented by Herbert Kitschelt, we should expect exactly the opposite. Media logic could be expected to favour individual politicians who tell exciting stories, rather than official statements by representatives of hierarchical organisations. The parties and their representatives must struggle to reach a more volatile electorate and one way to do that successfully is to distinguish oneself in relation to others (Kitschelt 2000). By this token, mediatisation becomes a force for fragmentation.

In the next section, we elaborate on mediatisation and its possible effect on MPs and political parties. We then discuss the overarching analytical framework and in this section we also present our case selection and our methodological tools. In the empirical section of this chapter, we study the effect of mediatisation on policy-making according to the interviewed MPs in Sweden and Finland and address the question: is mediatisation perceived to have a homogeneity-creating or a fragmenting effect on parties? This question is analysed in relation to three dimensions: the policy *content*; the policy *form*; and whether the policy represents an adaptation used mainly by the elite or by the party's mid-level. We end the chapter with some concluding remarks.

MEDIATISATION AND PARTY CHANGE: A FORCE FOR HOMOGENISATION OR FRAGMENTATION?

In cartel parties, according to Katz and Mair (see Chapter 1 in this book), power is expected to become concentrated at the very top of the party elite. Party leaders are expected to forge a consensus that goes beyond the divisions usually characteristic of politics. One likely consequence of this substantive consensus is that parties should increasingly be seen as similar to one another, as organisational and even ideological differences between them shrink (Blyth and Katz 2005). One factor that cartel party theory points to as promoting consensus is adaptation to a common media logic (Katz and Mair 1995, 2002).

According to the cartel party theory, initial differences between parties in terms of how party representatives use the media should decline over time. What can be expected is a greater degree of professionalism in using the media, with 'spin doctors' who have similar backgrounds and values setting the agenda for all main parties. The professional media advisors available to party leaders and the surrounding party elites all package the political message in the same way and emphasise the same issues across ideological divides, in order to capture headlines. Control by the party elite is important: to control the political message, the party elite controls the media resources, making it more difficult for more junior MPs to reach out to the public with individualistic messages. To sum up, politics has become more mediatised and, as a result, party leaders with the support of media advisors have taken control of party messages and adapted politics to media logic, making politics more similar across party boundaries (Bjerling 2013). We can therefore expect to see policy homogenisation, which can be seen as an indicator of cartelisation.

As a result of the process described here, MPs could be expected to regard mediatisation as in line with homogenisation. The theoretical foundation in the mediatisation literature for the expectation of a perceived homogenisation effect stems from descriptions of the media as the creators of a 'common horizon of experience' (Hjarvard 2008: 127; cf. Giddens 1984). According to this sociological literature, the media have dissolved local cultures in favour of one common culture. This research tends to have its point of departure in historical institutionalism, viewing the mediatisation process as one that entails making cultures and institutions in which all actors must relate similarly to one another. The media have become an autonomous actor, with its own logic and norms (Hjarvard 2008: 110, 116). In the sense that all actors wanting to take part in a mediatised conversation must understand and relate to common institutions and cultural references, it is possible to expect a more mediatised society to be a less pluralistic society, in which more homogeneous policies are favoured or at least expected.

According to some researchers, the primary driving force behind both of these trends – the concentration of power and the convergence of the parties – is the parties' increasing financial dependence on the state (Gidlund and Koole 2001; Koß 2011). However, the increased importance of the mass media (Strömbäck 2009) and media logic, along with other societal changes that reduce the ability of parties to influence politics in a particular direction (Blyth and Katz 2005; Katz and Mair 2009), are also expected to contribute to internal power concentration and increasing similarity within parties. The parties, to an increasing extent, rely on advice from centrally employed spin doctors and communications officers with similar backgrounds and world views. Despite their different party affiliations, these media advisors tend to frame all political messages in a similar way. One aspect of this worth mentioning is the focus on the personal or even the private, that is, the personalisation of politics. As media logic tends to favour the personal narrative (Strömbäck 2008; Campus 2010), these media advisors 'spin' individual politicians rather than ideological and policy conflicts. According to this argument, the personalisation of the political message can be expected to function as an intervening variable that advances policy homogenisation because it leaves less room for political conflict (de-ideologisation) and less room for a plurality of political issues in general. Personalisation also implies, moreover, that the party elite can control the message to an even greater extent than before, because the media can be expected to feature well-known party representatives.

This view of the merging of parties and the state in Western democracies has not gone unchallenged. A party researcher who has formulated well-founded criticism of the assumptions of cartel party theory is Herbert Kitschelt. One of his claims is that party elites have not become more alienated from voters; in fact, the opposite is true: they have become even more sensitive to the preferences of voters. The reason for this, according to Kitschelt's argument, is simple: parties cannot control voters as they could in the past, when party loyalty was more common. Parties are therefore forced to follow the preferences of an ever-more-volatile electorate (Kitschelt 2000: 163). Given this view of voters as increasingly volatile, there is reason to expect politicians to be responsive and to emphasise their own distinctiveness.

In addition, Kitschelt argues that if parties' ideologies are increasingly similar, which is not entirely certain, this is more likely to be a product of external factors outside the party system than of internal factors such as cartelisation. The complexity of the international political system or the economy might lead to increased ideological convergence, as states are left with limited manoeuvring room. Kitschelt argues that cartelisation is not a prerequisite for this type of development (Kitschelt 2000: 169f). Kitschelt's critique could be said to be twofold: (1) he is not convinced that ideological convergence indeed exists; and (2) if we do observe convergence, it may depend on other causal mechanisms than those predicted by cartel party theory.

Kitschelt's criticism of cartel party theory is based on assumptions that make an increase in mediatisation likely, even though he does not explicitly problematise the phenomenon. If we follow the consequences of Kitschelt's argument, it is perfectly reasonable to imagine that a general increase in individualisation and a willingness of politicians to emphasise their distinctiveness might include a development in which individual party members create their own media platforms and channels. If this happens, the ability of party elites to control their members will decline. If parties are unable to control individual party representatives, we can expect greater divergence and fragmentation in media relations. In view of Kitschelt's criticism of cartel party theory, mediatisation can be assumed to have taken place, and still greater fragmentation can be expected to occur as a result of this mediatisation. According to this argument, every member can act as his/her own entrepreneur and take advantage of the opportunities provided by a mediatised society to reach out to a public audience. Instead of homogenised politics, we should instead expect the opposite: fragmented politics.

By fragmentation, we here refer to a process whereby mediatisation provides actors at different levels of a formerly more hierarchical political system with the opportunity to make use of a diversified landscape of media channels. We can expect different actors to emphasise different issues and 'news'. The leadership of a party can no longer control the flow of information or decide who should or should not make a statement. We end up with a more fragmented political landscape with different politicians at different levels and with different policy preferences all striving to make their voices heard. This development fits into a more postmodern understanding of mediatisation, in which the opportunities for interaction are growing and we can expect a growing 'differentiation of what people perceive to be real' (Hjarvard 2008: 111).

New forms of communication make it easier for individuals to communicate on many different stages simultaneously and follow different norms on different stages. In an article on the abilities that stem from internet activities, several possible effects are discussed:

> The general assumption of researchers interested in hypertextual online journalism is that if hypertext is used innovatively it would provide a range of advantages over print journalism: no limitations of space, the possibility to offer a variety of perspectives, no finite deadline, direct access to sources, personalized paths of news perception and reading, contextualization of breaking news, and simultaneous targeting of different groups of readers – those only interested in the headlines and those interested in the deeper layers of information and sources. (Steensen 2011: 313)

Here, Steensen is discussing the possible fragmentation of both news production and news perception, with the diversification increasing among both news producers and consumers. When the new media environment fragments, the power of the media might also be reduced (Bennett and Iyengar 2008).

Previous research gives us strong reasons to support the claim of an ongoing process of the mediatisation of politics. However, turning to the consequences of this process, we are in a considerably weaker position from which to draw any certain conclusions, as views differ so greatly. It is our intention to investigate which of these views gains support according to the politicians' own perceptions of mediatisation.

In the next section, we first discuss our analytical framework and various theoretical expectations. Second, we discuss the cases and the comparative research design.

Analytical Framework

In the empirical section, we investigate perceptions of mediatisation in relation to three dimensions that are relevant according to mediatisation or party theory: the policy *content*; the policy *form*; and whether the policy represents an adaptation used mainly by the elite or by the mid-level of the party.

According to the homogenisation argument based on cartel party theory, we should expect the policy content to be limited to a narrow agenda that is defined by professional media advisors to the political elite in symbiosis with the media. Furthermore, we should expect the debate to be single-minded, with little room for competing perspectives. All in all, we should see a process of mediatisation used by the elite, given the professionalisation of the political leaderships' usage of media. One possible effect of this elite-centred process could be that average MPs become critical of the rising power of the media and dissatisfied with their own opportunities to gain media exposure; while members of the party elite can be expected to be more positive (cf. Van Aelst et al. 2008; Van Aelst et al. 2010; Aalberg and Strömbäck 2011; Elmelund-Praestekaer et al. 2011: 387–8).

On the other hand, according to the fragmentation argument based on Kitschelt's critique, we should expect a wider range of policy issues to be covered today, compared to the timeframe before mediatisation. We should especially expect greater attention to the fate of different individuals with different life trajectories (personalisation), at the expense of more strategic issues. With the wider range of issues on the table comes more diversified debate and greater attention by politicians to 'new' policy challenges. Finally, we could expect average MPs to be positive about this development, as it provides them with new opportunities. We could also expect members of the party elite to be more worried about the loss of their power and ability to keep the political message coherent.

In Table 6.1, we summarise possible perceived effects of mediatisation according to the homogenisation and fragmentation perspectives.

To analyse the empirical answers, we used the analytical framework presented in Table 6.1. Answers highlighting the constraining role of media advisors as the extended arm of party leadership were interpreted as signs of homogenisation. Answers that, instead, emphasised a more diversified media agenda, a greater number of media channels – beyond the control of party leadership but accessible to individual politicians at various levels – and greater opportunities to gain coverage of stories and political initiatives concerning a variety of issues were interpreted as signs of fragmentation. On the other hand, problems getting media coverage of other issues than the one currently dominating the media agenda were interpreted as indicating homogenisation of the form of politics. Finally, answers that stressed the need for certain media skills in order to use the media productively, and thus the need for strategic media resources at the disposal of party leadership, were interpreted as signs of homogenisation. Answers that instead emphasised the opportunities to sidestep party leadership in media relations due to new technology and a new media landscape were interpreted as signs of fragmentation.

Table 6.1   Perceived Effects of Mediatisation

	Homogenisation	Fragmentation
Adaptation of policy content to media logic	Helped by professional media aides, party leadership is capable of regaining control of agenda by presenting issues in a way that fits media logic. Politicians formulate policy on an issue once media have focused on it.	Politicians want to show their distinctiveness to the voters. One way to do this is to focus on various individual fates or scandals. A range of ideologies leads to multiple stories being told.
Adaptation of policy form to media logic	There are few important media channels and one question at a time dominates their agenda, leaving limited room for competing perspectives.	Many important media platforms broadly cover foreign policy, and politicians can choose to pay increased attention to 'new' foreign policy issues.
Elite- or grassroots-centred adaptation	The parties are professionalised in using the media, which gives party leadership and their aides (spin doctors) greater power. New social media give party leadership same advantages as old media.	Given increased numbers of communication platforms, mid-level party members gain new opportunities to make their voices heard. New social media give mid-level party members advantages and lead to new perspectives being discussed.

Case Selection and Comparative Design

We chose to study perceptions of mediatisation and its consequences in the field of foreign policy. The reason for studying foreign policy in particular is that this is a policy area associated with consensus culture and a constrained policy space (Jerneck et al. 1988; Bjereld and Demker 1995, 2000). The conditions in this policy area are therefore favourable to the cartel party theory; if the theory does not apply here, we can question the validity of this part of the theory in other policy areas as well.

In our study, we follow our fellow contributors to this book and use Sweden – more specifically, the members of Sweden's Foreign Affairs Committee – as the main case. We also include a comparative aspect, by using Finland and the members of the Finnish Foreign Affairs Committee as a reference case. The idea behind this is to include a similar case that mirrors the Swedish political system in most relevant respects and therefore makes it possible to extend the same line of reasoning beyond a single case, not least because Katz and Mair (1995: 17) cite both Sweden and Finland as cases probably in line with cartel party theory.[2] Our comparison also means that we are concentrating on a specific parliamentary committee with relatively few members. By including a second parliamentary committee, we were able to expand our group of interviewees.

One aspect of political culture that differs between Finland and Sweden is the degree of consensus in the foreign policy context. Deviations from the consensus norm occur from time to time in Sweden but are almost non-existent in the Finnish case.[3] Whether this leads to any differences in how mediatisation and its consequences are described remains to be seen. If we take cartel party theory seriously, we can expect homogenisation to be the pattern in both the Swedish case and the Finnish reference case, with some minor signs of fragmentation in Sweden, probably as a result of the somewhat weaker consensus norm in foreign policy.

Elite Interviews

The analysis of how mediatisation is perceived is based on interviews with members of the Foreign Affairs Committees in the Finnish and Swedish parliaments.[4] We tried to interview all members of the Foreign Affairs Committees in both Finland and Sweden; those committee members who were not interviewed declined our interview request.[5] In the Finnish case, we also interviewed the chair of the Christian Democratic party, as this party does not have a seat on the Foreign Affairs Committee. In 2012 we interviewed fifteen of the eighteen members of the Swedish Foreign Affairs Committee and, in addition, four members of the European Union Affairs Committee.[6] All Swedish interviews took place in a semi-structured setting based on for-malised questions with the opportunity to ask follow-up questions. In 2012 and at the beginning of 2013 we interviewed seven of a total of seventeen members of the Finnish Foreign Affairs Committee. In early 2014 we inter-viewed one additional MP and the chair of the Christian Democratic party group, for a total of nine interviews. In the Finnish case, with one excep-tion, we had to rely on written interviews by email, given the difficulty of gaining access to the MPs. One obvious shortcoming is that the answers obtained in the oral interviews are more extensive, given our ability to ask follow-up questions.[7] The answers to the follow-up questions rarely changed the impressions from the initial answers, however, so these initial answers are comparable to those obtained from the email interviews.[8] Furthermore, to minimise the possible negative effects of the different interview modes, all the interviews were structured around the same questions, providing us with the opportunity to make a credible comparison. All oral interviews were transcribed by a professional transcriptionist and then analysed, together with the written interviews, by the authors of this chapter.[9]

Consulting the methodological literature on how many interviews are enough to reach a reasonable level of theoretical saturation yields a variety of answers, depending on the context. Guest, Bunce and Johnson (2006) advocate twelve interviews and claim that very few new themes emerge after the twelfth. Considering that Guest, Bunce and Johnson based this conclusion on their research in Africa with prostitutes working in many different environments, and that their thirty-four interview questions covered six themes, we think it is safe to argue that one needs fewer interviews with fewer questions to reach a fair level of saturation when interviewing people from a more homogeneous group. Guest, Bunce and Johnson (2006: 74, 77) also acknowledge earlier studies arguing that as few as four people can be sufficient under such circumstances. Similarly, Esaiasson et al. (2007: 292) summarise the methodological debate and, based on their review, recommend 'about ten interviews' for each group. However, they also argue that the litmus test is theoretical saturation and that it is impossible to determine beforehand when this will be reached. According to this argument, one has reached theoretical saturation when no new relevant arguments appear in the interviews (Esaiasson et al. 2007: 309). Given the highly homogeneous character of the answers from the Finnish interviews reported below, we are confident that we have reached such a level of saturation.

We now turn our attention to the empirical findings, and we discuss the results in three sections treating: perceptions of the adaptation of foreign policy *content* to media logic; perceptions of the adaptation of foreign policy *form* to media logic; and whether mediatisation is perceived as a process used by the elite or by average parliamentarians. In each section, we structure our discussion in relation to the overall question: is mediatisation a force of perceived homogenisation or fragmentation?

ADAPTATION OF FOREIGN POLICY CONTENT TO MEDIA LOGIC: HOMOGENISATION OR FRAGMENTATION?

Sweden

The adaptation of foreign policy content to media logic in the Swedish case was expected to be rather extensive and be characterised mainly by homogenisation but with occasional traits of fragmentation. The empirical data confirm such a mixed expectation. In this section, we elaborate on how homogenisation and fragmentation are discussed and how we should understand this mixed perspective.

Over time, the media vary the content of their reporting of foreign policy issues. At one particular time, the European Union may be a hot topic; a few weeks later, foreign aid issues could be featured instead (interviews with MPs Bernhardsson, S,[10] Ceballos, G, Habsburg Douglas, M, and Winbäck, L). Although the topics that are covered change over time, all the media tend to run in the same direction, leading to homogenisation of coverage (interviews with Ceballos and Forslund). Catastrophic events such as tsunamis or earthquakes are good examples of issues that tend to be widely covered by the media; after a while, however, the media leave the areas where the disasters occurred to cover other locations. The 'CNN effect', whereby major international media cover certain areas and then national media and politicians follow their lead, is well known. After a while, international media leave and national media also stop reporting. If Westerners are affected by a catastrophe, then the media coverage is more intense (interviews with MPs Forslund, S, and Thorell, S).

The fact that some issues or processes are considered too difficult for the media to cover and are passed over by politicians as well strengthens the sense that such adaptation to media logic favours homogenisation. Some issues are considered too complex and cannot be adapted to the media format (interviews with MPs Forslund, S, Habsburg Douglas, M, Malm, L, and Winbäck, L). Accordingly, some foreign policy issues are never covered by the media or national politicians, meaning that the content of foreign policy is homogenised by this limited coverage.

The fact that parties have prepared ready-made answers to questions about many issues in advance could be seen as offering them a way to regain control of the agenda. Of course, that depends on the degree to which the parties are proactive and on the degree to which they instead react to media coverage. When MPs described how the parties have a 'policy box' (a 'box' of ready-made answers regarding various policies) and discuss these policies only when the media landscape is right, then it is easy to perceive the adaptation to mediatisation in terms of homogenisation (interview with MP Forslund, S). This need for ready-made answers on a broad variety of policies was expressed by one MP:

> The media affects us by being an agenda-setter. We, the politicians, must formulate opinions on issues we otherwise would not have cared about. (interview with MP Malm, L)

In this, the media put pressure on the politicians to formulate certain policies despite the internal priorities of the parties (interviews with MPs Bernhardsson, S, Ceballos, G, Enochsson, CD, and Malm, L). When the media advisors in the parties are described as gatekeepers who control what political messages the MPs can release and when they can release them, elite control comes to mind and, with it, less room for political issues outside the priorities of the elite. Sometimes party leaders are asked, during an ongoing media campaign, about whether they find it acceptable to relate the party's position to that campaign when launching the party's position on the issue (interview with MP Pethrus, CD). Media advisors are sometimes described not as 'changing the message' but as tending to find a 'clearer' picture or advising politicians to 'drop' certain issues. Of course, this implies a certain level of control by the party leadership (interview with MP Lundgren, C). Sometimes the media advisors are described as attempting to exert more far-reaching influence by suggesting what issues the MPs should discuss; and disagreements can sometimes arise between the media advisors and politicians (interview with MP Ceballos, G). Both examples above indicate homogenisation, but to different extents.

However, there are also signs of perceived fragmentation. When a foreign policy issue affects individual Swedes, especially journalists, then politicians tend to pay close attention to the media's reporting. Individual fates are important for policy-making in these cases and different actors tend to focus on different individuals (interviews with MPs Ceballos, G, Enochsson, CD, Johansson, M, Malm, L, and Pethrus, CD). This can make Swedish foreign policy more fragmented.

In situations in which Swedish citizens are taken hostage or imprisoned for political reasons abroad, Swedish media interest tends to be extensive. On those occasions, media reporting is believed to provide individual politicians with unique policy positions – politicians can choose to emphasise the need for swift action. This is sometimes done with the knowledge and help of civil society, which is believed to lend credibility to certain types of media coverage (interview with MP Winbäck, L) and to be the source of certain types of news, for example, regarding control of arms exports (interview with MP Ceballos, G). Just to give one example: with media help, public interest groups dealing with immigration issues try to put their domestic priorities on the Swedish foreign policy agenda, and some politicians are inclined to comment on and lead the resulting campaigns (interview with MP Malm, L). This is more in line with what might be expected to happen according to the fragmentation perspective.

The foreign policy agenda is described as more diversified and as involving more actors than it did just twenty years ago. Although some media actors are deemed important, their opportunity to dominate the agenda is described as more limited today. Public services, such as national TV, help uphold the quality of news reporting (interview with MP Johansson, M).

Other interviewees believed that the actions of politicians themselves can be a counterweight to media homogenisation, in the sense that politicians, with the help of other groups, can put other topics and regions on the political agenda. The larger parties, at least, with more MPs, more support staff and more know-how, can present a wider range of issues to the public:

> You should not be affected only by the current media stories. You should pay attention to longer-term issues. You can get the upper hand over the media on issues about which you are well informed. Then you can affect what they write. (interview with MP Thorell, S)

In sum, mediatisation is believed to have a mixed effect on foreign policy content in Sweden in terms of both homogenisation and fragmentation.

Finland

According to our theoretical expectations, mediatisation in Finland should in general be perceived as leading to the homogenisation of foreign policy. To the extent that mediatisation is at all acknowledged, these expectations are met. Generally, the Finnish MPs interviewed made hardly any references to media influence on the content of Finnish foreign policy. Although most of the MPs could identify a mediatisation process operating in politics in general, they still emphasised that Finnish foreign policy is an exceptional area in which the media exerts very limited influence.

One MP asserted: 'Finnish foreign policy can be characterised by words such as continuity and stability. ... Media influence is not very great because of the long tradition of consensual Finnish foreign policy and the present coalition government' (interview with MP Orpo, NCP). This typical statement reflects the general view of the MPs interviewed. Another MP concluded, 'In foreign policy issues [the media's] role is quite small' (interview with MP Kiviniemi, C), and in the words of a third MP, 'The media influence in Finnish foreign policy is not extensive. The media follow and report foreign policy decisions but don't have a special influence on specific decisions' (interview with MP Komi, C). A fourth MP acknowledged the lack of media influence and also argued that this is fortunate (interview with MP Donner, SPP).

Few interviewees diverged from this general rule of emphasising consensus and the lack of media influence together with mediatisation. MP Johannes Koskinen (SDP) started by emphasising the Finnish foreign policy consensus but, nevertheless, identified the advent of 'clear spillover effects from media coverage in other countries', resulting in influence from the media concentrating 'on current international affairs and incidents'. Peter Östman, chair of the Christian Democratic party, also acknowledged this and argued that this is a special challenge for small parties with divergent views outside the mainstream consensus (interview with MP Östman, CD).

When explicitly asked about how the media influenced Finnish foreign policy, MPs maintained their scepticism of media influence on foreign policy content. Some examples offered in the responses of several MPs, however, concern decisions on strategic and security issues, such as the possibility of EU membership (Finland became a member in 1995), future NATO membership and other forms of security–political co-operation, such as the Nordic Defence Cooperation (NORDEFCO) organisation. These examples all relate to traditional foreign policy areas, emphasising the strategic needs of the state, rather than the focus on catastrophes and the well-being of individuals expected from a mediatised foreign policy agenda.

To conclude, most Finnish MPs interviewed could identify the general mediatisation of politics, except in relation to Finnish foreign policy, which is an area in which policy goals are instead characterised by ideals such as consensus and continuity. When the media do play a role, it is within the boundaries of a traditional foreign policy agenda. Longstanding tradition in foreign policy matters and broad coalition governments both support these ideals. These findings suggest a certain political culture as a possible countervailing force to the mediatisation that makes the ongoing homogenisation of foreign policy possible. We therefore have no reason to argue that mediatisation causes either homogenisation or fragmentation; it is rather the longstanding political culture that upholds Finland's homogeneous foreign policy, despite any media pressure. We continue this discussion by turning to the form of Finnish and Swedish foreign policy.

ADAPTATION OF FOREIGN POLICY FORM TO MEDIA LOGIC: HOMOGENISATION OR FRAGMENTATION?

Sweden

The adaptation of foreign policy form to media logic in the Swedish case was expected to be characterised by homogenisation with some occasional traits of fragmentation. The results of the study indicate that fragmentation is the most prevalent feature overall, but some homogenisation features were evident when we investigated the internal party arena.

In terms of foreign policy form, MPs have rather elaborate views of how they must adapt to media logic (interviews with MPs Bernhardsson, S, Granlund, Ceballos, G, and Habsburg Douglas, M). As MP Habsburg Douglas put it:

> Of course you have to adapt to media logic. To be more credible, you talk about your own experiences ... and it becomes easier to sell a certain foreign policy. (interview with MP Habsburg Douglas, M)

Adaptation to media logic implies a greater emphasis on conflicts and personal experience, which leads to foreign policy news being taken out of context (interviews with MPs Bernhardsson, S, Ceballos, G, and Malm, L). Media logic could, in these cases, facilitate unintentional fragmentation.

A central remark on adaptation to media logic at the intersection of form and content is the belief that foreign policy must be based on an ideological foundation. A firm ideology is a necessary condition if one wants to formulate a credible foreign policy (interviews with MPs Ceballos, G, Enochsson, CD, Habsburg Douglas, M, Johansson, M, Thorell, S, and Winbäck, L). The bigger parties are believed to be like big maritime vessels, whose direction cannot be changed very easily, not even in response to particular media reactions (interview with MP Thorell, S).

If their ideologies are equally important to all parties, media adaptation will probably be expressed as both fragmentation and homogenisation simultaneously, determined by what particular aspect parties are compared on. Adaptation to media logic could be interpreted as fragmentation when comparing the parties: if different parties have different foreign policy ideologies, the result is many different foreign policy voices. However, such adaptation to media logic could also be interpreted as homogenisation if the internal life of parties is the basis of the comparison, as parties' ability to control their own MPs through party ideology could lead to fewer competing perspectives (cf. interviews with MPs Forslund, S, and Winbäck, L). However, in general, this conclusion implies a rather strong critique of the cartel party theory and its prediction of the de-ideologisation of politics.

When we compare these results with our theoretical expectations, we see that the cartel party theory receives support in relation to the first premise, that media logic can lead to greater homogenisation within parties, but this assumes a strong role for ideologies, which runs counter to the cartel party theory's assumption of the de-ideologisation of politics. The theory also predicted greater homogenisation between parties, but this is not supported by the responses of the Swedish MPs interviewed. There are still reasons to believe that we see a multitude of voices when we take the whole party arena into account. The MPs perceive the parties in Sweden to have different foreign policy ideologies that matter for the formulation of foreign policy.

Finland

We found few, if any, signs of the mediatisation of Finnish foreign policy content. Turning to the form of foreign policy, the impression is the same, although some signs of such influence were apparent in the MPs' responses.

The MPs cited various examples of how the rhythm and dissemination of foreign policy have changed over the years. One member of the Foreign

Affairs Committee identified the media's tendency to run polls using more or less objectively formulated questions: 'especially on the Internet, this is a cheap way to start or promote foreign policy debates' (interview with MP Koskinen, SDP). Another MP argued that the media challenge MPs to answer questions about foreign policy decisions, noting that the role of the media as critical observers has become increasingly established in foreign policy as well as in other areas (interview with MP Komi, C).

MP Pertti Salolainen (NCP), a former deputy prime minister, ambassador and BBC correspondent, said that the media 'can change the atmosphere, making certain decisions more likely or creating hesitancy towards a certain proposal', though he seriously doubted whether the media influence the content of foreign policy decisions. MP Johannes Koskinen (SDP) agreed, saying that the media are 'raising issues for politicians to react to, often in a populist or simplifying way'. Koskinen also argued that 'since the constitutional powers of the President of Finland were reduced in favour of parliamentarism, the scope [for media influence] has been widened'.

The last observation is especially important. Until the year 2000 Finnish foreign policy was largely the responsibility of the president in the Finnish semi-presidential system. This, together with the consensus tradition and broad coalition governments, dampened foreign policy debate, according to the MPs. But in 2000 the constitution was changed, turning Finland's government into a more traditional parliamentary system and reducing the power of the president. With parliamentarianism, more divergent perspectives were facilitated. This, together with the perceptions that 'foreign policy is discussed more nowadays than in Cold War times' (interview with MP Kiviniemi, C) and that 'the overall discussion environment has maybe become [a] more open one' (interview with MP Komi, C), may, at least in the long run, break up the consensus culture of Finnish foreign policy. However, the MPs maintained that the consensus norm is still strong and is perceived to affect the form of foreign policy as well. One senior member of the Foreign Affairs Committee argued that even after the constitutional amendments in 2000, foreign policy is still decided in co-operation between the president and the government, with only a minor role for parliament (interview with MP Donner, SPP), leaving less room for public debate in the media. Or, as another parliamentarian described the situation: 'Finnish foreign policy has long been based on the consensus principle. That means that the media have also followed the consensus built by decision makers'. But the same MP added, 'in recent years, the media have been more active in questioning foreign policy achievements and goals' (interview with MP Komi, C).

According to the perceptions of the MPs interviewed, the expected homogeneity persists in Finnish foreign policy but some initial signs of a mediatised form of foreign policy, with more openness and divergent perspectives, can be seen on the horizon. We might say that even the homogeneous case of Finland may be approaching a more fragmented foreign policy debate in the near future, at least if we trust the perceptions of MPs. We are, however, not there yet.

It is important to note the rather high level of mediatisation perceived by Finnish MPs in general, as reported in some other studies. Lengauer et al. (2013: 182, 186) demonstrate that Finnish MPs ascribe considerable power to the media; and Donges, Håkansson and Lengauer (2013: 205) conclude that Finnish MPs mostly acknowledge mediatisation. These results are in line with our own, as several of the Finnish MPs interviewed acknowledged the mediatisation of politics in general but not in the foreign policy area. One parliamentarian said, 'the media influence is rather significant in Finnish domestic politics, but in foreign policy issues its role is quite small' (interview with MP Kiviniemi, C). Another MP argued that the mediatisation of foreign policy is 'not as extensive as it is in many other fields of political life' (interview with MP Koskinen, SDP), while a third MP claimed that the 'mediatisation of politics in general is a fact … however, the media influence in Finnish foreign policy is not extensive' (interview with MP Komi, C). The Finnish consensus norm in foreign policy, rooted in constitutional conditions, may be an important part of the explanation for the lower levels of perceived mediatisation of Finnish foreign policy.

Let us now examine the relationship between mediatisation and the internal structures of parliamentary party groups.

ELITE-LEVEL OR MID-LEVEL ADAPTATION BY PARTIES: HOMOGENISATION OR FRAGMENTATION?

Sweden

According to our theoretical expectations, adaptation to mediatisation would be exploited mainly by average parliamentarians in the Swedish case. Whether the adaptation to media logic is considered a process exploited by the elite or by average parliamentarians was discussed by the Foreign Affairs Committee members in relation to the use of social media.

New social media are sometimes placed within the broader context of technological change. New technologies in general and new social media in particular, are believed to increase the opportunities to become quickly informed about events taking place far away. This new technology makes it possible to comment and reflect on these events as they take place. This is sometimes explicitly interpreted as leading to fragmentation, as so many different actors can contribute to the same discussions from widely divergent perspectives (interviews with MPs Lundgren, C, and Härstedt, S). It is also believed that politicians can be influenced and inspired by the variety of content available on new media: one clear example being the recognition of Western Sahara (interview with MP Runeson, S).

This means that media hegemony is declining and that more diverse stories are being told. As the media picture is becoming more fragmented, politicians now have opportunities to present more nuanced views on a range of questions. Politicians can choose to profile their party, to develop ideas and to investigate how new ideas are accepted and perceived (interviews with MPs Bernhardsson, S, Enochsson, CD, and Forslund, S), although this is not so easily done when they are part of a government coalition (interview with MP Lundgren, C). The fact that new media users themselves can create news could make more voices heard when it comes to foreign policy issues (interviews with MPs Habsburg Douglas, M, Runeson, S, Thorell, S, and Winbäck, L):

> Today, many more people have opinions on developments in the world, not just on things that take place in their hometown or in Sweden. The level of knowledge is much higher today. … So, I think that many more people have influence over how the parties act to address foreign policy issues today than they did twenty-five years ago. (interview with MP Runeson, S)

The facts that the (new) media facilitate the spread of information and that more people now have a say in Swedish foreign policy are easily interpreted as signs of fragmentation.

Backbencher MPs are somewhat more accustomed to using these new media techniques (interviews with MPs Ceballos, G, Forslund, S, Habsburg Douglas, M, and Runeson, S), although even some very elite party members, such as the Swedish Foreign Minister at the time of the interviews, are well acquainted with Twitter and blogs (interviews with MP Ceballos, G, Forslund, S, and Malm, L).

In sum, both homogenisation and fragmentation elements are found when we examine whether adaptation to the media is centred on the party elite or on mid-level MPs. According to more nuanced views, the central tendency today is the growing influence of average parliamentarians. The example of the Foreign Affairs Minister is the only one that supports the homogenisation perspective, meaning that this perspective is not as central as the fragmentation perspective.

Finland

As our results in relation to the first two research questions posed in this chapter cast serious doubt on the claimed mediatisation of Finnish foreign policy, especially as regards the content of foreign policy, a discussion of who are the driving forces of adaptation to media logic would be beside the point. However, there are still reasons to return to the question of the relationship between mediatisation and homogeneous or fragmented political structures. We do so with a focus on homogeneous, hierarchical structures as constituting a firewall *against* mediatisation, rather than a force *for* mediatisation and of adaptation to media logic.

The respondents point to one reason, expressed in two ways, why mediatisation has had a hard time gaining a foothold in Finnish foreign policy. This reason, which is related to the homogeneous structures found in this area, is the persistent consensus norm in Finnish foreign policy. This norm has its roots in the semi-presidential system, in which the president was largely in charge of foreign policy, in place until the year 2000. In this system, the president could safeguard national consensus and dampen debate, a role he or she still possesses even though the powers of the presidency are more limited today (cf. interview with MP Donner, SPP, above). The consensus has been strengthened from time to time by grand coalition governments involving most of the major established parties.

Based on this consensus norm, some MPs referred to the political culture itself, in which a strong emphasis on seniority in foreign policy decisions has made it harder to implement sudden and dramatic changes that would be in line with the often short-sighted media logic. One MP claimed that recently (arguably, since the constitutional changes), the Foreign Affairs Committee has become more professional and today includes the most senior MPs and functions, 'almost like an upper house' (interview with MP Salolainen, NCP). The norm of seniority seems to have persisted despite the constitutional changes. This norm is obviously a serious obstacle to backbench MPs who are trying to make use of the opportunities of a mediatised society; instead, the consensus is safeguarded by a political elite – previously the president but now senior MPs.

To conclude, there are few signs of either an elite- or a mid-level party process of mediatisation. There are, however, strong signs of an elite-driven defence against media logic in general.

CONCLUSION

Does mediatisation primarily function as a force for homogenisation, which suggests a process of de-ideologisation and that party elites retain their grip over policy implications, as posited by cartel party theory? Or is mediatisation a force for fragmentation, which implies greater opportunities for ideological variation as well as greater opportunities for individual MPs to profile their own distinctiveness with the help of the media, as suggested by Kitschelt's critique of cartel party theory?

This puzzle has been investigated in this chapter by comparing perceptions of mediatisation among MPs in Finland and Sweden. Both Finland and Sweden were expected to manifest strong homogenisation effects but, as Finland's foreign policy consensus is even stronger than Sweden's, we expected the homogenisation effect to be even stronger in the case of Finnish foreign policy.

Before drawing conclusions about how mediatisation was perceived by the MPs we interviewed, we should first emphasise that the perceived level of overall mediatisation varied significantly between the two cases. While the Swedish MPs acknowledged the presence of mediatisation in politics in general and in foreign policy more specifically, almost all the Finnish MPs acknowledged the mediatisation of politics in general but not in the foreign policy area. In our empirical analysis, we returned to the strong Finnish consensus norm as an obstacle to mediatisation.

Nevertheless we found some, although limited, indications of the mediatisation of Finnish foreign policy, as perceived by the members of the Finnish Foreign Affairs Committee. These results indicate that, to a greater extent than their Swedish peers, the Finnish MPs perceive mediatisation in terms of homogenisation, with the media supporting a traditional foreign policy consensus, while the Swedish MPs gave more mixed answers and see mediatisation as having both homogenisation and fragmentation effects. Despite the similarities between Sweden and Finland, there are also indisputable differences.

This means that both the proponents of cartel party theory and its leading critic, Herbert Kitschelt, can be said to be correct regarding the consequences of mediatisation, but in different respects. Cartel party theory is possibly more accurate regarding extreme consensual systems like the Finnish foreign policy decision-making system; Kitschelt is possibly more accurate regarding political systems in which there are at least some initial differences in ideology and policy formulation. This implies that Kitschelt's theory probably has a broader empirical significance than the cartel party theory. Cartel party theory is applicable only to Finnish foreign policy, an extreme consensual case with few equivalents. Kitschelt's theory applies better to Swedish foreign policy, also a consensual issue area but not such an extreme case as the Finnish one. This suggests that Kitschelt's theory is probably more applicable to a wide array of countries and issue areas than the cartel party theory.

To understand the potential role of mediatisation in politics in general and in party politics in particular, we argue that it is crucial that future research take political culture into account (cf. Brommesson and Ekengren 2013). The two cases and the interviews with MPs reported here give us ample evidence of the role of political culture in the foreign policy area, evidence that can help us understand differences in perceptions of mediatisation between two countries that are similar in so many respects. We also argue that the present results indicate that cartel party theory, as well as other party theories, should take account of cultural variables to a greater extent, if they are more fully to uncover the limits and merits of other variables (cf. Barrling 2014).

APPENDIX 1. INTERVIEWS WITH MEMBERS OF PARLIAMENT

Sweden

Bo Bernardsson (S), 15 May 2012
Bodil Ceballos (G), 29 May 2012
Anneli Enochsson (CD), 21 March 2012
Kennet Forslund (S), 25 April 2012
Marie Granlund (S), 21 May 2012
Walburga Habsburg Douglas (M), 25 April 2012
Kent Härstedt (S), 29 May 2012
Mats Johansson (M), 30 May 2012
Kerstin Lundgren (C), 25 September 2012
Fredrik Malm (L), 9 January 2013
Desireé Pethrus (CD), 9 January 2013
Carin Runeson (S), 25 April 2012
Olle Thorell (S), 24 February 2012
Christer Winbäck (L), 30 May 2012

Finland

Jörn Donner (SPP), 7 Feburary 2014
Mari Kiviniemi (C), 6 February 2013
Katri Komi (C), 28 January 2013
Johannes Koskinen (SDP), 4 March 2013
Petteri Orpo (NCP), 21 February, 2013
Pertti Salolainen (NCP), 7 December 2012
Peter Östman (CD), 11 March 2014

APPENDIX 2. INTERVIEW QUESTIONS

Power and Influence

- What actors do you think influence Swedish/Finnish foreign policy the most?
- In what ways do they exert influence?

Mediatisation

- There is a lot of talk about the ongoing mediatisation of politics in general. Would you consider the media influence on Swedish/Finnish foreign policy to be extensive?
- Do you have any specific examples of situations in which foreign policy decision-making has been affected by the media?
- What media affect foreign policy the most?
- Why do the media affect foreign policy?
- Do you think that the media influence has changed over time?

Strategy

- Do you use the media to influence foreign policy decision-making?
- How do you do that?
- Would you say that the media influence affects whether your party acts on certain issues? Is the same true of the government?
- Mediatisation, among other things, means that you simplify, polarise, dramatise and personalise. Do you use these strategies yourself to get breakthroughs in the media?

Ideology

- Another way to form foreign policy is to emphasise ideology. Have you encountered situations in which your ideology conflicts with what is deemed necessary according to the media agenda?
- How do you handle those situations?

NOTES

1. According to Nino Landerer's (2013) critique, it is questionable whether we can speak of a single media logic, so we should instead focus on many different logics. He argues that the common denominator of many media logics is competitiveness and marketisation. However, we agree with Strömbäck and Dimitrova (2011: 33) in arguing that the 'norms that govern the media overall are often more important than what distinguishes one form of media from another'.

2. Finland and Sweden in many ways share the same foreign policy context. Both are non-aligned, post-neutral members of the EU, situated in the same Nordic geographical area (Möller and Bjereld 2010). Sweden and Finland both relied on a policy of neutrality during the Cold War but have gradually adapted to new conditions in recent decades (Miles 2000; Ojanen, Herolf and Lindahl 2001; Rieker 2004; Möller and Bjereld 2010; Koivula and Sipilä 2011). Finland and Sweden share many

characteristics of political culture, partly as a result of the two being one state until 1809. In addition, since the constitutional changes made in 2000, Finland is no longer classified as a semi-presidential system but as a parliamentary system like Sweden (Nousiainen 2001). Both countries have a consensus culture (but see Chapter 5 in this book, regarding changes in the conflict/consensus dimension in the Swedish Parliament), in which the parties have been devoted to co-operation and negotiation to solve political divergences (Moring 2006: 86; Bågenholm and Demker 2007: 45; Tenscher, Mykkänen and Moring 2012: 151).

The media cultures in Finland and Sweden exhibit many similarities. Of course, as Daniel Hallin and Paolo Mancini (2004: 67) have demonstrated quite convincingly, media systems and political systems cannot be understood entirely separately. However, considering media culture in terms of the newspaper industry, political parallelism, professionalisation and the role of the state in a media system, Hallin and Mancini (2004: 67, 70, 143–96) demonstrate that both Finland and Sweden neatly fit into the 'North/Central European or Democratic Corporatist' ideal-type model (cf. Pfetsch et al. 2013: 36).

3. Previous research articulates competing expectations as to the consequences this consensus norm may have for the level of mediatisation. In an earlier interview study with policy elites in Finland, Reunanen, Kunelius, and Noppari (2010: 304–5) found support for the existence of a viable consensus culture as a local resource used to protect networks from mediatisation. In another project examining different aspects of mediatisation, Pfetsch et al. (2013) interviewed Finnish politicians about their perceptions of issues related to mediatisation. These interviews were conducted amidst a political scandal in which the foreign minister had to resign. Under these circumstances, Pfetsch et al. found support among Finnish politicians in general for the existence of a high level of perceived mediatisation. On the other hand, Tom Moring (2006: 94) has demonstrated that mediatisation effects on Finnish voting behaviour in national and European elections have been rather limited.

4. It is worth emphasising that we are examining *perceptions* of mediatisation as we believe that these have substantial consequences for actors' various actions, for example, how they address foreign policy issues.

5. A list of all politicians interviewed, with their party affiliations, can be found in Appendix 1.

6. Nothing indicates that our results would be different if we had interviewed only members of the European Union Affairs Committee.

7. Appendix 2 summarises the questions posed to interviewees. The oral interview with Perti Salolainen confirms that more complex answers were obtained in oral interviews, though there is no obvious difference in content.

8. In addition, because the interviewees were not only respondents but also informants, we deem the difference between the written and oral interviews to be minor. We therefore think that the differences in the answers from the Swedish and Finnish MPs represent genuine differences and are not simply the result of different interview techniques.

9. We examined MPs' perceptions at a particular time in history. Of course, it would have been better if we could have examined perceptions on several occasions,

in order to draw more certain conclusions regarding changes over time and to fully study the process claim implicit in mediatisation. However, as we measured perceptions of mediatisation on only one occasion, we instead asked about perceived changes over time. Although this is not as robust as having measured perceptions on several occasions, we still regard this as the most feasible option and robust enough for present purposes. In this, we rely on Reunanen, Kunelius and Noppari (2010: 304), who claim that perceptions of change are a good proxy for a longitudinal study.

10. For party names, see the List of Parties and Abbreviations above.

Chapter 7

Party Cartelisation or Gender Politicisation?

Helena Olofsdotter Stensöta and Anna Högmark

Theory on political cleavages holds that the inclusion of new social cleavages in politics is connected to the politicisation of new problems. In this chapter, the hypothesis derived from cartel party theory, that conflict in politics is diminishing over time, is examined in contrast to expectations derived from studies of women representatives.

The cartel party theory posits that political conflict should decrease over time, due to the development and dynamics of parties (for an outline of the theory, see Chapter 1 in this book). While political conflict between parties was considerable in the mass-party era in the early twentieth century, the declining importance of the grassroots marks the evolution of cartel parties. This development is interpreted as though the impetus for policy change has increasingly shifted from the grassroots to within the party itself (Katz and Mair 1995, 2009).

A quite different expectation can be derived from studies of women representatives in politics, however. Focus in this field of research is on when, how and why women politicians represent women's interests (Celis et al. 2008). Research has concluded that increased representation by women in politics has been connected to the politicisation of new issues, many of which are related to care, such as childcare, the six-hour working day and other care-and-career policies.

If we assume that the political interest of a specific group is not fully developed as the group first enters politics, but rather develops over time, an idea that is present in the work of Anne Phillips (1998), then we might hypothesise that an increase in women representatives in politics would increase policy conflict.

From these two bodies of theory, the following contrasting hypotheses can be derived regarding the development of political conflict in parliament over time:

Hypothesis 1: Political conflict in parliament should decrease over time.
Hypothesis 2: An increased proportion of women in parliament should increase the level of political conflict.
Hypothesis 2a: The relationship between women and conflict varies depending on:
  i. the subject area (e.g. the economy or social issues) of politics; and
  ii. whether or not women are in powerful positions.

We used a unique dataset of a total selection of parliamentary committee reports[1] in Sweden from 1971 to 2012, excluding election years, to test these two contrasting expectations.

Sweden is an interesting case from the gender perspective, as it is highly placed in many international rankings on gender equality. According to the World Economic Forum, in 2014, Sweden ranked fourth in gender equity (scoring 0.82, with Iceland in the lead with a score of 0.86)[2] and can therefore be considered a country suitable for the exploration of the impact of gender equality on external features.

The findings suggest that an increasing proportion of women in parliament is correlated with increasing levels of political conflict, after controlling for term of office and the time in office of the Alliance of right-wing parties This runs counter to the cartel theory hypothesis. It is more difficult to find reasons for the correlation between women representatives and levels of conflict, as the findings do not reveal systematic patterns. As a general conclusion, we note that it is not only in policy areas traditionally understood as the province of women that the presence of women is associated with higher levels of political conflict. In two traditionally male-dominated standing committees, Defence and Finance, an increasing number of women members correlates with increasing conflict.

PREVIOUS RESEARCH

Scholarly interest in representation by women has been motivated by three main questions (Pitkin 1967): first, the dynamics of fair access to political power, which is a question of 'descriptive representation'; second the question of when, how and why women represent women's interests, which is a question of 'substantive representation'; and, third, the question of women's symbolic representation.

Indeed, research on women's substantive representation has convincingly demonstrated that there is a small but consistent difference between female and male MPs in the way they represent women's interests across a broad range of political issues and in various contexts: women in legislatures have, on average, slightly more leftist attitudes than do men, are more supportive of environmental policies and care-and-career policies and are more opposed to pornography. The effect of gender is small but consistent and holds when controlling for ideology, party and constituency effects. Furthermore, the gender effect seems to be valid across institutional systems and types of welfare state (Celis 2006; Childs and Krook 2009; Kittilson and Schwindt-Bayer 2012; Lovenduski and Norris 1993, 2003; Narud and Valen 2000; Poggione 2004; Schwindt-Bayer and Mishler 2005; Skjeie 1992; Swers 2001; Wängnerud 2009).

The theoretical expectation that women represent certain interests was originally inspired by Marxist theory paying attention to structural divisions in society related to work (Diamond and Hartsock 1981). Elaborating on this idea, we can connect research that identifies social stratification as important for the formation of political interests with research on women's representation. An underlying theoretical idea in social stratification research is that the organisation of any interests corresponding to a group of people with marked characteristic experiences entails the politicisation of new problems. Just as organised labour market interests meant the politicisation of labour market issues, so women's emerging participation in politics could mean the politicisation of new political issues (e.g. issues related to public engagement in child-rearing) previously considered apolitical and 'private', and about which people were not expected to disagree much.

The impetus to research on gender and politics would be that women form a new type of cleavage that politicises such 'new' issues, for example, problematising the division between a 'private' family sphere that was once considered non-political and a 'public' political sphere. This private/public divide addresses issues of care and career in which women have a greater interest than men.

Lipset and Rokkan (1967) highlighted that the party system became frozen in the Nordic countries before full democratisation (in the form of all adults having the right to vote). During the twentieth century, the importance of social cleavages to voting was considerable in the Nordic countries, but it has declined over time, which is related to increased mobility both between social classes and geographically, along with increased urbanisation and secularisation (Oskarson 1994). This transition, in which long-term social group membership has been replaced with shorter-term considerations as reason to vote for a particular party, has been labelled 'dealignment' (Dalton, Flanagan and Beck 1984; Hagevi 2015a).

In previous feminist research, Nina Raaum (2005) discusses the development of women's representation in Norway by using Rokkan's model from 1967 of four levels of institutional thresholds: (a) legitimisation, including articulation of values and interests; (b) incorporation, including the right to vote and to exercise this right; (c) political representative presence in large numbers; and (d) political power. This provides a framework for describing the development of women's representation and discussing how to understand why women received the vote about two decades later than men in the Nordic context and why it was not until the late 1970s that the numbers of women representatives reached levels rising above the 'token' status of 20 per cent. Dahlerup and Freidenvall (2006) have also examined the politicisation of women in the Nordic context and argued that gender representation in the Nordic countries has increased along an incremental path, meaning it proceeds gradually and in small steps.

THEORY

Previous research on gender and politics has been oriented towards such questions as whether women bring *new* issues on to the political agenda and/or put a stronger emphasis on particular issues. Whether women MPs contribute to increased conflict in parliament generally has not been examined. However, if we assume that politicisation by new groups is a dynamic process that develops over time, we can expect that increased female representation may have broader consequences. More specifically, we might expect that policy areas not primarily marked by gender may also disclose patterns of increasing conflict as the number of women representatives increases.

The Swedish case is particularly interesting in relation to this question as, according to Freidenvall (2006), increased gender representation in Sweden has proceeded as a top-down project, which resembles how cartel party theory pictures party innovation and addresses the question of grassroots-induced *versus* leadership-induced changes. If we assume that parties' strategies are intended to attract voters, we can regard the recruitment of women as a strategy with that goal. However, if these recruited women, once in office, increase conflict, this would mean that the impact of women runs counter to expectations. Instead of strengthening the parties, these women in office might diminish party strength by creating more conflict. In relation to cartel party theory, we can ask whether some strategies characteristic of cartel parties may, in this case, have contributed to the undermining of the cartelisation process. If so, it would seem that recruitment of more women has become a cuckoo in the nest for political parties.

EMPIRICAL SECTION

Research Questions

The empirical analysis aims to answer the following question: does an increasing proportion of women in parliament increase the likelihood of political conflict in parliament? In relation to cartel party theory, we ask whether its hypothesis of decreasing political conflict finds support from a gender-sensitive analytical perspective. In relation to gender research, we ask whether the proposition that the gender cleavage may lead to new types of conflict applies to areas other than those traditionally connected with the gender divide, such as social policy and care-and-career policy.

We use a unique dataset consisting of a total sample of committee reports from the Swedish Parliament between 1971 and 2012, except in election years, which gives us 4,650 units of analysis (Loxbo and Sjölin 2016; see Chapter 5 of this book).[3] The dataset excludes reports of the European Union Affairs Committee, as this committee does not prepare government bills for decisions by Parliament as do the standing parliamentary committees (see Chapters 1 and 5 of this book). The study measures the reservations made by MPs (with few exceptions, affiliated with the parties in parliamentary opposition to the government), attached to the committee reports produced after the preparing of government bills. A reservation in a committee report is a sign of conflict between government and opposition, while the absence of such a reservation is a sign of parliamentary consensus.[4]

Dependent Variables

We use three dependent variables to measure the level of conflict.

1. *Any type of reservation.* This dichotomous variable distinguishes all committee reports produced on government bills to which *any type of reservation* is attached (ranging from reservations demanding minor changes in the bill to ones calling for full rejection of the bill) (1) from reports with no reservation attached (0). Half the sample, 2,652 committee reports, have such reservations attached to them.
2. *Any type of reservation across the left–right political divide.* This variable distinguishes all committee reports on government bills with attached reservations that are signed by parties *across the left–right political divide*; it is dichotomous, distinguishing any type of reservation across the divide (1) from no reservation (0). We have coded as reservations across the left–right political divide all committee reports in which the Greens ally themselves with either left- or right-wing parties on a reservation and

all co-edited reservations, including from New Democracy (in the early 1990s) or the Sweden Democrats. This coding might be controversial as it has been argued that the Greens can be connected to the left since at least 1996, especially at the voter level (Oscarsson 1998). However, as the present analysis actually concerns MPs and not voters, and because some researchers argue that the 'green' dimension cuts across the left–right political divide, we choose this operationalisation. Furthermore, as the question of gendered representation concerns whether gender is a separate dimension from the left–right political divide, it is defensible not to play down challenges to this divide but rather to acknowledge them fully. In 634 cases, such reservations are attached to a committee report according to this generous operationalisation.[5]

3. *Rejection.* This variable distinguishes whether any party has rejected the committee report on government bills entirely (1) or whether no such rejection has occurred (0). Hence, it is a strong measure of conflict. There are 559 committee reports on government bills out of a total of 4,650 in the sample that have reservations from at least one party that reject government bills in this way.

Table 7.1 describes the dependent variables.

Table 7.1   Description of Dependent Variables (absolute numbers per term of office)

Term of office	Parliamentary committee reports with any type of reservation	Parliamentary committee reports totally rejected by at least one party	Parliamentary committee reports with reservations across left–right political divide	Total number of parliamentary committee reports
1971–3	128	13	8	258
1974–6	135	20	13	299
1977–9	296	30	5	686
1980–2	385	55	6	773
1983–5	237	31	31	359
1986–8	221	31	36	315
1989–91	214	54	129	289
1992–4	196	39	2	378
1995–8	132	29	55	199
1999–2002	163	31	50	230
2003–6	152	77	47	240
2007–10	225	121	164	345
2011–12*	168	28	88	279
Total	**2,652**	**559**	**634**	**4,650**

Note: Table 7.1 shows absolute numbers of Committee Reports. The Swedish Parliament had 350 legislators until 1976, when the number was reduced to 349 to give an uneven number. All standing committees are included while the European Union Affairs Committee is excluded. There were sixteen standing committees until 2006, when the number decreased to fifteen.
*We do not have data for the whole last term of office.

Independent Variables

The main independent variable is the number of women representatives. It is measured in three ways:

1. *Proportion of women in parliament.* This variable measures the representation of women in parliament as the percentage of seats held by women. Women's share of seats in the Swedish Parliament has constantly increased over the period examined, except for the term of office starting in 1991. This was compensated for through an increase in the number of women MPs in 1994. However, the last measure from 2010 indicates a small decrease from 2006, and women still do not account for 50 per cent of MPs. The proportion of women has fluctuated between 14 per cent (1970–1) and 47 per cent (2006).
2. *Proportion of women in standing committees.* Although the proportion of women in parliament has gradually increased, this increase is not equally distributed across the standing committees. There was, and still is, although to a lesser extent, a rather strict division between women and men in the Swedish parliamentary landscape regarding the standing committees on which they serve (Wängnerud 2015). Women were formerly often represented in the Cultural Affairs, Social Insurance, Health and Welfare, and Justice committees, whereas women's representation lagged in the Transport and Communication, Finance, Defence, Taxation, and Industry and Trade committees. This unequal distribution resulted from both parliamentarians' own choices and strategic decisions made by the parties. We use the proportion of women as a percentage of delegates in standing committees as the measure, with the value ranging from 0 to 71 per cent.
3. *Women as chairs of standing committees.* Women's presence in powerful positions is often lower than in parliament as a whole. This variable accounts for whether a man (0) or a woman (1) occupies the position of standing committee chair. Fully 81 per cent of committee reports were presented with a man as the chair of the related committee.[6]

Table 7.2 describes the independent variables.

As we are interested in whether and how women's representation differs between standing committees, as a way to address women's and men's traditional policy interests/political culture, it is interesting to note in detail the variation in women's representation between standing committees. Table 7.3 shows the years when women first accounted for 40 per cent of the membership of specific standing committees and the years in which committees first had female chairs.

As Table 7.3 shows, there are considerable differences between standing committees in terms of the achievement of gender equality. The earliest

Table 7.2 Description of Independent Variables: Numbers of Women Representatives

	1971–3	1974–6	1977–9	1980–2	1983–5	1986–8	1989–91	1992–4	1995–8	1999–2002	2003–6	2007–10	2011–12
Parliament	14	21	23	26	27	31	38	33	40	43	45	47	45
Standing committees	15	16	19	23	26	28	36	34	42	47	47	45	43
Chairs of standing committees	6 (1)	13 (2)	6 (1)	0 (0)	13 (2)	19 (3)	25 (4)	31 (5)	38 (6)	44 (7)	25 (4)	47 (7)	40 (6)

Note: Women's presence in parliament is measured in per cent. Women in standing committees are measured as the mean per cent in all standing committees during each term of office. Women as chairs of standing committees are measured in per cent, with the absolute numbers of women shown within parentheses.

Table 7.3   Detailed Description of Women's Representation in Standing Committees

	Founding of Standing Committee	Year Women First Constituted 40 per cent	Year of First Female Chair
Environment and Agriculture	1970	1994	2002
Constitution	1970	1991	1994
Cultural Affairs	1970	1979	1982
Defence	1970	2006	2006
Finance	1970	1998	1994
Education	1970	1991	1991
Finance	1970	1998	1988
Foreign Affairs	1970	1994	1994
Justice	1970	1988	1970
Health and Welfare	1970	1982	1998
Social Insurance	1970	1982	1985
Tax	1970	1998	No
Transport and Communication	1970	2006	1994
Internal Affairs/Labour Market	1970–6/1976	– /1982	– /1982
Law/Civil Affairs II	1970–2006/2006	1988/2006	1991/2006
Civil Affairs I/Housing	1970–85/1985–2006	– /1994	1973/ –

Note: Fourteen standing committees have existed throughout the period. The last three committees' names changed during the period examined; information for the old and renamed committees is separated by /.

standing committees in which women constituted 40 per cent of membership were the Cultural Affairs (1979), Health and Welfare, Social Insurance (1982) and Justice (1988) committees. The last standing committees in which women constituted 40 per cent of membership were the Defence (2006) and the Transport and Communication (2006) committees. Similarly, we see variation between committees in the first year a woman was standing committee chair, ranging from 1970 (Justice), 1982 (Cultural Affairs) and 1985 (Social Insurance) to 2006 (Defence). These figures line up fairly well with the established conception of 'women's' *versus* 'men's' policy areas, with strong women's representation occurring earlier in typical women's policy areas; the exception is Justice, which, although not such an area, achieved female leadership and representation early on. Separated by lines in the table from the other standing committees are three committees that changed their names during the period.

Analysis: Likelihood of Conflict and Women's Presence in Parliament

This analysis is performed as a logistic regression because the dependent variables are dichotomous, distinguishing conflict from no conflict. We start by examining how the likelihood of conflict, in all three degrees, is affected by the general level of women representatives in parliament. The analysis controls for term of office (T1). In addition, the emergence of the Alliance, which was in power between 2006 and 2014 in Sweden, is generally considered to have changed how parliament works. Since the emergence of the Alliance, the latitude to present motions that straddle the left–right political divide has diminished considerably; the parties, especially the dominant Moderates, have become more centralised – so the critique runs (Pålsson 2011). By comparing the 1972–2005 and 2006–12 periods, we can explore this assertion (T2).

If we start by examining Model 1 (T1), Table 7.4 shows that there are significant relationships between the number of women in parliament and the likelihood of reservations being attached to a committee report in all three operationalisations. There is an increased likelihood of *any* type of reservation being attached to a committee report and, similarly, an increased and significant likelihood of a committee report being rejected in its entirety when there is an increased presence of female legislators. The last column also shows an increased likelihood of reservations across the left–right political divide as the number of women in parliament increases. In Model 2 (T2), Table 7.4 shows that controlling for the Alliance makes the relationship between any type of reservation and the proportion of women in parliament insignificant. By contrast, this control strengthens the relationship between, on the one hand, the number of women representatives and the total rejection of government bills by one party or more and on the other hand, the incidence of committee reports with reservations across the left–right divide. The effect of women is, however, very much smaller than the effect of the Alliance.

The findings regarding the total rejection of government bills and the incidence of committee reports with reservations across the left–right divide at first seem to support the idea that women representatives increase political conflict generally. However, several factors apart from the increasing proportion of women in parliament and term in office that change over time are likely to affect the results. As can be seen in the bottom row of Table 7.4, the explained variance (Pseudo R^2) for the null model, capturing only the effect on the dependent variables of controlling for term of office, is as high as when the share of women is included. Hence, the analysis does not support the idea that the level of conflict in parliament is raised by the increase in women representatives.

The analysis proceeds by examining the relationship between women's representation and levels of conflict in individual standing committees and by exploring the effect of women in powerful positions, that is, female committee chairs, which is shown in Table 7.5. Here, only one dependent variable is presented, the broadest: the likelihood that a committee report has any type

Table 7.4   Likelihood of Conflict/Co-Operation Evidenced in Committee Reports with Different Levels of Female Representatives in Parliament (bivariate logistic regressions, logit)

	Any Type of Reservation		One Party or More Totally Rejecting		Reservations Across the Left–Right Divide	
	T1	T2	T1	T2	T1	T2
Share of women in parliament	0.014* (2.46)	0.107 (1.29)	0.024* (2.14)	0.789*** (6.89)	0.086*** (6.99)	0.338*** (4.03)
Alliance (no Alliance is ref. cat.)		−2.890 (−1.08)		−23.706*** (−6.35)		−7.816** (−2.87)
Control, term of office (dummy)	Yes	Yes	Yes	Yes	Yes	Yes
Prob > chi²	0.00	0.000	0.00	0.000	0.00	0.000
Pseudo R^2	0.033	0.033	0.089	0.089	0.270	0.270
Null model, control term of office (dummy), Pseudo R^2	0.033	–	0.089	–	0.270	–

Note: *** $p \leq 0.001$; ** $p \leq 0.01$; * $p \leq 0.05$. Z-values within parentheses.

of reservation attached to it. The other two have also been examined but they show no significant results.

Table 7.5 shows specific standing committees for which there are significant relationships between the likelihood of any reservation being attached to a committee report, on one hand, and the proportion of women members and the presence of a female chair, respectively, on the other. There are three standing committees in which the proportion of women significantly increases the amount of conflict: Defence, Finance, and Environment and Agriculture. It is difficult to draw any conclusions about general mechanisms from these findings, but it is noteworthy that Defence – one of the last standing committees in which women achieved equality in representation and focused on a traditionally 'male' area – is represented here, as well as Finance, which did not achieve 40 per cent women's representation until 1998.

Looking at the relationship between the presence of female committee chairs and the likelihood that a committee report has any type of reservation attached to it, Table 7.5 shows that the presence of a female chair increases the likelihood of conflict in the Foreign Affairs and Cultural Affairs committees but decreases it in the Defence, Environment and Agriculture, and Civil Affairs/Housing committees. In regard to the committees where female chairs seem to curb conflict, we detect both Defence and Environment and Agriculture, where a female chair was appointed comparatively late (2006 and 2002), and Civil Affairs/Housing, where this happened early (1973). If

Table 7.5   Likelihood of Any Reservation Being Attached to a Committee Report Per Standing Committee (logistic regression, logit)

	Finance		Defence		Foreign Affairs		Cultural Affairs		Environment and Agriculture		Housing	
Fem. repr.	0.026*	0.037*	0.141**	0.141**	0.025	−0.035	−0.035	−0.035	−0.012	0.047*	−0.014	0.049
	(2.26)	(2.38)	(2.83)	(2.83)	(0.79)	(−1.22)	(−0.70)	(−0.70)	(−0.56)	(2.17)	(−0.98)	(1.35)
Fem. chair		−0.523		−3.715*		2.026*		1.466*		−2.015**		−2.914*
		(−0.87)		(−2.23)		(2.09)		(0.09) (1.69)		(−2.65)		(−1.85)
Term of office control	yes	yes	yes	yes	yes	yes	yes	yes	yes	yes	yes	yes
Pseudo R^2	0.071	0.071	0.094	0.094	0.087	0.087	0.049	0.049	0.050	0.050	0.100	0.100
Prob. > chi²	0.000	0.000	0.038	0.038	0.084	0.084	0.184	0.184	0.143	0.143	0.000	0.000

Note: First row shows female representation in standing committees; second row shows presence of female chairs.
*** $p \leq 0.001$; ** $p \leq 0.01$; * $p \leq 0.10$. Z-values within parentheses. The presence of a female chair is not significant in the Cultural Affairs and Housing committees at the 0.05 level.

we turn to where the female chair seems to increase conflict, Foreign Affairs and Cultural Affairs, these committees had their first female chair in the period between 1982 and 1994. Apart from the finding that there is a connection between the number of women and the level of conflict in traditionally male-dominated standing committees as well, patterns are inconclusive. This goes also for the two additional descriptive tables on female committee chairs and level of conflict, over time and per standing committee where likewise no systematic patterns are observable.

In sum, the analysis has shown in detail how women's representation has developed and increased over time within the Swedish parliament and its standing committees. It has also shown that there is a positive correlation between a higher number of women in parliament and the likelihood of conflict operationalised in three ways. As the variable 'women' does not add explicatory power to the model, it suggests that the driving force lies somewhere else; there is no indication that women increase conflict, and hence politicisation more generally.

In regard to the separate standing committees, the results are also inconclusive. Worth noticing is that an increased share of women is associated with increased conflict in traditionally 'male' areas such as Defence and Finance, which can be taken as an indicator of a possible politicising effect not being restricted to traditionally female areas. In regard to the correlation between female chair and the likelihood that a committee report has any type of conflict attached to it, there are few conclusive results.

CONCLUSION

The general finding that increased representation by women in the Swedish Parliament is correlated with increased political conflict can be seen as a critical observation in relation to the cartel party theory in two ways: first, against the general hypothesis of the cartel party theory that political conflict should diminish over time; and, second, against the notion that social cleavages lose power to shape politics. If we think of the increased representation of women as the political formation or institutionalisation of a new cleavage, that of gender, then it becomes clear that the historical development is more complex than cartel party theorists have imagined. From this perspective the cartel party theory is rooted in the development of *one* particular cleavage, the left–right divide, and therefore it cannot serve as a general description of party and party system development. In this, the analysis identifies certain shortcomings in the cartel party theory when it comes to describing change.

The analysis further attempted to find more general patterns between women's presence and levels of conflict, but the results were inconclusive. It was noted that the positive relationship between women and the likelihood that any type of reservation was attached to a committee report was found also in typically 'male' policy areas such as Defence and Finance; no systematic patterns could be established, however.

Above we used the metaphor of a cuckoo in the nest to describe the effect of more women legislators on political parties: party leaderships invited women to be representatives in order to strengthen the party but instead invited more conflict. This metaphor mirrors the correlation found in the material but no actual mechanism linking women to more political conflict generally could be established.

APPENDIX

Table A 7.1   **Proportion of Committee Reports with Reservations, Divided by Male and Female Chairs Per Term of Office, 1970–2010 (%)**

	1970	1973	1976	1979	1982	1985	1988	1991	1994	1998	2002	2006	2010	Total
Male chair	50	44	45	50	66	71	73	51	67	73	60	66	62	56
Female chair	47	50	19	-[a]	68	65	77	53	66	69	75	64	58	61
Total	50	45	43	50	66	70	74	52	66	71	63	66	60	57
Difference, male – female	3	–6	26	-[a]	–2	6	–4	–2	1	4	–15	2	4	–5

Note: [a] In 1979 there were no female chairs. Difference: male chair – female chair; negative values indicate higher levels of conflict with female chair. Number of reservations, male/female chair: total, 3,776/878; 1970, 239/19; 1973, 251/48; 1976, 634/52; 1979, 773/0; 1982, 325/34; 1985, 252/63; 1988, 197/92; 1991, 263/115; 1994, 106/93; 1998, 124/106; 2002, 183/57; 2006, 257/92; 2010, 172/10.

Table A 7.2   **Proportion of Committee Reports with Reservations, Divided by Male and Female Chairs Per Committee, 1970–2010 (%)**

	Male Chair	Female Chair	Total	Difference, Male–Female
Environment and Agriculture	59	58	59	1
Constitution	47	71	50	–26
Cultural Affairs	57	81	55	+24
Defence	44	61	45	–17
Industry and Trade	68	74	69	–6
Education	72	71	72	1
Finance	41	62	44	–21
Foreign Affairs	41	46	43	–5
Justice	54	49	51	5
Health and Welfare	58	88	61	–30
Social Insurance	70	83	74	–13
Transport and Communication	53	64	54	–11
Total	56	64	58	–8

Note: Difference: male chair–female chair, negative values indicate higher levels of conflict with female chair. Number of reservations, male/female chair: total, 2734/702; Environment and Agriculture, 218/33; Constitution, 201/28; Cultural Affairs, 123/70; Defence, 158/13; Industry and Trade, 369/43; Education, 247/48; Finance, 356/68; Foreign Affairs, 123/39; Justice, 184/222; Health and Welfare, 253/26; Social Insurance, 188/81; Transport and Communication, 314/31.

NOTES

1. In Swedish, *utskottsbetänkanden.*

2. World Economic Forum 2015.

3. The dataset of parliamentary committee reports was compiled by Karl Loxbo and Mats Sjölin in the research project Party Government in Flux (Loxbo and Sjölin 2016).

4. Reservations attached to committee reports rarely survive the final parliamentary vote.

5. The variable is calculated by adding together the dichotomous variables for reservations supported by parties from both sides of the left–right political divide. In practice, this includes all bills in which the Greens, New Democracy and Sweden Democrats were active.

6. Some of the standing committees have changed or been combined: in 1975, the Internal Affairs Committee was transformed into the Labour Market Committee, while in 1983, the former Civil Affairs Committee was transformed into the Housing Committee. In 2006, the Law Committee merged with the Housing Committee to become the Civil Affairs Committee.

Chapter 8

Party Culture and Cartelisation

Exploring the Inner Life of the Parliamentary Party

Katarina Barrling

The proponents of the cartel party thesis claim that parties' increasing dependence on state resources and their tendency to be office-seeking weaken their organisational identities and, correspondingly, reinforce inter-party collaboration and even collusion (e.g. Katz and Mair 1995, 2002, 2009; Mair 1997; Blyth and Katz 2005). What about possible restraining counter-forces? In this chapter, we address one such possible restraining force, namely, *party organisational culture*, and argue that it might hold party cartelisation in check. We also investigate whether the party groups in the Swedish Parliament have undergone the kind of cultural change that the cartel party thesis might lead us to expect.

Without focusing on the main implications of cartel parties' emergence that are claimed by the theory's proponents (see Chapters 2 to 7 in this book), it is fully possible to discuss the 'radius of action' of cartelisation and its limits. The argument here is that any discussion of cartelisation would gain from taking into account party organisational culture, which could probably restrain cartelisation but which has been overlooked in this area of research. This is surprising, because party organisational culture – broadly defined here as the party's collective identity and social norms – could be assumed to offer resistance to the tendencies of cartelisation (e.g. Kitschelt 1994; Koole 1996; Abélès 2000; Esaiasson and Heidar 2000; Chabal and Daloz 2006; Barrling 2013). Even Katz and Mair themselves (2009: 760) mention party organisational culture, though without considering it as a possible check to cartelisation.

The empirical basis of this study is an *investigation of party cultural change within the party groups (defined as the members of the parliamentary party) of the Swedish Parliament*. If we find that the organisational cultures of parliamentary parties appear to resist the pressure to change that close collaboration might bring, this would constitute a part of the party identity that is difficult to change and that would thereby obstruct the kind of ends–means rationality that cartelisation presupposes.

Even though cartelisation between established left- and right-wing parties may not be a general trend in Swedish politics (see Chapters 3, 5 and 7 of this book), the Swedish case still offers useful examples of collaboration. Since 1998 all parties that were in parliament at the time have engaged in far-reaching collaboration within political blocs (see Chapter 1 in this book). First and foremost is the renewed and more organised collaboration between the four right-wing parties (*Alliansen*, or Alliance) since 2004, which constituted the basis of the cabinet between 2006 and 2014. Second, the Social Democrats collaborated in a formalised way with the Green and the Left parties (though they were not included in the government): initially, when the Social Democrats governed from 1998 to 2006 and the other two parties acted as 'support parties', and then when the Social Democrats were in opposition from 2008 until the parliamentary elections in 2010. The far-reaching collaborations within the left-wing bloc and, more particularly, within the right-wing bloc have been institutionalised to such an extent that they can be presumed to encourage a tendency towards uniformity within each bloc that cartelisation is said to promote in all established parties across the left–right divide (cf. Blyth and Katz 2005). The expected mechanism is that, during this long period of intense collaboration, the parties in each bloc will have been exposed to pressure to converge in order to make government procedures work more smoothly (cf. Harmel and Janda 1994), factors that should advance party cultural change by reducing individual MP autonomy and the party's ideological consistency – both factors that could be assumed to obstruct collaboration.

A previous study (conducted in 1998–2002) demonstrated that the cultures then exhibited by the respective parties of the left- and right-wing blocs differed in important respects (Barrling Hermansson 2004; see further details later in this chapter). If we can demonstrate that the organisational cultures of these parties with experience of close collaboration with each other have not become more similar and/or that these parties have not changed their cultures in a manner consistent with what I call *the logic of cartelisation*, then we find support for the conclusion that party organisational culture is a force restraining cartelisation. Cultural variation between the parties also permits investigation of whether certain organisational cultures are more resistant to cartelisation than others (cf. Koole 1996).

Finally, as the actions of individual parties are in themselves insufficient for the formation of party cartels, which demands continuous co-ordination between different party elites (Krouwel 2012: 271), it is important not only to look at separate parties but, as I do here, also to consider the relations between them.

To conclude, the more specific research questions are the following:

1. Has there been any change in the organisational cultures of Swedish parliamentary parties in the periods 1998–2002 and 2012–2013?
2. If such changes have occurred,

    i.   Have they brought the cultures of the different parties closer to each other?
    ii.   What aspects of the different party organisational cultures have been touched by them?
    iii. Are they in agreement with the logic of cartelisation?

In this chapter, I investigate whether party organisational culture might restrain tendencies towards cartelisation.

THEORETICAL CONSIDERATIONS

In the context of this study, a key statement of the cartel party thesis is the following:

> For now, it seems, we remain with a reality that is defined by a set of mainstream parties that are largely indistinguishable from one another in terms of their main policy proposals, and that are closer to one another in terms of their styles, location, and organizational culture than any one of them is to the voters in the wider society. (Katz and Mair 2009: 760)

There are two points to make here. First, this kind of far-reaching generalisation about parties resembling each other is a part of the thesis that has been heavily criticised. Second, Katz and Mair acknowledge that party organisational culture is an important element when considering how different parties approach each other. However, they tend to disregard the issue that organisational culture is not very easy to change, and that it should therefore – if we were to line up elements obstructing cartelisation – be one of our 'prime suspects'. Even when expressing self-criticism, the authors of the cartelisation thesis tend to treat the issue of party organisational culture as if it were an isolated and easily perceived variable, which can be assumed to be susceptible to cartelisation in a rather straightforward manner. The problem is that organisational culture is not a straightforward 'variable' or 'factor' but rather a world view that infuses the attitudes and the behaviour of party representatives in a number of ways, informing how they value reality and also how they perceive it. Organisational culture restricts their radius of action and sometimes prevents them from making – or even detecting – choices that might seem rational from a strictly analytical point of view. Culture offers an account of behaviour through shared world views that make some actions more likely than others. It determines the actual freedom of group members, their expectations about how they are to act, and the means by which they are able to obtain social status. Organisational culture could therefore be expected to restrain the kind of ends–means rationality that the cartel party thesis presupposes; and it is likely to be tenacious to such an extent that it resists the pressures of far-reaching cartelisation (e.g. Kitschelt 1994; Koole 1996; Chabal and Daloz 2006). The further argument, which is developed below, is that a group's culture is difficult to change and this must be taken into account when analysing the prerequisites for cartelisation.

Political parties can best be described as a form of micro-society whose rationality is bounded. The opportunities of political parties to act in the ends–means rational manner predicted by the cartel party thesis are limited. Instead, culturally oriented views held by parties – such as social norms, allocation of status, and views of responsibility and social interplay – are in fact crucial for understanding party behaviour (e.g. Jensen 1993; Abélès 2000; Esaiasson and Heidar 2000; Chabal and Daloz 2006; Barrling 2013). Even studies that adhere to a rationalist perspective, such as Panebianco's (1988) seminal work on party organisation, point to the difficulties attached to the 'management' of organisational culture. Moreover, a study on organisational cultures within parliamentary party groups shows that even when the party leadership is aware of and admits to the drawbacks of their own group's culture, they still face difficulties in changing even their own attitudes in ways that would be strategically favourable, if such an adjustment conflicts with the cultural norms of their own group. We find a telling example in the case of the Moderates. For many years, the party was aware that it embraced a cultural ideal that could be perceived by voters as technocratic and insensitive, which was therefore detrimental to the party's ability to attract voters. Even though the Moderates understood that this norm reduced the possibilities of them gaining more votes, the norm was so strong that it hindered individual MPs from behaving in a different, more sensitive manner, as such behaviour could threaten the MPs' intra-party cohesion (Barrling Hermansson 2004). In the conflict between the cultural norm and ends–means rationality, the norm prevailed.

To conclude, cartel party theory requires development regarding the influence of organisational culture on how a party works. What do we mean, then, by culture, and how does the concept relate to the inner life of the political party? This issue will be developed in the following section.

The Cultural Perspective

The overall perspective applied here adheres to Geertz's semiotic definition of culture as the historically transmitted pattern of the socially determined meanings of various phenomena in a given group (Geertz 1975; cf. King et al. 1994). The core of the approach is to consider culture to be a system of meanings, the task then being to identify and interpret the meanings a given group ascribes to various phenomena (Chabal and Daloz 2006). Indeed, culture has been recognised for some time as a key to a better understanding of party politics (Kitschelt 1994; Heidar and Koole 2000; cf. Panebianco 1988 on identity incentives). What the concept of culture does is offer an account of how behaviour is filtered through the world views shared by a group, world views that make some actions more likely than others. Culture thus determines the actual freedom of group members, expectations of how they are to act and the means by which they are able to obtain respect and social standing. Culture also shapes a given group's interpretation of the behaviour of out-groups (Panebianco 1988; Chabal and Daloz 2006). By analysing culture, we learn what a specific event or type of behaviour signifies for a specific party: why it is supported or opposed, why it may cause difficulties within the group and so on. Cultural views determine how the party views itself and its surroundings in fundamental ways and, consequently, also offer resistance to the kind of ends–means rationality that is a prerequisite for cartelisation.

This cultural perspective is in accordance with the view that parties differ in ways that go beyond ideological dissimilarities. Consequently, instead of trying to determine what constitutes the party type of a particular period, party research would gain by asking why and under what circumstances some parties develop in different directions (Koole 1996; Krouwel 2012). Party scholarship has frequently suggested whole new types of political parties and, over time, the number of models has multiplied to the point of confusion, often resulting in a loss of explanatory power. In an extensive comparative study, Krouwel (2012) rejects this abundance of models. Instead of inventing new models, he claims, party research would gain by analysing ideological, organisational, and electoral development and change. Furthermore, party change is neither uniform nor linear but often divergent, and there are many examples of parties reverting to old habits and structures (Koole 1996; Krouwel 2012: 267).

These insights are fully consistent with the cultural perspective on politics and what it claims about culture biasing views in ways that are not always straightforward. This suggests that, rather than expecting any party to have reached the final stage of cartelisation, it would be more useful to consider whether some parties in particular are vulnerable to cartelisation tendencies; that is, whether certain party organisational cultures facilitate cartelisation while others make cartelisation more difficult. Correspondingly, there are reasons to believe that overall pressure for cartelisation poses more of a threat to some party organisational cultures than to others.

A previous study of parliamentary party culture (Barrling Hermansson 2004) demonstrates that party culture could be said to revolve around a

number of dimensions, two of which are particularly relevant to cartelisation: *views of political responsibility* and *the autonomy of individual MPs
vis-à-vis their own group*. Each of these dimensions displays two contrasting
ideal-type positions. In the first dimension, views of political responsibility, the party culture can be classified as tending towards either pragmatism
or idealism. The second dimension touches on how individual MPs view
independence, which is dependent on the group culture being collectivistic
(MPs' independence and radius of action are low) or individualistic (MPs'
independence and radius of action are high). The assumption here is that the
party leadership is approved as an agent representing the group as a collective (Barrling Hermansson 2004). For this dimension, the party organisational
culture can be classified as tending towards either individualism or collectivism. In the following section, we will explain to what degree the party cultural traits described above can be assumed to be compatible with the logic
of cartelisation.

ANALYTICAL FRAMEWORK

Using earlier findings regarding the organisational cultures of parliamentary party groups as an empirical point of departure, I suggest an analytical
framework concentrating on the compatibility between different party cultural aspects and what I term 'the logic of cartelisation'. From the theoretical
statements on cartelisation presented above, I derived cultural positions that
would be favourable to cartelisation; I then compared these with the various
cultural traits displayed by parties in 2012–2013 *versus* 1998–2002.
   Given the theoretical description of the cartel party as a de-ideologised,
professionalised and centralised organisation governed by the party elite, we
can infer that, to fit with the logic of cartelisation, the party's organisational
culture should manifest the following characteristics:

- a pragmatic rather than idealistic orientation, as pragmatism leaves more
  latitude for de-ideologisation and professionalism than does idealism;
- a collectivistic rather than individualistic orientation, as less space for the
  individual implies better opportunities for a top-down regime.

Summing up the results of the earlier study (Barrling Hermansson 2004), we
find the distribution along these dimensions shown in Table 8.1.
   The collectivistic cultural traits of the Moderates, the Centre Party, the
Christian Democrats and the Social Democrats fit with the logic of cartelisation, and so does the pragmatism of the Centre Party, the Christian Democrats, the Greens and the Social Democrats. If collectivism and pragmatism
persist, they are not as such signs of cartelisation, though they do not hinder

Table 8.1 Observed Party Culture, 1998–2002

	Pragmatic vs Idealistic Orientation	*Individualistic vs Collectivistic Orientation*
Moderates	IDEALISTIC	Collectivistic
Liberals	IDEALISTIC	INDIVIDUALISTIC
Centre Party	Pragmatic	Collectivistic
Christian Democrats	Pragmatic	Collectivistic
Greens	Pragmatic	INDIVIDUALISTIC
Social Democrats	Pragmatic	Collectivistic
Left Party	IDEALISTIC	INDIVIDUALISTIC

Note: Capital letters indicate those cultural traits that are *not* in accordance with the logic of cartelisation and would be expected to obstruct cartelisation.

cartelisation. Conversely, if there are cartelisation tendencies, the individualism of the Liberals, the Greens and the Left Party would have been tempered. Furthermore, the idealism of the Liberals, corresponding to that of the Moderates and the Left Party, would have given way to a more pragmatic attitude to political work if the process of cartelisation had proceeded unrestrained. The two parties in which the conflict between the logic of cartelisation and the culture identified in the reference study (Barrling Hermansson 2004) is the most extensive are the Liberals and the Left Party, these being both idealistic and individualistic.

To refine the discussion thus far, there are two possible opposing outcomes. The first would be that the party cultures have altered in ways that are fully consistent with the logic of cartelisation (thereby also becoming more like each other); more specifically, this would imply that all of the cultural traits in capital letters in Table 8.1 have changed. The underlying mechanism facilitating such a change during the period under investigation would be collaboration between the parties combined with their holding office or, as is the case with the so-called supportive parties, being close to office. The opposite extreme would be a result in which the party cultures have not changed at all, that is, that even those cultural traits that are in conflict with the logic of cartelisation have not changed. It is unlikely that the final result of the empirical investigation would be as clear-cut as these two extremes describe. Rather, we would expect different parties to be affected in different ways and to different degrees. The purpose of considering these two most extreme possible results is only to illustrate the range within which the results might be found.

Finally, when considering new parties (in the Swedish case, the Greens), an additional point should be made. Here, increased pragmatism and/or collectivism, at the expense of idealism and/or individualism, are not necessarily signs of cartelisation tendencies but might just as well be evidence of normalisation, that is, normal stages in the life cycle of a party (Panebianco 1988) or of adaptation to the conditions of being in government.

MATERIALS AND METHODS

The empirical investigation consists of a diachronic study in which the party cultures in 2012–2013 are contrasted with those observed in 1998–2002 (Barrling Hermansson 2004). The studies compared are similar in both methods and materials. If we find that the organisational cultures of the parliamentary party groups in each bloc have not been affected in a manner consistent with the logic of cartelisation, and that the different party cultures have not become more like each other, then we have stronger support for the conclusion that party organisational culture offers a constraint to cartelisation than we would have had we chosen a case in which cartelisation was less likely to emerge.

The party cultures observed during 1998–2002 were rooted in the parties' histories, at least some 20–30 years previously (Barrling Hermansson 2004). Inversely, the period from 2002 until today, although relatively short, includes a number of events that would be expected to bring about pressure for change and which would also favour the logic of cartelisation, such as change of government; new coalition and collaboration arrangements; leadership change; large-scale electoral defeats; demands for ideological and party cultural reconsideration; and the increased importance of the mass media (cf. Harmel and Janda 1994). In addition, the rapid electoral success and entrance into national parliament of the Sweden Democrats has caused convergence among all of the mainstream parties on immigration policy (Loxbo 2015), a fact that could also be expected to promote cartelisation tendencies. To present a valid comparison, the material is chosen to be consistent with the earlier study. The material consists of discursive interviews with a total of thirty-five MPs – five from each party. All of the MPs – with the exceptions of Mikaela Valtersson (Greens), Anna König Jerlmyr (Moderates) and Stefan Attefall (Christian Democrats) – are in parliament and most of them have had experience of several terms in parliament. The qualitative method applied is that of thick description (Geertz 1975; King et al. 1994) and follows the same principles of elite interviewing as those applied in the reference study (Barrling Hermansson 2004; cf. Berry 2002).

The party cultures were investigated with regard to two dimensions, *political responsibility* and *the autonomy of the individual MP*, with the extreme values of the two dimensions being considered ideal types. Each ideal type represents a certain view of how proper political work is defined. We shall elucidate this in the following section.

Definitions and Operationalisation

The concepts are operationalised correspondingly to the reference study of the 1998–2002 period (Barrling Hermansson 2004: 252–60, 281–4). The interview questions are open ended and their aim is to capture the identity and social norms of the given party group. Their connections to the two dimensions of this study are presented in Table 8.2 (each question was followed up by the query 'Has there been any change in this regard?').

The first dimension, *political responsibility*, concerns how a group – given the political capacity it possesses – should conduct itself in order to influence political decisions in a morally and ideologically legitimate way. On this point, the discussion concerns, for example, questions of whether the party should use its parliamentary position to negotiate compromises with other parties, or whether such deal-making undermines the aim of respectability in parliamentary work. According to the pragmatic ideal type, politics is regarded as situation dependent and action oriented, which calls attention to the importance of obtaining actual results in response to policy. Expressions that indicate pragmatism are, besides the word itself, descriptions that stress the need for co-operation, collaboration, compromise, realism, result-orientation, constructive solutions and the like.

The other ideal type of this dimension represents a view of political work that highly values ideological consistency, with what is considered moral behaviour in politics *not* being context dependent. This ideal type is linked to terms related to being faithful to party ideas and ideology, such as loyal, true, idealistic, consistent, steady, reliable, uncompromising and predictable.

The second dimension, individual MP autonomy, reflects whether the group views itself as collectivistic or individualistic. This theme concerns how much latitude individual MPs have to act on their own discretion such that they can create individual political profiles. In the collectivistic ideal type, the individual is deeply incorporated into the group, whereas the individualistic ideal type describes a group in which the individual has considerable personal freedom in relation to the group. In the case of a party that allows its individual members to act freely and to attract considerable attention – even when such behaviour is perceived by the group as harmful to the collective – the demand for individual subordination is extremely low. In contrast, in the case of a party that does not allow such liberty to individual MPs – even when the party as a collective gains thereby – the demand for individual subordination is extremely high.

The operational definition of individualism is descriptions by MPs of a group in which an MP can act independently (also above and beyond his or her own area of responsibility) and criticise the group and its leadership (either in camera or in public), and in which the leadership has to seek the support of the group before taking action. Collectivism, in contrast, is operationally defined as a group in which the individual MP cannot act without the support of the group (often, but not necessarily, represented by the leadership) or criticise the group and its leadership (especially not in public), and

Table 8.2   List of Questions, by Dimension

Political Responsibility	Autonomy of Individual MP
How does your group define 'sense of responsibility'?	How would you describe the 'degrees of freedom' of individual MPs? Does the group allow her/him to maintain a high profile? Even if this implies criticising one's own group (i.e. one's party and/or government)?
Are there policy issues that are too important to expose to political conflict?	If the group cannot reach a joint decision, what do you do?
Does your group possess traits of which you are particularly proud?	Does your group possess traits of which you are particularly proud?
Inversely, does your group have any shortcomings, disadvantages?	Inversely, does your group have any shortcomings, disadvantages?
What does it take to be considered competent by the group?	What does it take to be considered competent by the group?
What does it take to convince the group? Are certain arguments considered more valid than others?	What does it take to convince the group? Are certain arguments considered more valid than others?
To obtain social status and prestige within the group, how should one behave?	To obtain social status and prestige within the group, how should one behave?

Note: Partly, I identify the party's position on the two dimensions by asking questions that lie very close to the dimension as such, that is, concerning how the group defines responsibility and the extent of the individual MP's autonomy. However, to obtain a more comprehensive picture of how deeply rooted the attitudes related to these dimensions are, the positions are also investigated by looking at more fundamental cultural aspects, such as what the parliamentary party group is proud and less proud of; how it defines competence and valid arguments; and how MPs should behave in order to obtain social status and prestige within the party group. Both dimensions might be expressed through these cultural aspects and, for that reason, similar questions are instruments for measuring the party's attitude *vis-à-vis* each dimension.

in which the mandate for leadership to take action on behalf of the group as a whole is far-reaching (on the condition that leadership is considered to be a legitimate representative of the group at large).

PARTY ORGANISATIONAL CULTURES, 1998–2002

Political Responsibility

The results of the empirical study of the 1998–2002 period indicate that it was the parliamentary party groups the Moderates, the Liberals and the Left Party that came closest to the ideal type of viewing responsibility as a matter of ideological consistency. In the two first parties, a strictly professional attitude to political work was also emphasised (Barrling Hermansson 2004: 261–5). The MPs of the Left Party also believed that experience of belonging to an oppressed class (such as the proletariat) implied deeper political understanding of a kind that neither could nor should be called into question (Barrling Hermansson 2004: 270). In contrast, the parliamentary party groups of the Social Democrats, the Christian Democrats, the Centre Party and the Greens embodied an ideal that tended towards the pragmatic ideal type, expressing a practically oriented view in which what is politically right depends on the situation.

The Autonomy of the Individual MP

During the 1998–2002 period, the parliamentary party groups of the Moderates, the Social Democrats, the Christian Democrats and the Centre Party tended towards a more collectivistic norm, this tendency being particularly pronounced in the first two parties. Here, it was often difficult for the individual MP to maintain a high profile, even when the party would have gained from having such a nonconformist member. The demand for individual subordination to the group was also true for the Christian Democrats and the Centre Party, although there was a difference in that these parties were more tolerant of independent-minded MPs. In the last two parliamentary party groups, it was possible to dissent and be forgiven, which was much more difficult in the parliamentary party groups of the Moderates and the Social Democrats (Barrling Hermansson 2004: 290–2). In contrast, MPs from the Liberals, the Left Party and the Greens tended towards substantially less collectivism. In all three of these parties, the radius of action of the individual MP was described as substantial, thereby being much closer to the individualistic ideal type. Here, the cultural norm not only allowed but also encouraged a critical stance, not least with respect to the leadership of one's own group, a tendency that was particularly pronounced in the Left Party. A revealing example is the following: for an important debate in parliament, although the party leader, Gudrun Schyman, had expressed a wish to represent the party, the parliamentary party group side-stepped her and appointed another MP instead to represent the party in the debate (Barrling Hermansson 2004: 215–17, 292–8). Regarding the individualism of the Greens, a story told by one disillusioned member of the party leadership provides a telling example. As he told the story, when the party leadership criticised some MPs for frequently arriving late to important group meetings, their reproach was regarded as authoritarian and intrusive. Furthermore, when the leadership demanded that the tardy MPs stay late to compensate for the lost time, their request was perceived as provocative (Barrling Hermansson 2004: 233).

Figure 8.1 summarises all seven parties' distribution along the two dimensions.

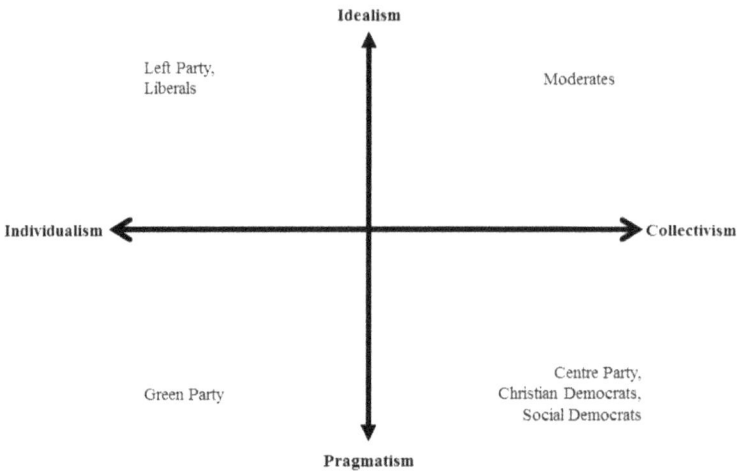

Figure 8.1   The positions of parliamentary party groups on two dimensions, idealism–pragmatism and individualism–collectivism. *Source*: Author's own.

When we contrast the different parties, we find that the differences between their cultures are pronounced. Figure 8.1 shows the parties' relative tendencies regarding the four ideal types. Looking at the cultural distribution of Swedish political parties, we can see that it is not organised along formal left–right political lines, dramatically so given that Swedish politics, since the advent of democracy, has been dominated by the left–right spectrum. The Liberals are culturally closest to the party viewed as their chief ideological opponent, the formerly communist Left Party. At the same time, culturally, the Social Democrats have more in common with the two non-socialist parties, the Centre Party and the Christian Democrats, than they do with the parties with which they co-occupy the ideological left. Bearing this in mind, we now turn to the question of whether this pattern has changed.

PARTY ORGANISATIONAL CULTURES, 2012–2013

Moderates

When investigating organisational change, the case of the Moderates is particularly interesting, because the party has been the object of its leadership's deliberate attempt to reshape it from the ground up, leadership change being the main explanatory factor (Harmel and Janda 1994). Fredrik Reinfeldt, leader of the Moderates from 2004 to 2014, and his circle had an extensive reform agenda when he took office as party leader, one objective of which was to fundamentally reshape the party culture, to achieve a more pragmatic and co-operative orientation. Reinfeldt also wanted to create a more sensitive party culture, a party more apt to listen to and respond to the electorate (Reinfeldt 2015: 142–5). In accordance with this, he was a founder of the renewed right-wing bloc collaboration in 2004. He then had the chance to develop a more pragmatic side to the party upon forming a coalition government in 2006, given that being in government, especially a coalition government, necessarily entails a more pragmatic attitude than when in opposition (Müller and Strøm 2010).

As for the first dimension, *political responsibility*, the new attitude cultivated in the group by its leadership is also reflected in the answers given by the MPs interviewed. All five noted that the party had adopted a more pragmatic perspective on ideological matters and that this trait was reinforced by the party's role in government, which made compromise necessary, due both to the requirements of coalition government and to the legal and budgetary restrictions surrounding government as such. Maria Abrahamsson (M) mentioned that, to be regarded as a skilful politician, it is important to be able to manoeuvre so that the 'dangers' of government are avoided, especially those connected with minority government. Being the largest party in government, she noted, the Moderates must be prepared to shoulder certain responsibilities. There is also enthusiasm for and dedication to being in government, as governing a country is not just about being some sort of think tank. Rather, it implies a need to find practical solutions, although this certainly steals attention away from ideological development and creativity. In that way, the party in government also becomes more defensive than it is in opposition, which is not surprising, Abrahamsson concluded. A similar description was given by Henrik von Sydow (M), who described the situation in terms of the party's having adopted a more professional attitude to parliamentary work, for example, concerning organisational structure, meetings, media and forming the basis for political decisions: 'The focus is on what we ought to do, more than on having certain opinions'. It is therefore also more important today to be able to show how ideas can be transformed into practical solutions and finally implemented, that is, instrumental arguments have become more important. Von Sydow considered this change to be partly, though not exclusively, due to being in government. According to him, it is also important to remember that the Moderates, given their size, resemble a medium-sized company, and therefore they must find efficient ways to work.

There has been a distinct change in orientation in this regard within the Moderates, whose former ideological consistency has been replaced with a more pragmatic attitude. However, there are two important points to make here. First, the change reflects what seems to be a fundamental trait of the Moderates' culture, namely, the demand for consistency and for being aware of the party's function in parliament. While the 'old' Moderates were

consistent ideologues, the 'new' Moderates are consistent in their pragmatism. In this sense, the demand for consistency remains and it seems only
reasonable that the party has adopted a more pragmatic attitude, as that is
what is demanded of a party that aspires to, or is in, government. So far, the
change does not reflect a change in culture as much as it does a change in
role. This interpretation is also in accordance with the description given by
several MPs in the reference study, in which leading MPs emphasised that the
opposition role demands ideological consistency while being in government
requires compromise, collaboration and pragmatism (Barrling Hermansson
2004: 94–100).

Regarding the second dimension, *the autonomy of the individual MP*, the
top-down change in the Moderates also indicates that the hierarchical structure, combined with strong collectivism and leadership, remained unbroken,
an interpretation that also finds support in the interviews. All the interviewees
described a group in which the leadership was strong and the individual MPs
were expected to subordinate themselves to the group will. However, the
strong hierarchy of the group does not imply that there was no latitude at all
for individual MPs, nor that their opportunities did not vary over time. For
example, according to Anna König Jerlmyr, the party group's considerable
increase in size after the elections of 2006, and the larger proportion of new
MPs that resulted, did in fact create more opportunities for newcomers to be
heard and to participate in the development of new policies. Furthermore,
Thalén Finné stated that the latitude for discussion was larger than some
ten years previously, though it is not entirely clear whether this opinion was
simply because she personally had become more experienced. However,
Thalén Finné also considered the party whip to be very strong when a decision was finally reached, and that there was no room for deviating opinions
when voting. None of the MPs contradicted the highly critical account given
by a former MP, Anne-Marie Pålsson, in a book that has attracted considerable attention, of a strongly collectivistic group that makes few allowances
for the individual; though the interviewed MPs noted that there was no other
way for a party group of this size to function, especially when in government
(Pålsson 2011). All the interviewees affirmed how important it was to adapt
to parliamentary processes, behave in a punctilious manner and never 'give
rise to surprise' (Abrahamsson). Though the interviewees were generally
accepting of their party's strong collectivism, some criticism was expressed.
Two MPs, Abrahamsson and de Pourbaix Lundin, remarked that the 'new'
Moderates' image of being a party of 'listeners' was more valid in relation to
the public than when it came to internal decision-making, though this pattern
should also be understood as an expression of the need to display awareness
of the responsibilities of the leader of a coalition and a government. Though
there has been a certain renewal – represented by the many new, young MPs;

by the new group leader, Anna Kinberg Batra, who has a more attentive leadership style than that of her predecessors; and by a certain ideological shift – the strong position of the leadership (at the time, the leadership of both the parliamentary party group and the cabinet, especially Prime Minister Fredrik Reinfeldt and Minister of Finance Anders Borg) remained as strong as ever (Abrahamsson).

Left Party

The strong individualism and demand for ideological consistency reported in the reference study makes the Left Party one of the two-party cultures that are least in accord with the logic of cartelisation (the Liberals being the other). As for the dimension *the autonomy of the individual MP*, all MPs indicated that the Left Party's organisational culture remains strongly individualistic. In contrast to the findings of the reference study, there were fewer conflicts and factions than ten to fifteen years previously. The level of internal discussion and criticism, however, remained the same. According to Josefin Brink, self-criticism could be described as something of a 'general sport'. The group was characterised by a widespread urge to question and criticise (almost constituting an 'illness', she said) to such a degree as to be detrimental to the group. This criticism particularly concerned the leadership: as soon as someone has been chosen for a high position, he or she becomes 'fair game', Brink explained (or, in the words of group leader Hans Linde, there is 'difficulty recognising "star quality"'). Although such conduct, according to Brink and Linde, is an expression of the sound idea of MP independence and of freedom of judgement, it is not an ideal situation for the party. Another MP, Kent Persson, stressed the ongoing discussion of how party members should aim to work *with* instead of *against* each other, noting that it was not always beneficial to the group to expose its internal workings in op-eds in the leading Swedish newspaper, nor to protect the 'none has the right to tell me what to do' attitude. Another recurrent interviewee opinion was that the individual MP had almost too much freedom, because of the small size of the group (nineteen people) so that one person was usually in charge of the whole agenda for her or his parliamentary committee (there are sixteen committees in the Riksdag).

Concerning the other dimension, *political responsibility*, the MPs' views were unanimous, though more complex. On the one hand, they suggested that there was a more pragmatic orientation today than fifteen years ago; on the other hand, their views also reflected a culture in which ideological consistency is still much more highly valued than pragmatism. A shift that has taken place, though, is that the group is now more favourable towards being in government, while the reference study found resistance to this, as it implied being co-opted by establishment structures. Group leader Hans Linde here stressed that the party was now prepared to enter government, but not at any cost. He said that there was a widespread belief that compromise went too far during the collaboration with the Social Democratic government in the late 1990s and early 2000s and that the party had thereby risked losing its ideals. As a consequence, the group was now wary of going too far in the direction of prag-matism. A revealing story about the difference between the Left Party and the Social Democrats in this regard was told by the former Left Party leader, Lars Ohly, who was closely involved in co-operation with the Social Democrats, both in government and in opposition. For the Left Party, he said, compromise could never be considered intrinsically good but only a necessary evil. The government party had difficulties accepting that, even after having agreed to a compromise, the Left Party would stick to its original policy line in public and declare that it would continue to strive to reach its goals on such issues.

Liberals

The Liberals could be described as the Left Party's cultural cousin. Here, too, in the former study, we found individualism (though with a somewhat less critical stance) combined with a preference for ideological consistency. As in the case of the Liberals' cousin on the left, we can observe a certain degree of change, although fundamental cultural traits appear to have persisted.

Beginning with *the autonomy of the individual MP*, all interviewees described a group in which individual latitude was still great. One MP, Eva Flyborg, even said that there has been a 'revolution' in this respect, because of a new generation taking its place in the party group, a generation that does not accept old hierarchical structures. The other MPs' statements did not con-tradict the account of this MP, though they did not go nearly as far.

The interviewees generally described a group in which there was latitude for discussion, MPs were markedly involved in the policy-making process in relation to government, and members felt free to make their voices heard and to criticise the group as well as the leadership. A telling example was when the group leader, Johan Pehrson, asked how an MP ought to behave to be perceived as competent, made fun of his own authority: 'Then you must obey me. JOKE! JOKE!'

Several MPs also noted the importance of the leadership of party leader Jan Björklund on this point. He was described as unpretentious and open, giving individual MPs the opportunity to take part in party decision-making. Barbro Westerholm claimed that Björklund's military background was an advantage: 'If you don't have the troops on your side, then you cannot win the war, and that is his technique, to bring the troops with him, to listen to the troops, [to find out] what they have seen in the bushes'.

On the other hand, the interviewees' accounts reveal that more party discipline is called for during voting and, according to the MPs, this was entirely due to the party's position in government. The increased importance of group loyalty arising from being in government, however, was balanced by increased influence during the policy process. All MPs said that they were involved at an earlier stage than before, and long before decisions were made in government. Although individual MPs' influence during the policy process appears to have grown, their capacity to obstruct the party whip when voting has diminished. The MPs were aware that the situation was partly in conflict with the party's high regard for individual autonomy but considered the process of involving MPs at an early stage of the policy process to be a good way of striking a balance.

Considering the dimension of *political responsibility*, it appears as though ideological consistency is more valued than pragmatism. However, there is also understanding of what government in coalition requires in terms of compromise, not only in relation to other parties but also in relation to the bleak reality of administration. The general perception was that being in government and the organised collaboration in the right-wing bloc have profoundly altered how the party reflects on issues of political responsibility. Group leader Johan Pehrson commented on the qualities of the Moderate Minister of Finance, Anders Borg, who exposed the budget not only of the red–green opposition but also of the Liberals – filled as it was with 'wishful thinking' – thereby forcing Pehrson's own party to begin thinking not only about ideals but also about expenditure. His fellow MP, Ulf Nilsson, framed this as the party now being forced to think and react on two levels: the level of the party itself and that of the right-wing bloc. However, there is not enough evidence to say whether there has been a change of culture in this respect: the party is still highly ideological and, according to the accounts given, being in government could roughly be described as an exceptional case that demands a sacrifice – for the greater good, to be sure, but it is still perceived as a sacrifice.

Greens

Like other Green parties, the Swedish Greens have an anti-establishment and anti-party legacy in which idealism rather than striving for office is the governing logic (Kitschelt 1994; Dumont and Bäck 2006). Considering the overall tradition of its party family, the Greens could be expected to be particularly susceptible to cartelisation tendencies, in view of the growing pragmatism of Green parties (cf. Barrling Hermansson 2004; Ljunggren 2010). Interestingly, the follow-up study demonstrates that the growth of pragmatism found in the reference study has apparently slowed, during a period when we might have expected the opposite (see Barrling 2014).

As for the dimension of *the autonomy of the individual MP*, the overarching result is that individualism remains strong in the Green parliamentary party group and all interviewees described a highly individualistic group culture. In the words of Per Bolund, the opportunities for MPs to make their voices heard during group meetings are 'limitless' and such behaviour is appreciated and even encouraged. On the downside, this conduct tends to render group meetings lengthy and sometimes inefficient; on the upside, decision-making gains in legitimacy. As in the Left Party, there is tolerance of internal criticism communicated in public. Also as in the Left Party, there is a tendency to be particularly critical of the party leadership. Therefore, it is not a winning argument to cite the support of the party leaders (who, in the Greens, are two spokespersons – in Swedish, *språkrör* – with definite term limits), but rather the opposite.

As for potential change, Ulf Holm said that, notwithstanding the high standing of individual MPs, there may have been change since 1988 when the party first entered parliament. Then, the group's distrust of parliamentary work was more profound than it is now. His fellow MP, Mehmet Kaplan, suggested that the attitude in this regard varies with the parliamentary situation and that the autonomy of individual MPs is somewhat restricted when the party is part of the parliamentary majority. However, these restrictions mainly concern voting in parliament, not overall behaviour within the party group as such. The relatively weak position of the leadership is also reflected in the procedure used when the group cannot reach a consensual decision. If compromise is impossible, then voting is still the standard solution and, unlike in any other party group, the method is frequently applied. According to experienced MPs Holm and Valtersson, making a decision on the issue in question would never be delegated to the leadership of the party's parliamentary group or even to the party's MP in the committee preparing the associated bill (see Barrling 2014: 111).

The development of the *political responsibility* dimension is particularly interesting. To develop in accordance with the logic of cartelisation, the Greens ought to have proceeded more pragmatically, especially as the party has participated in far-reaching collaboration with other parties (cf. Blyth and Katz 2005). However, the evolution of the Greens appears to be more complex: it is not that 'pragmatisation' has stopped, but it seems to have been obstructed and is now more disputed than it was in 2002. All the Green interviewees stated that the group is more pragmatic today than it was when new in parliament (1988–2001), and that the general tendency is towards a more pragmatic orientation, attributable to the desire to have actual influence on policy. However, several interviewees also proclaimed that there now is more distinct tension within the group in this respect: some MPs are striving for more pragmatism in political work, whereas others consider pragmatism a threat to the fundamental identity of the party and wish to return to more fundamental values, such as ideological consistency. Holm also holds that, during the last three elections, the external party organisation has grown in importance at the expense of the parliamentary group (at odds with the cartel party thesis; cf. Krouwel 2012), a process furthered by the weakened uniformity of the parliamentary party group. The party is thus less pragmatic than its current public image would suggest and it is a social setting in which the strongest possible argument is still: 'But our Congress has decided!' In the interviews, both Holm and Valtersson described this general pattern and they both considered that there was still a strong demand for party representatives to be 'green enough', not only ideologically but also as regards lifestyle issues.

Centre Party

The reference study found the Centre Party to be the most pragmatic of them all and, moreover, to be a party with a collectivistic rather than individualistic tendency (though it is less hierarchical than the Moderates or Social Democrats). The party's organisational culture is thus in accord with what we describe as the logic of cartelisation, that is, its culture is such that the preconditions for cartelisation would be more favourable than in the aforementioned parties. Given the Centre Party's decade of far-reaching government collaboration within the right-wing bloc, it would be interesting to examine whether its cultural traits have been reinforced.

As for the dimension of *the autonomy of the individual MP*, all Centre Party MPs interviewed stated that the party culture still displays a collectivistic tendency. In this case, collectivism is expressed primarily in descriptions of the group as 'homogenous' (Torstensson) and united by a need to stick together, rather than by the requirement that the MPs subordinate themselves to the group, although this would ultimately be the consequence. According to Centre MPs with a long-term perspective, there has been a change in that there is more latitude for discussion within the group today than some ten to fifteen years ago. However, unlike in the Liberals or, even more so, in the Left and Green parties, the aim of such discussion is not to allow criticism of ideas, the leadership or the group, but rather to facilitate deliberation; the Centre Party undoubtedly values compromise and trade-offs more than voting as solutions when the group holds diverging opinions. For a telling example of the difference between a collectivistic culture, such as that of the Centre Party, and an individualistic culture, particularly pronounced in the Left and Green parties, let us consider the following case related by Åsa Torstensson and Annika Qarlsson. One MP was perceived as going too far in criticising the Centre Party leader Maud Olofsson. The situation was not very dramatic and could have arisen any day in the Left Party or the Greens without provoking any reaction. However, in the more collectivistic setting of the Centre Party, openly expressed disapproval was considered disloyal to the party leader and therefore also to the group overall. Interestingly, Torstensson also noted a certain tendency towards relaxation in this respect; she said that the group reaction might have been quite different – and more accepting – had the incident occurred five years later. Qarlsson believed that the group might be heading towards a more individualistic culture, because of a new generation entering parliament, but that this transformation had not yet taken place. When I asked Rickard Nordin, the youngest Centre MP, to comment on these conjectures, his short answer was that he firmly believed that the group needed unity in order to function and that its members were therefore highly dependent on each other. Interestingly, Nordin, new in parliament and one of the assumed proponents of the 'new individualism', in this statement contributed what could be described as an archetypal description of Centre Party culture, summarising descriptions made ten years earlier. Some tendencies towards potential long-term change can be found but the old norms still operate to such an extent that they also infuse the answers given by the representatives of the generation said to be the bearer of this potential change.

Considering the *political responsibility* dimension, the accounts given by the Centre MPs are well in line with the party culture observed a decade ago. The general impression is of a group that puts a high value on compromise: actions should accordingly be evaluated in relation to their actual consequences, rather than their ideological consistency. Interestingly, the story the Centre Party MPs told of their years in government resembles that of their Liberal counterparts. However, the Centre Party MPs also stressed the difference between the years when the right-wing bloc held the government with a parliamentary majority (2006–2010), and the later government period when the right-wing bloc had only a minority of the seats in parliament (2010–2014). During the first period, MPs' influence was circumscribed, while during the minority government the parliamentary group increased its influence, the government being more dependent on a 'faithful' group, which, in the case of the Centre Party, implied greater MP involvement in government processes. The change is interesting because it provides a significant example of the Centre Party's far-reaching appreciation of negotiation and compromise. During the first period, the group increasingly exhibited what we might call 'compromise fatigue'. Torstensson, experienced as an MP and a minister, recalled feelings of surprise over this fatigue, she asked: 'Why did we develop this reaction now?' The Centre Party is used to both leading and compromising, but only rarely in a majority position, so minority government is a 'tradition' in the party, she explained. Still, the group displayed fatigue and disappointment because it could not understand 'what was in it for us'; here, Torstensson added that she was convinced that the party would do the same thing again, that compromise was still held in high regard. She also commented that after the elections of 2010, the situation changed to one of minority government, and that to cope with the new situation, leadership chose to involve the parliamentary group in actual negotiations as well (as we also saw in the case of the Liberals). Although the level of compromise did not decrease, it was as though 'being let into the negotiation room' energised the MPs: now they could exercise what they felt was their talent, negotiating with the other parties in the right-wing bloc. 'It is fun to negotiate', Torstensson concluded.

Social Democrats

During the years of right-wing government, the Social Democrats felt great confusion at being in opposition after twelve consecutive years in government. Several MPs even noted that it was not until their party had been defeated the second time, in 2010, that its representatives really grasped that it was no longer 'the ruling government party of Sweden'. This unfamiliarity with being in opposition also influenced what used to be one of the main traits of the group: the demand for absolute group loyalty. This weakened sense of party loyalty was exacerbated by feeble and short-lived party leaderships, first of Mona Sahlin and later of Håkan Juholt, which, implied a veritable crisis, as MP Eva-Lena Jansson put it. As for the dimension of *the autonomy of the individual MP*, it appears as though the difficulties the party group experienced have somewhat weakened the hierarchical order of the party. As two MPs described it, suddenly there was no one to remind the group of its collectivistic norm, or to demonstrate it, and so there were no sanctions for going against the norm (Johansson and Ygeman).

However, notwithstanding difficulties such as media leaks and disloyal behaviour in the group, all MPs interviewed said that the collectivism of the group remained relatively powerful. While commenting on the still-marked norm of loyalty, Anders Ygeman noted that it was not only disloyal to criticise the Social Democratic group in the open but also unnecessary: 'We share the same goal, we all want to win the elections – it would be a pity to obstruct that'. However, he perceived the party's structure as less hierarchical than that of the Moderates and said that this could partly explain why the group, when facing problems, has sometimes had difficulties remaining unified. His fellow MP, Morgan Johansson, considered that, notwithstanding the party's considerable size and internal controversies, it has nevertheless managed to hold together. Johansson suggested that an egalitarian ideal within the group coexists with an authoritarian one, the latter needing to be managed by a strong leader in order to function, as was the case under the former party leader Göran Persson. The pattern is not the same as in the Moderates, where MPs might be chastised during group meetings, but it still combines comparatively strong group pressure with a demand for MPs to provide input. It would not be true to say that the years in opposition have fostered greater individualism, though, as Johansson pointed out, society's individualistic *Zeitgeist* is sometimes difficult for a party with collectivistic ideals to accommodate. He also emphasised the norm of not speaking too much during group meetings and, when speaking, of being thoroughly prepared and well acquainted with the topic. According to Johansson, when MPs voice opinions, it is important to convey natural authority and seriousness, and certainly not to sound as though 'you're giving a speech on International Worker's Day'. Johansson's account is well in line with those of several other MPs. A telling comment about the value of choosing one's words and time was made by Björn von Sydow: 'Oh, that deputy hasn't said anything in a couple of months, now that s/he does, it is probably important!'

Though the party is collectivistic, the interviews indicated that the Social Democrats are still less hierarchical than the Moderates. Eva-Lena Jansson compared the relationship between the parliamentary party group and party leadership to that between parliament and government, in that the leadership must seek support in the parliamentary group, where it only sometimes wins. She noted that the greater the difficulties facing the party, the more important the role of the party group. Though discussion behind closed doors might be heated, there was still a norm of sticking together and not criticising the party outside the group. Speaking in 2012 Jansson said that party discipline was still strong, though less so than when the party was in government.

Concerning the dimension *political responsibility*, all MPs described a party culture in which pragmatism prevails. Morgan Johansson noted that a crucial skill is 'the craft of politics', being able to get things done and transform political ideas into policy, a capacity that requires a certain pragmatism. Johansson also noted that it was still more important to manifest the potential for government than for active opposition. This point, he said, recalls the Moderates: when it comes to handling difficult issues, the smaller parties have the luxury of doing what is considered to be the 'right thing', which Björn von Sydow captured when he noted that the latitude for idealism has indisputable limits in a party such as the Social Democrats. Both Johansson and von Sydow stated that the smaller parties, well aware that they were never likely be in a position to fully implement their ideas, do not have to concern themselves with practicalities. Parties have different goals, Johansson and von Sydow added, and the goal of these smaller parties might be that of changing the political agenda, an honourable purpose to be sure but not the main aim of the Social Democrats. Johansson concluded: 'In the Social Democrats, you would never hear anybody say, "We should work not in order to realise our policies, or not to aim for office". I've never heard a Social Democrat say that our goal does not need to be holding office'. However, there is also the danger of staying too long in office, both Johansson and von Sydow continued, in which case the party becomes a 'machine', occupied with government technique and forgetting to develop policies and ideas.

Hillevi Larsson is one of those who maintain that the Social Democrats are a highly pragmatic party. Unlike the Centre Party, however, compromise is not seen as having intrinsic value; rather, it is tactical considerations that determine how far to go: 'In those policy areas where the party has strong electoral support, one should not compromise – it's as simple as that', Larsson says. As for the view of compromise, the words of another MP, Eva-Lena Jansson, support the belief that compromise is not considered to have any intrinsic value. The slightly more positive attitude towards compromise that the party had adopted has been somewhat diminished because of disputes with the Left and Green parties and by the number of 'shut doors' these implied. In a sense, though, she said, another side to pragmatism has been strengthened, as a period of not being involved in collaboration with the Left and the Greens made it possible for the Social Democrats to hold 'softer' ideological positions and to be less critical of industry. Another factor in favour of pragmatism, Jansson added, is that even though the years in opposition led to feelings of bewilderment (a description affirmed by all Social Democratic MPs interviewed), they also had a positive side. Loosened ties to the state apparatus have rendered the party less defensive and tempered its tendency to invariably defend the state and affirm that everything is in good order. There has also been more sincere humility since losing the elections for a second time, in 2010; before that, there was more of a sense of waiting to regain power, as if, Jansson explained, it actually 'belonged to us'.

Christian Democrats

There are similarities between the Christian Democrats and the Centre Party as regards the dimension of *political responsibility*. Both groups emphasise the need for accommodation in order to gain influence and they share the view that politics without influence is pointless. However, while the Centre Party's emphasis is on negotiation and compromise, the Christian Democrats stress consensus, for which a necessary condition is behaving in a friendly and approachable manner. All of the interviewees maintained that this was a fundamental cultural trait of the party. There is a crux, though, indicated by MP Désirée Pethrus, in that the party preferences on some issues (such as family policies) are sometimes controversial in modern liberal society and the party therefore risks being perceived as too conservative by the public. There is a paradox here, Pethrus added: on one hand, the party has strong ideological convictions [comparable to those of the Left Party: author's note]; on the other hand, the party's strong consensual ideal sometimes overcomes the former, so that the party accepts losing more than it perhaps needs to.

During its years in government, the Christian Democrat party had many opportunities to seek consensus through its collaboration within the right-wing bloc. All the MPs stressed that the party had an incontestable duty to be loyal to its government coalition, even when there was strong disagreement, and they said that this duty was executed in practice. However, there has been some internal criticism implying that the party might sometimes be too compliant and should actually behave more assertively. In this regard, former party group leader Stefan Attefall claimed that the younger generation has tended to be more combative.[1]

As is well known, conflicts within parties can unquestionably rival those between parties in intensity and it should be emphasised that the Christian Democrat party has certainly had opportunities to put its consensual ideal into practice within the parliamentary party group itself. It is telling that Christian Democrats make it a point of honour to avoid voting in the group.[2] Voting is considered to create winners and losers, thereby engendering division and disunion, and should therefore be avoided. This outlook on consensus gives the group leader an especially important role, because s/he is the one who has the role of weighing various opinions together, identifying the common denominator and presenting the group with a solution on which all can agree (Pethrus, Attefall, Andersson).

Concerning the dimension of *the autonomy of the individual MP*, all Christian Democratic MPs emphasised that being in government entails less latitude for individual MPs to act freely. However, none of them indicated that this reflected any more pervasive change in culture rather than a temporary adjustment in behaviour. An experienced MP, Stefan Attefall, also noted that the situation was the same during the right-wing governments of 1991–1994 and 2006–2014. We also find examples of the opposite tendency: certain situations might increase MPs' autonomy, such as during the discussion of a new party leader, when MP Mats Odell presented himself as rival candidate to the incumbent party leader, Göran Hägglund. During the period preceding the Christian Democratic party congress that re-elected Hägglund, there was more latitude for individual MPs to raise their profiles, this time in favour of one of the two candidates (Andersson, Szyber).

Caroline Szyber said that there is a certain latitude in the Christian Democratic party for MPs to criticise their party but that, to be met with respect, they must demonstrate that they have made an effort to influence party opinion first. She also noted that it is mandatory to combine personal commitment with the ability to display responsibility for party policy as a whole, not only in relation to isolated political issues. It must, Szyber continued, be crystal clear that critical MPs are acting for the sake of the party as a whole. She added that, although MPs do have some autonomy, this is a case of freedom within limits. These limits should be regarded as providing support rather than as restrictions, helping MPs orient themselves in their daily parliamentary work. In general, too much freedom of action is not appreciated by the group. There are, however, rare examples of MPs introducing parliamentary bills against the will of the party leadership (Pethrus, Attefall), conduct that would hardly be approved of in the more hierarchical culture of the Moderates.

The Christian Democratic group provides a telling example of how different cultural aspects can interact and of how collectivism can come in different forms. Direct pressure on MPs to adapt themselves to the group is less strict and forceful than in the Social Democratic and, particularly, the Moderate parliamentary groups. In the Christian Democrats, the mechanism that favours collectivism instead derives support from the party norm of behaving in an agreeable and non-confrontational way – a norm linked to the dimension of political responsibility. The negative attitude towards voting within the group is indicative of this view: demand for consensus does limit the autonomy of individual MPs, even though it is implemented through a demand for agreeableness rather than rigorous subordination.

CONCLUSION

This chapter has examined and contrasted the organisational cultures of seven parties. It is now time to take a closer look at how these results relate to the cartel party thesis. If we compare the cultures observed in 2012–2013 with those observed in 1998–2002, we find two dissimilarities observable between the periods. The Moderates appear to have moved in a more pragmatic direction, whereas the idealistic side of the Greens has been strengthened. To qualify our conclusions, let us start by looking further into what has happened or – as in most cases – has not happened.

The only change that does not oppose the logic of cartelisation is that of the Moderates. However, as discussed earlier, that change appears to have been a result of the party's change of role from opposition to government rather than due to cartelisation. This conclusion is supported by the fact that the organisational culture of the Moderates (observed in 1998–2002) stresses the importance of politicians being aware of their function: there is a need for idealism in opposition, while a more pragmatic stance is needed when in government. Furthermore, we have found no signs of the parties of the right-wing bloc having adapted their respective cultures to one another; instead, we still observe variations on a theme. For example, the collectivism of the Moderates differs in form from that of the Centre Party, which, in turn, differs

Table 8.3   Observed Party Cultures, 2012–2013

	Pragmatic vs Idealistic Orientation	*Individualistic vs Collectivistic Orientation*
Moderates	Pragmatic	Collectivistic
Liberals	IDEALISTIC	INDIVIDUALISTIC
Centre Party	Pragmatic	Collectivistic
Christian Democrats	Pragmatic	Collectivistic
Greens	Pragmatic/IDEALISTIC	INDIVIDUALISTIC
Social Democrats	Pragmatic	Collectivistic
Left Party	IDEALISTIC	INDIVIDUALISTIC

Note: Capital letters indicate those cultural traits that are *not* in accordance with the logic of cartelisation and would be expected to obstruct cartelisation. Changes from the reference study (Barrling Hermansson 2004) are underlined.

from that of the Christian Democrats; the Liberals, in contrast, still embrace individualism. Furthermore, according to the interviewees from the Centre Party, there are even tendencies towards a strengthened idealism in the Centre Party, though this tendency is not yet very strong. These tendencies are particularly interesting because they contradict the cartel party thesis. The younger generation in the Centre Party has tended to introduce new perspectives – what might be described as a mild breeze of idealism, surprising in this archetypically pragmatic party. Interestingly, rather than having become more pragmatic during its years in government, the Centre Party has instead experienced a period of fatigue with its role as the Swedish champion of pragmatism. We found comparable descriptions of the Christian Democrats, though not as strongly expressed.

In the case of the Social Democrats, the pragmatic and collectivistic orientation remains, although the collectivism was disturbed, first, by several years in opposition and, second, by internal leadership crisis. It cannot be said that the party culture has changed, but it should be noted that the few slight alterations there are contradict the logic of cartelisation. For this party, the time in opposition simply appears to have made it more difficult to sustain a collectivistic outlook on parliamentary work. These tendencies are in line with those displayed by the Moderates, in that they corroborate the idea that office is more important than coalition as such in influencing culture, the Social Democrats having found themselves in both opposition and in 'shadow cabinet coalition' during those years.

Finally, the Liberals and the Left Party are especially interesting because, historically, these parties have possessed organisational cultures that are the most at odds with the logic of cartelisation, because they are both idealistic and individualistic. In the follow-up study, we observed a somewhat more nuanced view of these dimensions. The Liberal interviewees revealed an understanding of the special conditions under which a government works, conditions that require less idealism and demand that individuals subordinate themselves to the collective that the government represents. In the Left Party several years of right-wing government have fostered the opinion that a more pragmatic attitude might sometimes be necessary to avoid what the party perceives as the 'worst-case scenario' – a right-wing government. However, the idealism of the Left Party is still strong. Furthermore, though there have been efforts to play down the far-reaching individualism in the party, there are no signs of an individualism in decline. The prevailing individualism and idealism of the Left Party culture, as well as the strengthened idealism of the Greens, demonstrate that party cultures have not become more similar in the left-wing bloc.

If we return to the research questions posed at the outset, we find that there was some change between the 1998–2002 and 2012–2013 periods. We also find: (i) that there is no overall pattern of the parties converging; (ii) that the actual observable changes are increased pragmatism in the Moderates and, inversely, increased idealism in the Greens; and (iii) that the change in the Moderates fits with the logic of cartelisation, although the underlying reason for the change seems instead to be in line with a party culture adapting to holding office. The change in the Greens is clearly contrary to the logic of cartelisation.

The overall conclusion, however, is that the observed changes in attitudes are so in accordance with the fundamental cultural traits of the Moderates and the Greens that one cannot infer that they reflect any fundamental cultural change in either party. Instead, it seems reasonable to describe these changes, in the words of Krouwel (2012: 267), as examples of parties 'moving back to traditional structures and habits'. In the case of the Greens, this is a consequence of the party's longing for its idealistic origins; in the case of the Moderates, it is a result of the party's determination to uphold its cultural structures and habits (by adapting to the procedures and ways of thinking that the party's role requires). In sum, no signs of cartelisation can be detected in the cultural party patterns examined here.

APPENDIX: INTERVIEWS AND INTERVIEWEES

Centre Party

Anders W. Jonsson (group leader, starting 2011), 14 May 2012
Rickard Nordin, 24 October 2012
Annika Qarlsson, 12 March 2012
Åsa Torstensson, 18 April 2012
Solveig Zander, 12 February 2013

Christian Democrats

Yvonne Andersson, 26 April 2012
Stefan Attefall (group leader 2002–2010), 8 May 2012
Lars Gustafsson, 24 April 2013
Désirée Pethrus, 15 April 2013
Caroline Szyber, 12 March 2012

Greens

Per Bolund, 26 March 2012
Maria Ferm, 31 May 2012
Ulf Holm, 22 November 2012
Mehmet Kaplan, 16 May 2012
Mikaela Valtersson (group leader 2006–2011), 21 November 2012

Liberals

Eva Flyborg, 25 April 2012
Ulf Nilsson, 2 April 2012
Christer Nylander, 10 May 2012
Johan Pehrson (party group leader 2006–2014), 23 May 2012
Barbro Westerholm, 19 March 2012

Left Party

Josefin Brink, 26 April 2012
Hans Linde (group leader starting 2010), 23 April 2013
Lars Ohly (party leader 2004–2012), 20 April 2012
Lena Olsson, 7 June 2012
Kent Persson, 22 November 2012

Moderates

Maria Abrahamsson, 28 May 2012
Anna König Jerlmyr, 28 June 2012
Marietta de Pourbaix Lundin, 21 2012
Henrik von Sydow, 20 April 2012
Ewa Thalén Finné, 17 April 2012

Social Democrats

Eva-Lena Jansson, 23 November 2012
Morgan Johansson, 27 March 2013
Hillevi Larsson, 10 July 2012
Björn von Sydow (president of parliament 2002–2006), 9 January 2013
Anders Ygeman, 13 March 2013

NOTES

1. At the time of the interview, Attefall was a cabinet minister.
2. After this study was conducted, according to interviews with deputies carried out by Swedish Radio, the Christian Democratic parliamentary party group did, in fact, vote to replace the group leader Emma Henriksson with Andreas Carlson, an MP politically closer to Ebba Busch Thor (the newly elected Christian Democratic party leader, though never part of the parliamentary party group) (Garcia and Sandin 2015). It should be noted that a consensus-seeking culture does not imply a culture free from conflict. When conflict does arise in such a culture, it might induce even stronger antagonism than in a more hierarchical setting, as friction between group members in a consensus culture clashes with the ideal of sticking together and discontent in the group can have difficulties finding legitimate expression (Douglas 1982: 206, 1996: 43).

Chapter 9

Democracy and the Cartel Party

Henrik Enroth and Mats Sjölin

So far in this book we have concentrated on the matter of empirical support. In this chapter, our intention is to bring the normative aspects of the cartel party theory into sharper focus, in light of the findings presented and discussed in previous chapters. The cartel party theory is freighted with normative baggage, although much of it remains undeclared. There has been a certain ambivalence from the outset between an ostensibly descriptive account of historical mutations in the party form and a particular normative assessment of the same mutations. There has also been a certain reticence in spelling out the latter.

The original statement of the theory suggested that 'the rise of the cartel-party model as an empirical phenomenon is also associated with a revision of the normative model of democracy' (Katz and Mair 1995: 21). This revision has been depicted as a move away from a conception of democracy historically associated with the mass party and, Katz and Mair (1995: 6, 21) have suggested, with 'a particular, and now dated, ideal of social structure, neither of which is characteristic of postindustrial societies'. This has the semblance of a purely descriptive statement but there is no mistaking Katz and Mair's misgivings about these developments. In our current situation, they suggest, 'the significant element is what is missing' from the conception of democracy with which we have in effect been left: 'the currying of public favour by elites, rather than public involvement in policy-making'. 'Voters', in accordance with this latter-day conception of democracy, 'should be concerned with results rather than policy, which is the domain of the professional. Parties are partnerships of professionals, not associations of, or for, the citizens'; these partnerships are premised on 'the toning down of competition' (Katz and Mair 1995: 22–3). Democracy by way of parties can now, in supposed consequence, 'be seen as a means by which the rulers control the ruled, rather than the other way around' and 'a means of achieving social stability rather than social change' (Katz and Mair 1995: 22; cf. Mair 2005; Katz and Mair 2009). Democracy is no longer seen as 'a process by which limitations or controls are imposed on the state by civil society, becoming instead a service provided by the state for civil society' (Katz and Mair 1995: 22).

What there is by way of explicit normative argument in the cartel party theory can be found more or less in full in these remarks, spread over two of the twenty-three pages that constitute the original statement of the theory. The concerns that can be gleaned from these pages should by now be familiar: we have the professionalisation of political elites and the attendant convergence of ideology and policy; we have parties pursuing the professional self-interest of the elites supposedly controlling them, rather than acting responsively in relation to their nominal constituents. What remains less than clear is by what criteria these complaints are to be judged, not least given the meagre – or at best mixed – empirical support for the cartel party theory provided by the analyses in this book. If indeed 'the significant element' is missing from this picture, then we need first of all, a clearer view of the possible standards by which the democratic credentials of party politics can be meaningfully gauged.

To that end, and by way of background, we start by turning in the first section below to Robert Dahl's classic work in democratic theory, recalling in brief the attributes he famously associates with 'polyarchy' as an approximately democratic regime type. While Dahl's list of attributes has the virtues of clarity and simplicity in bringing out many of our entrenched intuitions about democracy, there is little to be learned from this list specifically about the nature and role of parties in a modern democracy. Therefore, having drawn from Dahl what we take to be general democratic values relevant to any discussion of modern representative democracy, we then turn to influential work in the field of party research, taking a closer look at two dominant and divergent accounts of what we should expect of parties in a modern democracy: the first puts a premium on parties' responsiveness to their constituents and the second emphasises accountability, parties here being seen as a means of holding governors to account. Thus equipped, in the second section we take a closer look at what the proponents of the cartel theory themselves make of the normative implications of their theory. We argue that the cartel theory selects and combines key elements from both models but it also goes well beyond the concerns introduced in these two standard models of party democracy, pointing instead towards a more radical critical or sceptical stance towards parties as mediators between voters and policy-makers. For Katz and Mair, the main cause for blame in this regard remains elite collusion. By way of conclusion, we suggest that in light of the findings presented in this book, what emerges most forcefully from a consideration of Katz and

Mair's work is not so much the threat of convergence and collusion as the very opposite: the entrenchment of conflict.

THE 'PARTY GOVERNMENT' AND 'CONSENSUS' MODELS

For Dahl (1989: 6–8), any assessment of the functions and practices of governments and political institutions must include a proper understanding of democratic norms and values. In *Democracy and Its Critics* (1989), Dahl identifies five normative criteria that a democratic process ought to satisfy. As is well known, these criteria are presented as ideal standards, never perfectly satisfied in actual political processes – hence the label 'polyarchy' for political regimes approximating what we customarily think of and speak of as democracies (cf. Enroth 2010a).

In a 'narrow sense', Dahl explains, a democratic process entails (i) effective participation and (ii) voting equality. Both these criteria concern the requirement that citizens have a say in the process of collective decision-making. For participation to be effective, 'citizens ought to have an adequate opportunity, and an equal opportunity, for expressing their preferences as to the final outcome'. Voting equality is, in essence, about choice. Citizens ought to have a real and effective choice between different outcomes and an equal opportunity to make choices, and their choices should be counted as equal.

For a process to qualify as 'fully democratic', Dahl continues, two additional criteria must be met: (iii) enlightened understanding, meaning that democratic processes ought to provide citizens with an adequate understanding of the consequences of policies for themselves and others; and (iv) control of the agenda. Finally, a democratic process ought to satisfy (v) the criterion of inclusion, that is, 'the demos should include all adults subject to the binding collective decisions' (Dahl 1989: 120).

Although Dahl (1989: 110, 116–17) stresses that the criteria for a democratic process do not specify any particular institutional design or decision rule, such as the majority principle, he also identifies a number of institutions in a polyarchic regime (Dahl 1982: 10–11). At the most general level, those institutions centre on 'the continuing responsiveness of the government to the preferences of its citizens' (Dahl 1971: 1). Specifically, citizenship should 'include the right to oppose and vote out the government' (Dahl 1989: 221), so institutions promoting public contestation and political competition are needed. Opposition and the right to participate are essential dimensions of democracy (Dahl 1971: 4–6), and a clear-cut distinction – in theory and practice alike – between government and opposition is one of its key presuppositions.

Like so many theorists of democracy, Dahl is notoriously taciturn on the nature and place of parties in a polyarchic regime. For a corrective, we can turn to literature on comparative government, in which it has long been acknowledged that political parties play a vital role in the functioning of modern parliamentary democracies (see, for example, Castles and Wildenmann 1986; Dalton, Farrell and McAllister 2011). Political parties are the hub of democracy, around which political decision-making processes are worked out. There is no agreement, however, as to just *how* a liberal democracy with strong political parties might fulfil the requirements of a fully democratic process, for instance, regarding the values of responsiveness, choice and political competition, or on the matter of how to strike a balance between those values.

Here, it may be useful to distinguish between three arenas in which parties operate: the electoral arena, where we expect parties to seek vote maximisation; the parliamentary arena, where parties seek to maximise parliamentary influence; and the internal arena, where party cohesion is variously at stake (Sjöblom 1968: 73–87). Approached in this manner, the cartel party theory is a theory of (i) the relationships between parties and voters in the electoral arena; (ii) the relationships between parties in the parliamentary arena; (iii) the relationships between the party elite and the rank-and-file members in the internal arena; and (iv) party behaviour in and across these different arenas.

Moreover, we can consult two competing normative models of the role of parties in modern democracies: the 'party government' model and the 'consensus' model of party democracy. A major difference between these models is 'the contrast between the view that elections are a mechanism to hold government accountable and the view that they are means to ensure that citizens' views and interests are properly represented in the democratic process' (Thomassen 2014: 1).

According to the classic formulation of the *party government model*, parties rule when in government and oppose the government's measures when in opposition; in both capacities they must be accountable to voters. Elections should offer voters an effective choice between a limited number of general political programmes presented by cohesive parties, which should, ideally, leave voters with two distinct directions for government to take (Schattschneider 1948; Ranney 1954: 11–13; Katz 1986: 4–5). It is assumed in this model that parties that win elections will also be able to implement their policies. Political power must therefore be concentrated in the parties in government and there should be no co-operation between government and opposition in the parliamentary arena (Thomassen 2014: 2). The task of the opposition parties is to criticise the government, not to influence its policies (Sjölin 1993: 153–4). Voting, in this model, is retrospective, allowing voters to assess and sanction government behaviour after the fact (Holmberg 2014b:

133, 135; cf. Mansbridge 2003, 2011). Herein, according to the model, lies the essence of accountability (Ranney 1954: 12; Lewin 2007: 3–4).

The *consensus model* of democracy challenges several core elements of the party government model. For its foremost proponent, Arend Lijphart, the consensus model is not only an alternative and equally legitimate type of democracy (Lijphart 1999: 6) but also one that is more likely to fulfil the normative criteria in Dahl's theory. The consensus model, in short, 'tends to be the "kinder, gentler" form of democracy' (Lijphart 1999: 275–7, 301). In contrast to the party government model, the consensus model stipulates that 'rules and institutions aim at broad participation in government and broad agreement on the policies the government should pursue' (Lijphart 1999: 2). Elections should present voters with a wide range of choices among parties in a multi-party system offering a variety of policy alternatives (Huber and Powell 1994: 299). Elections are mainly future oriented and voting is prospective in outlook. The primary purpose of elections is to achieve responsiveness in the relationship between voters and parties in parliament (Lewin 2007: 95; Holmberg 2014b: 133, 135). Moreover, there 'is no deterministic relation between the election outcome and the formation of the government' in this model (Thomassen 2014: 3). Negotiations are needed to form a majority government and the value of responsiveness demands that the majority should not monopolise political power. Government formation as well as parliamentary decision-making should therefore aim for inclusiveness, broad co-operation and power-sharing (Lijphart 1999: 2–3, 90, 116). By way of negotiation and compromise, the opposition parties are included in and allowed influence over the policy-making process (Strøm 1986, 1990; Sannerstedt 1992; Sjölin 1993: 154–5).

This brief description of these two models cannot, of course, do justice to their complexities. The major differences between the models can be summarised in terms of the dichotomies outlined in Table 9.1.

A first and essential dividing line between the two models is the fact that they put a premium on different values in the democratic process. Proponents of the party government model take the value of accountability to be paramount in fulfilling the criteria of a democratic process. For advocates of the consensus model, the value of responsiveness is the gist of the democratic process instead (Lewin 2007: 96–7).

As a consequence of the difference in democratic values, the party government model focuses primarily on relations between parties and voters in the electoral arena to ensure accountability, whereas the consensus model focuses on party relations in the parliamentary arena as key to creating and maintaining responsiveness between voter preferences and public policies.

Another set of dichotomous contrasts between the party government model and the consensus model can be found in their normative views of relations

Table 9.1 Normative Models of Liberal Democracy and Political Processes

	Party Government Model	Consensus Model
Democratic values	Accountability is major democratic value	Responsiveness is major democratic value
Electoral arena: relations between voters and parties	Electoral arena is key to fulfilling values of democracy	——
• Electoral competition	Identifiable alternative governments; explicit pre-electoral coalition commitments	Wide range of party choice; absence of explicit pre-electoral coalition commitments
• Voting	Sanction model (retrospective voting)	Mandate model (prospective voting)
• Representation	Majority control vision	Proportionate influence vision
Parliamentary arena: relations between parties	——	Parliamentary arena is key to fulfilling values of democracy
• Government–opposition relations	• Concentration of power in government parties	• Inclusiveness, power sharing with opposition parties
• Policy-making style	• Conflict seeking (excluding)	• Consensus seeking (including)
• Decision-making process	• Voting to obtain majority	• Negotiations to obtain broad majority
Internal arena: relations within parties	• Intra-party democracy is counterproductive to party cohesion • Intra-party democracy contributes to mediation between voter preferences and public policy	

between parties in the parliamentary arena. The most important dividing line here concerns the distribution of power among parties in parliament. For proponents of the party government model, it is essential that elections yield not only strong majority governments but also 'governments that are essentially unconstrained by other parties in the policy-making process' (Huber and Powell 1994: 291); concentration of power in government parties is therefore necessary in this model. In contrast, the consensus model instead aims for the formation of broad multi-party governments and a 'balanced executive–legislative relationship', allowing power-sharing with opposition parties (Lijphart 1999: 90, 116).

Consequently, the policy-making style of the party government model is conflict-seeking in nature, excluding competitive opposition from parliamentary influence and ensuring a majority for government policies through decisions by vote. In contrast, in the consensus model, parties seek consensus between major parties in the parliamentary arena, the government often involving co-operative opposition parties in the formulation of policies worked out through negotiated broad agreements.

THE CARTEL PARTY AND MODELS OF DEMOCRACY

The visions of democracy presented above are ideal types and, specifically, polar types. The party government model and the consensus model represent the two end points of the accountability–responsiveness value dimension (Sartori 1976: 145–6). It is in the nature of political ideal types that they do not necessarily depict any existing political systems. Most liberal democracies display more or less distinctive features from both models, a combination that may also change over time (Katz 1986: 44; Hagevi 1998: 28–34, 251; Lijphart 1999: 116; Arter 2006: 13). We shall return shortly to the particularities of this combination in the Swedish case and to the changes it has undergone. Before doing so, however, we must take a closer look at what the cartel party theory takes from these models, and what its proponents make of the normative implications of their observations.

Like many of us, Katz and Mair select and combine elements from the two models. As to inter-party relations in the parliamentary arena, Katz and Mair's account is generally in the spirit, if not always the letter, of the party government model. It might be tempting to conclude from the cartel party theory that conflict is the normatively preferred state in the parliamentary arena, although this would probably be an overstatement. Katz and Mair do not so much explicitly propound conflict as they disapprove of co-operation and consensus, which appear in the theory as shorthand for elite collusion and cartelisation. This distrust of co-operation and consensus seeking was an essential aspect of the theory from the outset; indeed, this is part of what led Katz and Mair to single out Sweden as particularly fertile ground in this respect, cartelisation being 'likely to develop most easily in those political cultures marked by a tradition of inter-party cooperation and accommodation' (Katz and Mair 1995: 17).

As to party–voter relations in the electoral arena, the argument is more in the spirit of the consensus model but, again, by negative inference: parties are faulted for failing in their representative capacity and for not being adequately responsive to the concerns of their voters but this does not translate into an explicit preference for responsiveness as a normative criterion for party behaviour in the electoral arena. Needless to say, this does not translate into calls for co-operation and power-sharing in the parliamentary arena.

Making good normative sense of the cartel party theory is made more difficult by the possibility that 'Katz and Mair' may not necessarily speak with one voice or constitute an unchanging unit on this matter. Katz's earlier work, for instance, though decidedly tilted towards the party government model, contains references – evaluatively neutral rather than dismissive – to the consensus model as well to the kind of co-operative behaviour and readiness to compromise stipulated by this model (e.g. Katz 1986). In contrast, any mention of co-operation or consensus in Mair's later work is evaluatively negative in the context of collusion and cartelisation (e.g. Mair 2005, 2008) and the same is true of Katz and Mair's joint work (e.g. 1995, 2009).

The question of conflict and consensus nicely captures what Katz and Mair take from, as well as where they depart from, our two models. In line with the party government model, the ideal of accountability and the categorical distinction between government and opposition are invested with considerable normative force in the cartel theory but much the same is true of the ideals of responsiveness and influence associated with the consensus model. Most notably, these ideals are all enlisted in the service of Katz and Mair's overarching critique of what they take to be the power of elites in party politics. For Katz and Mair, as for so many students of modern democracy for whom elitism is an ever-looming threat, consensus tends to look suspect – a mere semblance, an elite ruse to paper over conflicts or power asymmetries within and between parties (cf. Bachrach 1962; Lukes 1974; Bachrach and Baratz 1975) and to further exacerbate parties' distance from the concerns of voters. By the same token, inter-party co-operation and a readiness to compromise are bound to look like collusion and cartelisation – again, it is claimed, an elite strategy to stifle competition and insulate professional politicians from any concerns that might be detrimental to their own, presumably shared, self-interest.

Mair's critique of the UK's New Labour may serve to illustrate the point. In a piece in *New Left Review* in 2000, Mair argued that since its coming to power in 1997, Labour had done much to 'dismantle this traditionally majoritarian system of government', moving the UK 'substantially closer to Lijphart's alternative model of consensus democracy' (Mair 2000: 24). However, the measures taken to that effect should not be construed as efforts to strengthen party rule as much as to 'marginalise' it, in effect 'to evade party – and hence partisanship – altogether' (Mair 2000: 26). The programme of New Labour, Mair points out, was conceived of by the party as 'the only alternative, and hence without partisan purpose', all the while stressing the need for 'closer Lib–Lab co-operation' (Mair 2000: 24). The upshot was a mode of 'governance' – the connotations of non-partisan administration in this word aptly convey what Mair has in mind – 'not intended as party democracy' (Mair 2000: 28). Rather, Mair concludes, New Labour amounted to nothing less than an 'assault on partisan politics' (Mair 2000: 28). What Mair staged in this piece was yet another performance of the old drama of the party to end all parties, or the party 'above all parties' (Arendt 1968: 38; Rosenblum 2008: 40). New Labour, in Mair's account, was pitting itself against a faction and – as a consequence, or at least the consequence Mair wishes to draw out – against the party as such resulting in institutionalised factionalism. In the end, what New Labour illustrated in this piece was not in point of fact a turn towards Lijphart's consensus model but a faux consensus without party, the morphing of party rule into elite administration (Mair 2000: 21).

Normatively, the cartel party theory is all about critique rather than standards for best practice. This in itself is certainly no cause for blame. Critique of power is an integral part of the Enlightenment tradition and thus, in Immanuel Kant's words, part of our means of 'release from our self-incurred tutelage' (Kant 1988: 462; cf. Foucault 1984). Critique of power is also preliminary for any standards of best practice in the world of human affairs. The critique of parties and party politics offered by Katz and Mair arguably misfires, however, when we take into account what has transpired in recent decades, not least in the case singled out by Katz and Mair as the most likely one for cartelisation.

In the literature on comparative government, the workings of Swedish democracy from the end of World War II up to at least the 1970s have been characterised as an example of the consensus model of democracy (Lijphart 1977; Elder, Thomas and Arter 1988). The consensual elements noted in Swedish politics are, first and foremost, 'a low intensity of conflict, together with a highly effective machinery for conflict resolution. The predominant style of policy-making is seen as concertative and deliberative, and the level of inter-elite agreement is high' (Elder, Thomas and Arter 1988: 182). This is the background understanding against which proponents of the cartel party theory have pointed to Sweden as a likely case of party system cartelisation (Katz and Mair 1995: 17, 2009: 755).

The image of Sweden as a consensual type of democracy has not been undisputed, however. Researchers have also emphasised elements of conflict and ideological differences between the political parties in the post-war era (Uddhammar 1993: 471–3; Hagevi 1998: 33–4, 251). Moreover, there is evidence to suggest that the mix of elements from the party government model and the consensus model has changed substantially in Swedish politics in recent decades. When Arter (2006: 270) summarised these developments some ten years ago, he concluded that 'all in all, Sweden is a majoritarian democracy', which roughly corresponds to what we have labelled the party government model, albeit 'with consensual legislative practice'. Looking now at the development of party relations in the parliamentary arena in recent decades, the nature and degree of consensus in legislative practice can no longer be taken as a matter of course, if indeed it ever could.

First, concerning policy-making style, in a study of committee reports
with reservations from one or more of the opposition parties in the
Swedish parliament (an established indicator for political conflict; see
Chapters 3 and 4 of this book) during the period 1919–1990, Anders Sannerstedt and Mats Sjölin (1992) demonstrated that the level of conflict
was comparatively low and stable from the 1950s until the 1970s. Only a
few years later, however, in the early 1980s, this pattern changed dramatically, with the proportion of committee reports with reservations rising
from one-third to almost two-thirds in 1990 (Sannerstedt and Sjölin 1992:
113). Likewise, when analysing reservations from the opposition parties in committee reports on government propositions in the 1970–2014
period, Karl Loxbo and Mats Sjölin have found that this upturn in the
level of conflict was consolidated in the 1990s and further strengthened
in the 2000s (Loxbo and Sjölin 2016; see also Chapter 3 of this book).

The frequency of reservations may not be a very discriminatory measure, as it does not account for the degree of policy disagreement between
the government and the opposition parties. However, Emil Uddhammar
(1993: 460–1) found a similar pattern when he analysed party positions on a
sample of parliamentary decisions from 1900 to 1990 that concerned social,
economic and regulatory policies related to the size of the Swedish welfare
state. Policy differences between government and opposition parties have,
by and large, been small. Once again, the 1980s stand out as a period with
greater differences between the parties' policy claims when compared with
the 1960s and 1970s. Furthermore, as Karl Loxbo and Magnus Hagevi demonstrate in Chapter 3 of this book, 'intense controversy over policy-making –
that is, when the opposition rejects government bills outright – has risen
markedly over time'.

A second relevant dividing line to consider between the party government model and the consensus model in this context concerns power relations between government and opposition parties, including the extent of
power-sharing and the propensity to resolve conflicts over policy by way
of negotiations in the parliamentary arena (cf. Elder, Thomas and Arter
1988: 11).

Swedish parliamentary committees are of special interest as important
sites for negotiation. The ability to reach compromise between government
and opposition parties has traditionally been considered a typical consensual
trait of Swedish politics (Sjölin 1993: 146–9; Sannerstedt 1996). Available
data on the outcome of committee deliberations on government propositions
and opposition party counterproposals indicate a steady decline in Swedish
governments' willingness to co-operate with the opposition (Loxbo and Sjölin 2016). In the 1960s, 1970s and early 1980s, committee majorities made
substantial changes and amendments in well over 20 per cent of all politicised

government proposals. In most cases these changes were also accepted by the government parties (Stjernquist 1966: 29–32; Sjölin 1993: 183, 193). In contrast, in the 1990s and 2000s, the proportion of committee reports in which the government made adjustments to counterproposals by the opposition more than halved (Loxbo and Sjölin 2016). The decline in power-sharing with opposition parties over time in Sweden has been reinforced by a strengthening of bipolar bloc competition between a bloc of red–green parties and a bloc of non-socialist parties. Bloc politics has increased since the beginning of the 1990s in the parliamentary and the electoral arenas alike (Arter 2006; Aylott 2011; Hagevi 2015b).

With the benefit of hindsight, we can certainly question the nature and strength of consensual democracy in Swedish politics in the 1960s and 1970s. History aside, all the empirical data on party relations we have reviewed indicates that parliamentary politics in Sweden has drifted away from the consensus model towards the party government model in the course of the 1990s and 2000s, again with the 1980s as something of a watershed decade. This is valid for all three categories of party relations in the parliamentary arena presented in Table 9.1. First, power-sharing with opposition parties has diminished and the power of governments over parliamentary policy-making has been strengthened. Second, changes in the policy-making style are manifest; the propensity to politicise issues in parliament and the level of inter-party conflict have been on the rise. Third, in the parliamentary decision-making process, negotiations to reach compromise across the bloc divide have declined. Parties increasingly rely on bloc voting in contests over policies in parliament. All in all, then, we need to consider what these changes mean for the normative assessment of the cartel party theory and the findings in this book.

IS ELITE CO-OPERATION A BAD THING?

In a working paper from 2005, Mair discusses what he takes to be the malaise of contemporary party politics, namely, 'popular withdrawal and disengagement from conventional politics, on the one hand, and … elite withdrawal into the institutions, on the other hand' (Mair 2005: 1). As he also noted in the same working paper, 'it seems pointless trying to establish where this process might have been initiated, and by whom' (Mair 2005: 21). 'What matters', he continued, 'is that it is mutually reinforcing, and that the ensuing gap between rulers and ruled – or, perhaps more accurately, between administrators and administered – is being stretched by the withdrawal that is taking place on both sides of the divide' (Mair 2005: 21).

In the statements and restatements of the cartel party theory, however, elite collusion is treated as a – if not the most – forceful driver of this process, with the consequence that, among other things, co-operation and consensus seeking are made to look inherently suspect, like fancy names for collusion and cartelisation. In a sense, little has changed in the past decade concerning the double withdrawal of which Mair speaks. This book has lent further support to the observation that parliamentary politics and those who pursue it have indeed been professionalised along the lines discussed by Katz and Mair, and there is little reason to believe that professional politicians are held in higher regard by their constituents now than they were ten years ago. In another sense, however, the whole stage on which this drama is being played out has changed dramatically and, with it, the normative pivot on which the drama itself turns. For Katz and Mair, as we have seen, the problem remains elite collusion, co-operation and the popular discontent or disenchantment such collusion supposedly breeds. But in the demonstrable absence of evidence of actual collusion that has also been established in this book, and in light of compelling evidence of waning consensus and waxing conflict, we are obliged to ask: what is the problem with co-operation and consensus seeking?

If indeed Mair's public withdrawal from politics is real, which seems hard to dispute, the main cause for concern today may not so much be self-serving strategies of collusion on the part of political elites, strategies of which evidence is scant at best, but rather the opposite: a shift in the balance between our two models of democracy such that the parliamentary and electoral arenas alike seem subject to increasing conflict, even antagonism. Placing the findings in this book in the context of broader contemporary developments, what seems most normatively troublesome at present in European and US party politics may not be the triumph of a culture of consensus and compromise, let alone the presence of collusion and cartelisation, but rather the entrenchment of conflict, with attendant partisan isolation and polarisation (see Theriault 2008).[1]

In the Swedish context, the break-up of the so-called December Agreement, mentioned in Chapter 1 of this book, may serve as an illustration. From this perspective, the defection of the Christian Democrats from the bloc-transcending agreement to contain the electoral success of the anti-immigration Sweden Democrats may suggest the vulnerability of any cartel to defection (Kitschelt 2000: 168; Blyth and Katz 2005: 39; cf. Chapter 2 of this book); it may also suggest a changing balance between the two models of democracy discussed here and their respective logics and values.

This question cuts to the core of party democracy and identifies an irreducible tension at its heart. As Katz and Mair – and indeed most people – recognise, partisanship, pluralism and conflict are essential to party politics, but not everybody recognises that partisan politics unmoderated by a readiness to compromise and seek consensus – a willingness to co-operate – will be but a continuation of the private pursuit of self-interest by other means (cf. Arendt 1958; Pitkin 1973, 1981). In a rare serious consideration of parties and partisanship by a political theorist, Nancy Rosenblum has suggested – in keeping with a long tradition of pluralist political theory – that politics 'exists only when the fact of pluralism is accepted and there is latitude for open agitation of groups with rival interests and opinions' (Rosenblum 2008: 6; cf. Laski 1919; Dahl 1956; Mouffe 2000; Connolly 2005). However, as most pluralists have in the end felt compelled to acknowledge, when politics becomes nothing but the open agitation of groups with rival interests and opinions, it soon lapses into political dysfunction and social disorder. At the time of writing, compelling illustrations of this point can be found on both sides of the Atlantic, in otherwise dissimilar party systems and political traditions. Pluralism, as its history clearly demonstrates, cannot go it alone. As early-twentieth-century critics of pluralist theory repeatedly remarked, plurality without at least the ambition to recognise – or forge – unity of some kind will breed social and political disintegration (Ellis 1920; Coker 1921; cf. Enroth 2010b). In short, if there is a problem today with co-operation and consensus seeking, it is not that we have too much of it.

Nor is this problem confined to the parliamentary arena. As Mair (2005: 21) suggested, there is 'a world of the citizens – or a host of particularized worlds of the citizens – and a world of the politicians and parties, and the interaction between these worlds steadily diminishes'. Our contemporary 'worlds' as citizens must indeed be cast in the plural, perhaps increasingly so. Particularisation carries on unabated, seemingly unstoppable. Not only political attitudes but also the very conditions of their formation, dissemination and communication increasingly seem subject to partisan division and polarisation, again on both sides of the Atlantic, albeit so far most patently in the United States. Media scholars have noted – and cautioned – that the production and consumption of information and news both follow and sustain demographic and social divisions, these being easily exploited for political purposes (e.g. Iyengar and Hahn 2009; Prior 2013; Melki and Pickering 2014). With the recent explosion of social media this tendency is likely to be exacerbated, leaving large swaths of the populations of modern democracies with no conceivable reason, or indeed impulse or even ability, to move out of their cognitive and ideological comfort zones. The disturbing upshot has been described, as Douglas Brommesson and Ann-Marie Ekengren note in Chapter 6 of this book, as a growing 'differentiation of what people perceive to be real' (Hjarvard 2008: 111).

In her fine work on partisanship, Rosenblum speaks of 'a disposition to compromise' belonging to the partisan – or at least to Rosenblum's vision of the partisan as a key figure in democratic politics. She also speaks of 'a democratic obligation that partisans assume' not to fall prey to the 'vicissitudes of targeted messages and slivered audiences and divisive issues of the moment'. Partisans, she suggests, 'resist fragmentation' (Rosenblum 2008: 360). At the time of writing, this suggestion seems wishful at best, in the parliamentary no less than in the electoral arena. Giovanni Sartori – ever insightful, even, or especially, when one does not entirely agree with him – noted many years ago that parties can 'go off course on two sides': on one side, the threat of 'excessive partisanship and/or a relapse into factionalism'; on the other, the menace of 'monopoly and/or unitarism'. *Pace* Katz and Mair, if there is presently cause for concern in this area, the latter menace has little do to with it. Parties, Sartori concludes, 'stay safely on course only when they manage to balance partisanship and impartial governing, loyalty to the party and loyalty to the state, party interest and general interest' (Sartori 1976: 65).

There is much to be said for this conclusion, even for those of us for whom notions of impartial governing and general interest do not come naturally. There is a balance to be struck and parties that at least make an effort to strike it responsibly may be more vital today than before, but the balance to be struck can be broached more helpfully than in Sartori's conception. More promising in this regard is what is implied by Rosenblum: that duality or tension is inherent in the very notion of partisanship, and thus party, a peculiarity reflected in the differences between our two models of party democracy. To the point here is also Hanna Pitkin's reminder, offered in America in the wake of the conflicts of the 1960s, that 'what characterizes political life is precisely the problem of continually creating unity in a context of diversity, rival claims, unequal power, and conflicting interests' (Pitkin 1973: 215). When we enter public life, Pitkin later added, whether out of 'personal need, fear, ambition or interest',

> we are there forced to acknowledge the power of others and appeal to their standards, even as we try to get them to acknowledge our power and standards. We are forced to find or create a common language of purposes and aspirations, not merely to clothe our private outlook in public disguise, but to become aware ourselves of its public meaning. (Pitkin 1981: 347)

What Pitkin describes is a transition that recent developments have made us less obliged or even able to make, whether as professional politicians or citizens, but it is a transition that is essential to party politics and one that must at least be attempted in order to make conflict publicly negotiable. In this, the two models of party democracy discussed in this chapter should be seen as complementary rather than opposed, as two incomplete parts of the same complex whole, or as two horns of a dilemma that can only be – and always must be – managed or made manageable but that cannot be resolved in any conclusive manner. The dilemma will play out differently in different political systems certainly, but it will make itself felt wherever parties play a central role in mediating between citizens and policy-makers.

NOTE

1. We note here the need to distinguish analytically, as Katz and Mair do not, between consensus and conflict, on the one hand, and convergence and polarisation, on the other (Hagevi 2014c: 162–4). In keeping with our two models of party democracy, our main concern here is with the dimensions of consensus and conflict. While both dimensions may certainly be normatively consequential, it should be pointed out that the relationship between conflict and polarisation is – or should be – an empirical rather than conceptual or theoretical one (Kitschelt 2007a: 533–4; Azmanova 2011: 387–8; cf. Chapter 10 of this book).

Chapter 10

Conclusions

Magnus Hagevi and Henrik Enroth

As a general statement about party development, the cartel party theory has severe problems. What is assumed to be the most devastating effect of cartelisation on representative democracy is the alleged erosion of the links between voters and parties, 'which are based on trust, accountability, and above all, representation' (Mair 1997: 153). Our findings in this book do not support such claims. Concerning public trust in parties and politicians, the study presented in Chapter 3 finds increasing rather than decreasing levels of trust, starting in the mid 1990s. By 2010 the level of political trust in Sweden was back to approximately the same level as in the early 1970s, the decade when Katz and Mair (1995) claim that cartel parties emerged. Regarding accountability and representation, issue congruence between voters and MPs on important left–right issues has not eroded, as Chapter 3 also demonstrates, and concerning issues not related to the left–right dimension, issue congruence has remained fairly stable. However, mainly due to what is often referred to as 'new politics' and to the growing conflict between holders of libertarian and authoritarian values, political representation regarding these issues decreased somewhat during the period under investigation. Instead of elite cartelisation, we found polarisation among the party elite and, relative to the party elite, convergence around the political centre at mass level (Holmberg 2014a). In short, there has been little deterioration of political representation, party elites are more polarised than their voters, and public trust in politics has increased – all phenomena that provide no support for the cartel party theory.

The studies presented here do provide support for some of the claims advanced by the cartel party theory, however. In Swedish politics from the 1970s/1980s up to the 2010s, we find some indications of policy convergence between parties, though not in issues related to European affairs. The number

205

of party members has decreased while public funding of political parties has increased, indeed replacing the parties' previous financial dependence on their members, as discussed in Chapter 3. A growing proportion of politicians are professional and employed full time or part time as politicians; and professional experience, explored in Chapter 4, is now all but essential for a political career. There is also support for the mediatisation of party politics, as demonstrated in Chapter 6. In the case of an extreme culture of consensus, such as that of Finland, mediatisation has increased the emphasis on consensus, which can be said to be consistent with the assumptions of cartel party theory. Still, with the exception of mediatisation in Finland, this confirmation of specific aspects of the cartel party theory is at the descriptive level only and refers to the general structure of political parties and the party system, rather than to the causal mechanisms posited by the theory (Kitschelt 2000).

As a test of the core propositions of the cartel party theory, therefore, these results are of limited value in themselves. The value of a theory in this context, we suggest, lies in its ability to explain events in accordance with the relationships between the variables identified in the theory, including the assumed causal relationships between them (see Popper 1989). Our empirical data do not illustrate the causality suggested by the cartel party theory (Kitschelt 2000: 169), meaning that the theory cannot satisfactorily explain the development of Swedish political parties over the period examined in this book.

ABSENCE OF CAUSAL RELATIONSHIPS

Some of the most crucial findings of our studies concern the lack of support for the cartel party theory's suggested explanations of party and party system change, that is, cartelisation, depoliticisation and declining internal party democracy. In addition, concerning the potential to initiate change in party politics, we find that Katz and Mair (1995) have underestimated the importance of new alternative conflicts in politics (see Chapter 7 of this book) and overestimated the importance of the increased professionalisation of party politicians (see Chapter 4 of this book). While gender conflict seems to have led to increased conflict between parties in the Swedish Parliament, MPs who make their political careers as professional politicians differ little from other MPs – aside from their professional careers. In addition, in the Swedish political system mediatisation seems to have fragmented, not homogenised, political communication (see Chapter 6 of this book). In the following sections, we elaborate on this lack of support for the explanations offered by the cartel party theory for party change in respect of cartelisation and depoliticisation, party democracy and representation and trust.

To recap, the cartel party theory consists of two interrelated core hypotheses (Katz and Mair 2009: 756–7; see Chapter 1 of this book). The first of these states that political parties are becoming increasingly removed from civil society and are, instead, converging with the state (Mair 1994: 7–8). This change is leading parties to become dependent on public party subsidies, effectively making the parties part of the state (Katz and Mair 1995: 15, 2009: 754–5, 759), while party members, as representatives of civil society, are, in practice, becoming rationalised out of existence (Mair 1997: 113–14; Katz 2001; Katz and Mair 2002). Instead of cultivating flourishing internal democracy, cartel party leadership establishes oligarchic control over party organisations (Katz and Mair 1995: 22, 2009: 759). Controlling their parties from the top, the leaders of cartel parties can free themselves from the policy demands of ideologically motivated grassroots members. Indeed, Swedish political parties have lost members while increasing the financial resources they obtain from public subsidies (see Chapter 3 of this book). However, we found no empirical evidence that intra-party democracy is in a spiral of decline over time (see Chapter 3 of this book). Instead, our findings suggest that proponents of the cartel party theory tend to idealise the democratic qualities of the mass party (cf. Enroth 2017), while seriously overestimating the control exercised by present-day party leaders. Even if we had found more extensive support for policy convergence between political parties in Sweden, our findings mean that decreased party democracy and increased oligarchic control of parties cannot explain such a shift.

According to the second of the two core hypotheses of cartel party theory (Blyth and Katz 2005; Mair 2007, 2013; Katz and Mair 2009; see Chapter 1 of this book), that parties collaborate, we should be able to observe an increase in consensual agreements and a decrease in policy conflict, particularly in policy-making relating to left–right issues and in European affairs. According to the cartel party theory (Katz and Mair 1995), such collaboration is one important explanation for policy convergence among political parties. While mainstream parties have not converged on European affairs issues (see Chapter 5 of this book), the same parties have converged to some extent to similar left–right positions (see Chapter 3 of this book). Still, we found no evidence whatsoever of cartel-like elite collaboration undermining ideological conflict between parties and depoliticising politics in the parliamentary arena. On the contrary, our analyses of parliamentary decision-making over time indicate exactly the opposite tendency, as shown in Chapters 3 and 5. Rather than withering away, policy conflicts between the major parties have increased over time, regarding both left–right issues and European affairs. Contrary to the claims of depoliticisation made in cartel party theory (Katz and Mair 1995, 2009; Blyth and Katz 2005; Mair 2007, 2013), this intensified parliamentary conflict reflects a desire among opposition parties to remain relevant in politics. Also, as shown in Chapter 8, long-established internal party cultures have remained essentially the same throughout the period under investigation, with few signs of cartelisation in evidence.

As discussed in Chapter 9, these findings also cast serious doubt on the normative assumptions of the cartel party theory. For Katz and Mair, the normative problem in this regard remains elite collusion and co-operation and the popular discontent or disenchantment such collusion supposedly breeds. In the demonstrable absence of evidence of collusion, however, and in light of extensive evidence of waning consensus and waxing conflict over time, the main normative concern that emerges from this book may be the potential entrenchment of conflict and possible polarisation of party systems rather than elite-induced consensus.

Taken together, then, given the lack of manifest causal relationships between the assumed explanations and the observed changes in Swedish party politics, the usefulness of the cartel party theory is very much in doubt. Simply stated, it appears that the theory does not explain the kind of political events it sets out to.

ALTERNATIVE EXPLANATIONS

What about party changes that *are* in accordance with the cartel party theory? Is the theory at least partially supported by developments in terms of increased public party financing, declining party membership among citizens and convergence between established parties? Once again, this is doubtful. Some of Katz and Mair's (1995) assumptions when they introduced cartel party theory were hardly predictions of the future but rather described developments in contemporary society. For instance, this is clear when it comes to parties' declining memberships and growing dependence on public subsidies (Gidlund 1983; Widfeldt 1997: 102). Such observations do not bolster the potential value of the theory because they do not explain or predict anything but only describe actual political changes. Even so, of greater importance is that other theories, not necessarily connected to the cartel party theory, offer very plausible theoretical explanations for these changes. Let us take a look at these explanations in more detail.

Policy Convergence

One possible explanation of policy convergence between parties, an explanation that competes with cartelisation, is the median voter theorem. Simply stated, this theory applies to parties wanting to maximise the number of votes they get. As voters are assumed to vote for parties based on the proximity of party policies to their views, parties should adopt the policies that most typical voters prefer or move towards these voters' views of policies and positions (Downs 1957). If most voters converge on the centre of the dominant issue dimensions in a polity, the theory explains decreased issue polarisation among parties. Although Katz and Mair (1995: 14) refer to the median voter theorem, they do not acknowledge that the basis of policy convergence among parties in this theory and in the cartel party theory are entirely opposite. The median voter theorem is based on fierce competition between parties for vote maximisation. In contrast, cartel party theory assumes collaboration and collusion between parties. Once again, since our studies demonstrate that conflict between Swedish parties has increased (see Chapters 3, 5, and 7 of this book), it seems plausible to conclude that competition between parties has also increased. Another sign of such competition is an increased number of 'party switchers' among Swedish – and European – voters (Oscarsson and Holmberg 2013; Hagevi 2015a), which means that a successful party can win the support of a greater part of the electorate. Policy convergence between parties can therefore be explained by competition, not collaboration, between parties (Kitschelt 2000: 164, 167).

One problem with applying the median voter theorem to Swedish politics is the multi-party system in Sweden. Downs (1957) imagines a two-party system; the existence of several parties makes it much more difficult to calculate the vote-maximisation strategies of parties. The problem is reduced somewhat if the multiple parties form two political blocs that compete with each other (Kitschelt 2007a: 533–5). Indeed, bipolar competition through bloc politics has become more common in European party systems (Bale 2003; Mair 2008), including the Swedish system (Aylott 2011; Hagevi 2015b; see Chapter 1 of this book). The idea of blocs is that they compete with each other to collect the most votes and, based on the election result, form the government. In the competition for vote-maximisation, a multi-party system with two competing blocs may work similarly to a two-party system. The development of bipolar competition intensifies conflict over the median voter and increases the conflict in the party system (see Chapter 5 of this book).[1]

Instead, electoral competition between parties, not collaboration to share power, may underlie the dynamics of change.

Individualisation

One pillar of the cartel party theory is that the role of party members has been reduced by rationalisation, because parties are controlled from the top (Katz and Mair 1995, 2009). However, individualisation theory offers a very different perspective on the decrease in the numbers of party members and the alleged decline of internal party democracy. Individualisation is a comprehensive process of social change such that more individuals are emphasising their independence in social relationships at the expense of collective communities (cf. Giddens 1991). Scholars describe Swedish society as among the most individualised in the world (Inglehart and Welzel 2005: 56–65; Schwartz 2006). For our purposes, two aspects of individualisation are of particular interest.

The first of these aspects concerns the reduction in party membership numbers. Citizens' party loyalty, together with their interest in becoming party members (or members of any kind of social movement), is reduced as the sense of collective belonging declines in the process of individualisation. With increasing economic development, welfare, education and reducing differences between social groups, the dominant identity within a certain social group (such as class and/or religion) is replaced with a multitude of competing identities, each of less importance to the individual. During this process, past interest conflicts between social groups decline and previous alignments between voters and parties break down (Dalton, Flanagan and Beck 1984; Franklin, Mackie and Valen 1992; Dalton 2010). This de-alignment based on individualisation leads to fewer citizens having strong identification with a party (Oscarsson and Holmberg 2013) and, therefore, to a smaller number of party members.

Second, individualisation can shed some light on the assumed lack of internal party democracy as well. Instead of perceiving a decline in the internal democracy of parties, individualisation theory points to increased conflict related to a general rebellion against authority on the part of citizens (Bjereld and Demker 2005). For individualistic citizens, it is far from obvious why they should obey the leaders of trade unions, churches and government or abide in party ranks according to a proclaimed hierarchy. Current party members, like other citizens, may be more critical and question authorities in ways many did not half a century ago (Inglehart 1997; cf. Moschonas 2002: 131). In this process, party leaders (along with leaders of interest organisations) may have lost a good deal of control over their members (Thomassen and van Ham 2015). In the era of individualisation, party members perceive it as their natural right to follow their own agenda and question the proposals of party leaders. This may foster criticism of traditional top-down control in parties and intensify intra-party conflicts. However, *pace* Katz and Mair, this should not be equated with reduced democracy in parties (Loxbo 2009). Instead, as seen in Chapter 3, parties may have responded to the demands of their individualised members and strengthened, not weakened, internal democracy during the period when Katz and Mair (1995) argue that cartel parties developed.

Public Funding of Parties as an Incentive for Party Fragmentation and Competition

Given the assumption that established parties form cartels against parties that challenge them (Katz and Mair 1995), a basic problem facing the cartel party theory is the growing fragmentation of party systems (Scarrow 2006: 630). Since the late 1980s the old, stable Swedish five-party system has expanded; by the end of the 2010s there were eight parties in Parliament. If the aim of cartel parties is to prevent competition from new parties, this strategy seems to have worked poorly. Indeed, one of many possible causes of party fragmentation is the public funding of parties; in contrast to the claims of cartel party theory, the public funding of parties may have increased the fragmentation of party systems.

Katz and Mair (1995: 15; see Bolin 2012: 95–97) assume that public funding of parties favours established parties at the expense of new ones. They assume that cartel parties implement public funding so they can conduct professional campaigns and other activities, while newly established parties do not receive public funding. Instead, new parties have to depend on civil society for support. According to this view, the established parties have a strong competitive advantage and are protected from challenges from parties not in the cartel. Still, empirical studies of these claims have not supported the cartel party theory (Pierre, Svåsand and Widfeldt 2000: 22; Scarrow 2006).

Citizens who are looking to start a new party can take the existence of public funding of parties as positive encouragement to put their plans into action. Party subsidies, and the remuneration of elected public officials, can act as what are called selective incentives for individuals who are willing to make the effort to form new parties (Downs 1957; Olson 1971). Like an entrepreneur operating in a free market, the so-called party contractor (Nownes and Neeley 1996; Erlingsson 2005: 100–4) meets demand in the voter market by launching a new party. However, the cost of forming a political party could be a disincentive to doing so. Erlingsson (2005: 100) argues that the party contractor may be motivated to assume this cost by the selective incentive of a hope of private gain. If Erlingsson's assumption is correct, then we would like to add both the existence and ever-increasing range of party support and politicians' remuneration as possible incentives for establishing new parties. The greater the gain a party entrepreneur can hope for in forming a new party, the more likely it is that this will happen.

Contrary to the prediction of the cartel party theory, then, public party subsidies can encourage, stimulate and incentivise, rather than impede, the launching of new parties (Kitschelt 2000: 171; Pierre, Svåsand and Widfeldt 2000: 22). Kevin Casas-Zamora (2005: 42–3) argues that, compared with established parties, it is more difficult for new parties to mobilise citizens as party members and to finance party activities. For instance, increasing individualisation in society (see above) makes it more difficult to involve people in political parties than it was when the established parties were created. Susan Scarrow (2006: 629) argues that public funding of parties provides new challengers with a degree of economic stability that they otherwise would be unable to count on. Other scholars have noted that public funding tends to form a larger share of the total income of small parties than of large parties (Sundberg 2002; Casas-Zamora 2005: 42). As new parties tend to be relatively small at the beginning, there is a good chance that they will benefit from public subsidies and that these resources will indeed be important when they are challenging established parties.

In Sweden, parties outside Parliament also receive public funding. If a party wins at least 1 per cent of the votes in a general election (the same applies to local and regional elections), at the next election the state pays for the printing and distribution of a number of ballot papers equal to three times the obtained votes in the previous election (Valmyndigheten 2015). If a party has won at least 2.5 per cent of the votes in one of the last two general elections, the party is entitled to obtain public funding at the national level (Swedish Parliament 2015). Local and regional politics may also be beneficial to the financial status of new parties. Before entering Parliament, new parties commonly achieve greater electoral success at the local and regional levels (Bolin 2012: 95). At the local level, total Swedish public subsidies to parties are about the same amount as at the national level, while regional-level subsidies are about half that amount. Adding to this, politicians at the local and regional levels are remunerated by the authorities they govern, and the level of this remuneration has risen sharply in recent decades (Hagevi 2014b: 36–9). Compared with the hypothetical case of the absence of party subsidies, local and regional politics can give new parties a relatively stable financial foundation before they are able to obtain representation at the national level (Kitschelt 2007b: 1190–1).

Public funding of parties can thus directly affect the level of competition in the party system. The structure of public subsidies can give parties incentives not to collaborate but rather to compete for voters. To the extent that the public funding of parties is allocated based not on power holdings or co-operation but on voter support (as in Sweden), this, along with the desire to gain power, will encourage parties to maximise their share of votes in competition with other parties (Kitschelt 2000: 168). Public subsidies could well constitute incentives to increase conflict, rather than co-operation, between parties.

POLICY POLARISATION AND CONFLICT

This work has identified some ideological convergence between parties over time (see Chapter 3 of this book) as well as increased conflict between parties (see Chapters 3, 5, 7 and 9 of this book). Scholars of party systems often regard policy polarisation and inter-party conflict as the same thing (e.g. Katz and Mair 1995: 19, 2009: 757; Layman et al. 2010; see also Katz and Mair 1996: 530). In essence, Katz and Mair (1995, 2009) argue that party systems have gone from policy polarisation and conflict to policy convergence and consensus.

However, there is reason to emphasise the differences between the degree of policy polarisation and the degree of conflict (Kitschelt 2007a: 533–4; Azmanova 2011: 387–8). Policy polarisation is related to the distance between two positions on an issue. A high degree of policy polarisation means that two parties have very different views, while a low degree of polarisation means that their positions are more similar (DiMaggio, Evans and Bryson 1996; Kitschelt 2007a: 533–4, 2007b: 1185). Conflict does not concern the extent to which the parties' positions are different from or similar to each other but whether the parties are collaborating or competing with each other (Azmanova 2011: 388). This distinction has been more or less implicitly made by several political scientists. Anthony Downs (1957; see also Laver 2005) argues that parties' competition for voters could lead to their positions becoming more alike. Arend Lijphart (1977, 1984, 1999, 2008) points out that parties separated by great ideological distance in highly segmented societies can work together to make decisions by consensus. If we compare several political systems, there might very well be a correlation between policy polarisation and conflict. A high degree of policy polarisation between parties can certainly give rise to strong conflict between them. Nevertheless, it could also be that reduced policy polarisation – convergence – does not reduce the degree of conflict between parties; instead, as in the Swedish case, the level of inter-party conflict could increase.

If we distinguish between the level of inter-party policy polarisation and the degree of inter-party conflict, we also create openings for other theoretical explanations of party system change besides the cartel party theory, some of which have been mentioned in this chapter. This means that even though parties may very well change their positions on issues and converge ideologically, they need not be co-operating, collaborating or colluding. At the same time, the level of conflict between parties may remain constant or even increase. As noted in Chapter 2, to use the cartel concept to cover convergence of this kind even in the absence of actual co-operation is to strain its acceptable usage, inviting theoretical ambiguity. In general, much would be gained empirically as well as theoretically by distinguishing more clearly and consistently between the concepts of ideological convergence, depoliticisation and collaboration, notions that tend to be conflated in the cartel party theory. In sum, we can certainly conclude that the cartel party theory has a hard time explaining key developments in the Swedish party system in recent decades, in spite of Sweden being presented by the authors of the theory as a case particularly amenable to cartelisation. As we have suggested in this chapter, however, there are other theories that may well fare better. Scholars of political parties may have more to gain from exploring new models and theories, or from re-examining current party politics using established models and typologies, such as catch-all parties (Kirchheimer 1966) and electoral professional parties (Panebianco 1988), together with basic theories of vote maximisation (Downs 1957).

NOTE

1. Mair (2007: 14) opposes the idea that bloc politics entails increased conflict between parties and is the opposite of cartelisation. According to Mair, the EU restricts the opportunities for parties to make decisions in national politics. Instead, party politics is concerned only with who will be elected. The increased importance of bloc politics, according to Mair, leads to a contest between two teams of political leaders with similar policies, resulting in opposition within the cartel. In Chapter 5 of this book, this assumption is dealt with in detail.

References

Aalberg, T. and J. Strömbäck. 2011. 'Media-driven men and media-critical women? An empirical study of gender and MPs' relationships with the media in Norway and Sweden'. *International Political Science Review* 32 (2): 167–87.

Abélès, M. 2000. *Un ethnologue à l'assemblée*. Paris: Odile Jacob.

Anderson, C. J. and P. Beramendi. 2012. 'Left parties, poor voters, and electoral participation in advanced industrial societies'. *Comparative Political Studies* 45 (6): 714–46.

Ansell, B. W. 2010. *From the Ballot to the Blackboard: The Redistributive Political Economy of Education*. Cambridge, UK: Cambridge University Press.

Arendt, H. 1958. *The Human Condition*. Chicago, IL: University of Chicago Press.

—— 1968. *The Origins of Totalitarianism*. New York, NY: Harcourt.

Arter, D. 2006. *Democracy in Scandinavia: Consensual, Majoritarian or Mixed?* Manchester, UK: Manchester University Press.

Asp, K. 1986. *Mäktiga massmedier: studier i politii opinionsbildning*. Stockholm, SW: Akademilitteratur.

Auel, K. and T. Christiansen. 2015. 'After Lisbon: national parliaments in the European Union'. *West European Politics* 38 (2): 261–81.

Aylott, N. 2011. 'Parties and party systems in the North'. In *The Madisonian Turn: Political Parties and Parliamentary Democracy in Nordic Europe*, edited by T. Bergman and K. Strøm, 297–328. Ann Arbor, MI: University of Michigan Press.

Azmanova, A. 2011. 'After the left–right (dis)continuum: Globalization and the remaking of Europe's ideological geography'. *International Political Sociology* 5 (4): 384–407.

Bachrach, P. 1962. 'Elite consensus and democracy'. *Journal of Politics* 24 (3): 439–52.

Bachrach, P. and M. Baratz. 1975. 'Power and its two faces revisited: a reply to Geoffrey Debnam'. *American Political Science Review* 69 (3): 900–4.

Bäck, H. and J. Hellström. 2015. 'Efter valet 2014: regeringsbildningen och det inställda extravalet'. *Statsvetenskaplig tidskrift* 117 (2): 261–78.

Bågenholm, A. and M. Demker. 2007. *Styrelseskick i elva länder + EU*. Lund SW: Liber.

Bale, T. 2003. 'Cinderella and her ugly sisters: the mainstream and extreme right in Europe's bipolarising party system'. *West European Politics* 26 (3): 67–90.

Ball, T. 1989. 'Party'. In *Political Innovation and Conceptual Change*, edited by T. Ball, J. Farr and R. L. Hanson, 155–76. Cambridge, UK: Cambridge University Press.

Barrling Hermansson, K. 2004. *Partikulturer*. Uppsala, SW: Uppsala Universitet.

Barrling, K. 2013. 'Exploring the inner life of the party: a framework for analysing elite party culture'. *Scandinavian Political Studies* 36 (2): 177–99.

―――― 2014. 'Från maskrosäng till tuktad rabatt? En studie av partikulturell förändring i det svenska Miljöpartiet'. *Statsvetenskaplig tidskrift* 116 (1): 95–122.

Bartolini, S. 2005. *Restructuring Europe. Centre Formation, System Building, and Political Structuring Between the Nation State and the European Union*. Oxford, UK: Oxford University Press.

Bengtsson, Å., K. M. Hansen, Ó. Þ. Harðarson, H. M. Narud and H. Oscarsson. 2014. *The Nordic Voter: Myths of Exceptionalism*. Colchester, UK: ECPR Press.

Bennett, W. L. and S. Iyengar. 2008. 'A new era of minimal effects: the changing foundations of political communication'. *Journal of Communication* 58 (4): 707–31.

Beramendi, P., S. Häusermann, H. Kitschelt and H. Kriesi, eds. 2015. *The Politics of Advanced Capitalism*. Cambridge, UK: Cambridge University Press.

Bergman, T. 1997. 'National parliaments and the EU Affairs Committees: notes on empirical variation and competing explanations'. *Journal of European Public Policy* 4 (3): 373–87.

Berry, J. 2002. 'Validity and reliability issues in elite interviewing'. *Political Science and Politics* 25 (4): 679–82.

Best, H. and H. Cotta, eds. 2000a. *Parliamentary Representatives in Europe 1848–2000: Legislative Recruitment and Careers in Eleven European Countries*. Oxford, UK: Oxford University Press.

―――― 2000b. 'Elite transformation and modes of representation since the mid-nineteenth century: theoretical considerations'. In *Parliamentary Representatives in Europe 1848–2000: Legislative Recruitment and Careers in Eleven European Countries*, edited by H. Best and M. Cotta, 1–28. Oxford, UK: Oxford University Press.

Beyme, K. von. 1996. 'The concept of political class: A new dimension of research on elites?' *West European Politics* 19 (1): 68–87.

Biezen, I. van, P. Mair and T. Pogunkte. 2012. 'Going, going … gone? The decline of party membership in contemporary Europe'. *European Journal of Political Research* 51 (1): 24–56.

Biezen, I. van and T. Pogunkte. 2014. 'The decline of membership-based politics'. *Party Politics* 20 (2): 205–16.

Bjarnegård E. 2013. *Gender, Informal Institutions and Political Recruitment: Explaining Male Dominance in Parliamentary Representation*. New York: Palgrave Macmillan.

Bjereld, U. and M. Demker. 1995. *Utrikespolitiken som slagfält: De svenska partierna och utrikesfrågorna*. Stockholm, SE: Nerenius och Santérus.

—— 2000. 'Foreign policy as battlefield: A study of national interest and party motives'. *Scandinavian Political Studies* 23 (1): 17–36.

—— 2005. *I Vattumannens tid? En bok om 1968 års auktoritetsuppror och dess betydelse i dag.* Stockholm, SE: Hjalmarson & Högberg.

Bjerling, J. 2013. *The Personalization of Swedish Politics: Party Leaders in the Election Coverage 1979–2010.* Göteborg, SE: Department of Journalism, Media and Communication, University of Gothenburg.

Blyth, M. and R. S. Katz. 2005. 'From catch-all politics to cartelisation: the political economy of the cartel party'. *West European Politics* 28 (1): 33–60.

Bolin, N. 2012. *Målsättning riksdagen: Ett aktörsperspektiv på nya partiers intrude i det nationella parlamentet.* Umeå, SE: Statsvetenskapliga institutionen, Umeå universitet.

—— 2015. 'Partikongresser och interndemokrat'. In *Partier och partisystem*, edited by M. Hagevi, 105–19. Lund, SE: Studentlitteratur.

Bonander, F. 2009. *Party Membership and State Subsidies: A Comparative Study.* Örebro, SE: Örebro University.

Borchert, J. 2003. 'Professional politicians: Towards a comparative perspective'. In *The Political Class in Advanced Democracies*, edited by J. Borchert and J. Ziess, 1–25. Oxford, UK: Oxford University Press.

Borchert, J. and J. Ziess, eds. 2003. *The Political Class in Advanced Democracies.* Oxford: Oxford University Press.

Bornschier, S. 2010. 'The new cultural divide and the two-dimensional space in Western Europe'. *West European Politics* 33 (3): 419–44.

Bratton, K. and L. Ray. 2002. 'Descriptive representation, policy outcomes, and municipal day-care coverage in Norway'. *American Journal of Political Science* 46 (2): 428–37.

Brommesson, D. and A.-M. Ekengren. 2013. 'What happens when a new government enters office? A comparison of ideological change in British and Swedish foreign policy 1991–2011'. *Cooperation and Conflict.* 48 (1): 3–27.

Budge, I. 2013. 'The standard right–left scale'. Unpublished paper, Essex, UK: University of Essex, available online at: https://manifestoproject.wzb.eu/down/papers/budge_right-left-scale.pdf (accessed 30 November 2015).

Budge, I., H.-D. Klingemann, A. Volkens, J. Bara E. and Tanenbaum. 2010. *Mapping Policy Preferences. Estimates for Parties, Electors, and Governments 1945–1998.* Oxford, UK: Oxford University Press.

Burke, E. 1931 [1827]. 'Speech to the Electors of Bristol'. In *Edmund Burke, Speeches and Letters on American Affairs*, intro. by H. Law, 68–75. London, UK: Everyman.

Burke, K. 1941. 'Four master tropes'. *Kenyon Review* 3 (4): 421–38.

Byeme, K. von 1996. 'The concept of political class: a new dimension of research on elites?' *West European Politics* 19 (1): 68–97.

Campus, D. 2010. 'Mediatization and personalization of politics in Italy and France: the cases of Berlusconi and Sarkozy'. *International Journal of Press/Politics* 15 (2): 219–35.

Carroll, L. 2001. *Alice's Adventures in Wonderland* and *Through the Looking-Glass and What Alice Found There.* London, UK: Bloomsbury.

Casas-Zamora, K. 2005. *Paying for Democracy: Political Finance and State Funding for Parties*. Colchester, UK: ECPR Press.

Castles, F. G. and R. Wildenmann, eds. *Visions and Realities of Party Government*. Berlin, DE: Walter de Gruyter.

Celis, K. 2006. 'Substantive representation of women: the representation of women's interests and the impact of descriptive representation in the Belgian parliament (1900–1979)'. *Journal of Women, Politics & Policy* 28 (2): 85–114.

Celis, K., S. Childs, J. Kantola and M. L. Krook. 2008. 'Rethinking women's substantial representation'. *Representation* 44 (2): 99–110.

Chabal, P. and J.-P. Daloz. 2006. *Culture Troubles: Politics and the Interpretation of Meaning*. Chicago, IL: University of Chicago Press.

Childs, S. and M. L. Krook. 2009. 'Analysing women's substantive representation: from critical mass to critical actors'. *Government and Opposition* 44 (2): 125–45.

Coker, F. W. 1921. 'The technique of the pluralist state'. *American Political Science Review* 15 (2): 186–213.

Connolly, W. E. 2005. *Pluralism*. Durham, NC: Duke University Press.

Cotta, M. and H. Best. 2000. 'Between professionalization and democratization: A synoptic view on the making of the European representative'. In *Parliamentary Representatives in Europe 1848–2000: Legislative Recruitment and Careers in Eleven European Countries*, edited by H. Best and M. Cotta, 493–526. Oxford, UK: Oxford University Press.

Dahl, R. A. 1956. *A Preface to Democratic Theory*. Chicago, IL: University of Chicago Press.

———— 1966a. 'Preface'. In *Political Oppositions in Western Democracies*, edited by R. A. Dahl, xiii–xxi. New Haven, CT: Yale University Press.

———— 1966b. 'Epilogue'. In *Political Oppositions in Western Democracies*, edited by R. A. Dahl, 387–401. New Haven, CT: Yale University Press.

———— 1971. *Polyarchy. Participation and Opposition*. New Haven, CT: Yale University Press.

———— 1982. *Dilemmas of Pluralist Democracy. Autonomy vs. Control*. New Haven, CT: Yale University Press.

———— 1989. *Democracy and Its Critics*. New Haven, CT: Yale University Press.

Dahlerup, D. and L. Freidenvall. 2006. 'Quotas as a "fast track" to equal representation for women'. *International Feminist Journal of Politics* 7 (1): 26–48.

Dalton, R. J. 2010. 'Ideology, partisanship, and democratic development'. In *Comparing Democracies 3: Elections and Voting in the 21th Century*, edited by L. LeDuc, R. G. Niemi and P. Norris, 143–64. London, UK: Sage.

Dalton, R. J., D. M. Farrell and I. McAllister. 2011. *Political Parties & Democratic Linkage. How Parties Organize Democracy*. Oxford, UK: Oxford University Press.

Dalton, R. J., S. C. Flanagan P. A. and Beck, eds. 1984. *Electoral Change in Advanced Industrial Democracies: Realignment or Dealignment?* Princeton, NJ: Princeton University Press.

De Sio, L. and T. Weber 2014. 'Issue yield: A model of party strategy in multidimensional space'. *American Political Science Review* 108 (4): 870–85.

Derrida, J. 1982. *Margins of Philosophy*. Chicago, IL: University of Chicago Press.

Detterbeck, K. 2005. 'Cartel parties in Western Europe?' *Party Politics* 11 (2): 173–91.

Diamond I. and N. Hartsock. 1981. 'Beyond interest in politics'. *American Political Science Review* 75 (3): 717–21.

DiMaggio, P., J. Evans and B. Bryson. 1996. 'Have Americans' social attitudes become more polarized?' *American Journal of Sociology* 102 (3): 690–755.

Dinas, E. and K. Gemenis. 2010. 'Measuring parties' ideological positions with manifesto data: A critical evaluation of the competing methods'. *Party Politics* 16 (4): 427–50.

Donges, P., N. Håkansson and G. Lengauer. 2013. 'Media logics and changes in news reporting'. In *Political Communication Cultures in Western Europe. Attitudes of Political Actors and Journalists in Nine Countries*, edited by B. Pfetsch, 196–218. New York: Palgrave Macmillan.

Douglas, M. 1982. *In the Active Voice*. London, UK: Routledge & Kegan Paul.

———— 1996. *Thought Styles: Critical Essays on Good Taste*. London, UK: Sage Publications.

Downs, A. 1957. *An Economic Theory of Democracy*. New York: Harper & Row.

Dumont, P. and H. Bäck. 2006. 'Why so few, and why so late? Green parties and the question of governmental participation'. *European Journal of Political Research* 45 (s1): 35–67.

Duverger, M. 1954. *Political Parties: Their organization and Activity in the Modern State*. London, UK: Methuen.

Ekholm, K. 2000 'Internationell handel och utlandsinvesteringar'. In *Marknad och politik*, edited by B. Södersten, 338–69. Stockholm, SE: SNS Förlag.

Elder, N., A. H. Thomas and D. Arter. 1988. *The Consensual Democracies? The Government and Politics of the Scandinavian States*. Oxford, UK: Basil Blackwell.

Eliassen, K. and M. Pedersen. 1978. 'Professionalization of legislatures: Long-term change in political recruitment in Denmark and Norway'. *Comparative Studies in Society & History* 20 (2): 286–318.

Ellis, E. D. 1920. 'The pluralistic state'. *American Political Science Review* 14 (3): 393–407.

Elmelund-Praestekaer, C., D. N. Hopman and A. S. Nörgaard. 2011. 'Does mediatization change MP–media interaction and MP attitudes toward the media? Evidence from a longitudinal study of Danish MPs'. *International Journal of Press/Politics* 16 (3): 382–403.

Enroth, H. 2010a. 'Robert Dahl'. In *The Sage Encyclopedia of Political Theory*, edited by M. Bevir, 349–50. London: Sage.

———— 2010b. 'Beyond unity in plurality: rethinking the pluralist legacy'. *Contemporary Political Theory* 9 (4): 458–76.

———— 2014. 'Representation och kartellisering'. *Statsvetenskaplig tidskrift* 116 (1): 149–58.

———— 2017. 'Cartelization versus representation? On a misconception in contemporary party theory'. *Party Politics* 23 (2): 124–34.

Erikson, R. S. 2015. 'Income inequality and policy responsiveness'. *Annual Review of Political Science* 18: 11–29.

Erlingsson, G. Ó. 2005. *Varför bildas nya partier? Om kollektivt handlande och partientreprenörer.* Lund, SE: Statsvetenskapliga institutionen, Lunds universitet.

Erlingsson, G. Ó., M. Hagevi and K. Loxbo. 2015. *Inget tyder på försämrad interndemokrati,* available online at: https://politologerna.wordpress.com/2015/02/13/inget-tyder-pa-forsamrad-interndemokrati/ (accessed 20 February 2015).

Erlingsson, G. Ó. and M. Persson. 2014. 'Ingen partikris trots allt?' In *Mittfåra och marginal,* edited by H. Oscarsson and A. Bergström, 407–20. Göteborg: SOM Institute, University of Gothenburg.

Esaiasson, P., M. Gilljam, H. Oscarsson and L. Wängnerud. 2007. *Metodpraktikan.* Stockholm, SE: Norstedts Juridik.

Esaiasson, P. and K. Heidar, eds. 2000. *Beyond Westminster and Congress: The Nordic Experience.* Columbus, OH: Ohio State University Press.

Esaiasson, P. and S. Holmberg. 1996. *Representation From Above: Members of Parliament and Representative Democracy in Sweden.* Aldershot, UK: Dartmouth.

Fakta om folkvalda: Riksdagen 1985–1988. 1986. Stockholm, SE: Riksdagens förvaltningskontor.

Fakta om folkvalda: Riksdagen 1988–1991. 1989. Stockholm, SE: Riksdagens förvaltningskontor.

Fakta om folkvalda: Riksdagen 1991–1994. 1992. Stockholm, SE: Riksdagens förvaltningskontor.

Fakta om folkvalda: Riksdagen 1994–1998. 1995. Stockholm, SE: Riksdagens förvaltningskontor.

Fakta om folkvalda: Riksdagen 1998–2002. 1999. Stockholm, SE: Riksdagens förvaltningskontor.

Fakta om folkvalda: Riksdagen 2002–2006. 2003. Stockholm, SE: Riksdagens förvaltningskontor.

Fakta om folkvalda: Riksdagen 2006–2010. 2007. Stockholm, SE: Riksdagens förvaltningskontor.

Fakta om folkvalda: Riksdagen 2010–2014. 2011. Stockholm, SE: Riksdagens förvaltningskontor.

Farr, J. 1989. 'Understanding conceptual change politically'. In *Political Innovation and Conceptual Change,* edited by T. Ball, J. Farr and R. L. Hanson, 24–49. Cambridge, UK: Cambridge University Press.

Finseraas, H. and K. Vernby. 2011. 'What parties are and what parties do: partisanship and welfare state reform in an era of austerity'. *Socio-Economic Review* 9 (4): 613–38.

Flanagan, S. C. and A.-R. Lee. 2003. 'The new politics, culture wars, and the authoritarian-libertarian value change in advanced industrial democracies'. *Comparative Political Studies* 36 (3): 235–71.

Foucault, M. 1984. 'What Is Enlightenment?' In *The Foucault Reader,* edited by P. Rabinow, 32–50. New York: Pantheon.

Franklin, M., T. Mackie and H. Valen, eds. 1992. *Electoral Change: Responses to Evolving Social and Attitudinal Structures in Western Countries.* Cambridge, UK: Cambridge University Press.

Freidenvall, L. 2006. 'Vägen till varannan damernas: om kvinnorepresentation, kvotering och kandidaturval i svensk politik 1970–2002'. Stockholm: Statsvetenskapliga institutionen, Stockholms universitet.

Frey, C. B. and M. A. Osborne. 2013. *The Future of Employment: How Susceptible are Jobs to Computerisation?* Oxford: Oxford University Engineering Sciences Department and the Oxford Martin School, Programme on the Impacts of Future Technology.

Gallager, M., M. Laver and P. Mair. 2011. *Representative Government in Modern Europe: Institutions, Parties, and Governments.* London, UK: McGraw-Hill.

Garcia, I. and E. Sandin. 2015. 'KD-strid om ny gruppledare'. *Sveriges radio,* available online at: http://sverigesradio.se/sida/artikel.aspx?programid=83&artikel=6192421 (accessed 14 November 2015).

Garsten, C., B. Rothstein and S. Svallfors. 2015. *Makt utan mandat: De policyprofessionella i svensk politik.* Stockholm, SE: Dialogos förlag.

Geertz, C. 1975. *The Interpretation of Cultures.* New York: Basic Books.

Giddens, A. 1984. *The Constitution of Society: Outline of the Theory of Structuration.* Cambridge, UK: Polity Press.

——— 1991. *Modernity and Self-Identity.* Stanford, CA: Stanford University Press.

Gidlund, G. 1983. *Partistöd.* Lund, SE: Liber/CWK Gleerup.

——— 1985. *Det kommunala partistödet: En studie av kommunernas och landstingens stöd till de politiska partierna.* Ds C 1985: 8. Stockholm: Liber/Allmänna förlaget.

Gidlund, G. and R. Koole. 2001. 'Political finance in the north of Europe: the Netherlands and Sweden'. In *Foundations for Democracy: Approaches to comparative political finance. Essays in honour of Herbert E. Alexander,* edited by K.-H. Nassmacher, 112–30. Baden-Baden, DE: Nomos Verlagsgesellschaft.

Giger, N. and M. Nelson. 2010. 'The electoral consequences of welfare state retrenchment: Blame avoidance or credit claiming in the era of permanent austerity?' *European Journal of Political Research* 50 (1): 1–23.

Gilljam, M. and T. Möller. 1996. 'Från medlemspartier till väljarpartier'. In *På medborgarnas villkor: En demokratisk infrastruktur,* 129–87. SOU 1996: 162. Stockholm, SE: Fritzes.

Gourevitch, P. 1986. *Politics in Hard Times: Comparative Responses to International Economic Crisis.* Ithaca, NY: Cornell University Press.

Green-Pedersen, C. 2012. 'A giant fast asleep? Party incentives and the politicisation of European integration'. *Political Studies* 60 (1): 115–30.

Griffin, J. D., B. Newman and C. Wolbrechta. 2012. 'Gender gap in policy representation in the US Congress'. *Legislative Studies Quarterly* 37 (1): 35–66.

Grimm, J. and W. Grimm. 1860. *Deutsches Wörterbuch, Bd 2.* Leipzig, DE: Verlag von S. Hirzel.

Guest, G., A. Bunce and L. Johnson. 2006. 'How many interviews are enough? An experiment with data saturation and variability'. *Field Methods* 18: 59–81.

Hacking, I. 1999. *The Social Construction of What?* Cambridge, MA: Harvard University Press.

Hadenius, S. 2008. *Sveriges politiska historia från 1865 till våra dagar: Konflikt och samförstånd.* Stockholm, SE: Hjalmarson & Högberg.

Hagevi, M. 1998. *Bakom riksdagens fasad.* Göteborg, SE: Akademiförlaget Corona.

────── 1999. *Professionalisering och deltagande i den lokala representativa demokratin: En analys av kommunala förtroendeuppdrag 1999.* Göteborg, SE: Cefos, University of Gothenburg.

────── 2000a. 'Parliamentary party groups in the Swedish Riksdag'. In *Parliamentary Party Groups in European Democracies: Political Parties Behind Closed Doors*, edited by K. Heidar and R. Koole, 145–60. London, UK: Routledge.

────── 2000b. 'Nordic light on committee assignments'. In *Beyond Westminster and Congress: The Nordic experience*, edited by P. Esaiasson and K. Heidar, 237–61. Columbus, OH: Ohio State University Press.

────── 2003. 'Sweden: between participation ideal and professionalism'. In *The Political Class in Advanced Democracies: A Comparative Handbook*, edited by J. Borchert and J. Zeiss, 352–73. Oxford, UK: Oxford University Press.

────── 2010. 'Vilka har någon gång varit offentligt förtroendevalda?' Paper presented to the conference *Statsvetenskapliga förbundets årsmöte* in Göteborg, Sweden, September–October.

────── 2012. 'Beyond church and state: private religiosity and post-materialist political opinion among individuals in Sweden'. *Journal of Church and State* 54 (4): 499–525.

────── 2014a. 'Förändrade villkor för riksdagens partigrupper'. *Statsvetenskaplig tidskrift* 116 (1): 5–20.

────── 2014b. 'Fyra decenniers partistöd'. *Statsvetenskaplig tidskrift* 116 (1): 21–44.

────── 2014c. 'Kartellisering i nytt ljus: Slutsatser'. *Statsvetenskaplig tidskrift* 116 (1): 159–69.

────── 2015a. *Den svenska väljaren 2014.* Malmö, SE: Gleerups.

────── 2015b. 'Bloc identification in the in multi-party systems: The case of the Swedish two-bloc system'. *West European Politics* 38 (1): 73–92.

────── 2015c. 'Survey 2014: teknisk rapport'. *Surveyjournalen* 2 (1–2): 59–67.

Hagevi, M. and K. Loxbo. 2015. 'Partierna och demokratin efter medlemsnedgången'. In *Demokratiutredningens betänkande*. SOU 2015: 100. 13–64. Stockholm, SE: Fritzes.

Hall, P. A. 2014. 'Varieties of capitalism and the euro crisis'. *West European Politics* 37 (6): 1223–43.

Hallin, D. and P. Mancini. 2004. *Comparing Media Systems: Three Models of Media and Politics.* Cambridge, UK: Cambridge University Press.

Harmel, R. and K. Janda. 1994. 'An integrated theory of party goals and party change'. *Journal of Theoretical Politics* 6 (3): 259–87.

Häusermann. S. and H. Kriesi. 2015. 'What do voters want? Dimensions and configurations in individual-level preferences and party choice'. In *The Politics of Advanced Capitalism*, edited by P. Beramendi, S. Häusermann, H. Kitschelt and H. Kriesi, 202–230. Cambridge, UK: Cambridge University Press.

Heidar, K. and R. Koole. 2000. 'Parliamentary party groups compared'. In *Parliamentary Party Groups in European Democracies: Political Parties Behind Closed Doors*, edited by K. Heidar and R. Koole, 248–70. London: Routledge.

Hellwig, T. 2014. *Globalization and Mass Politics: Retaining the Room to Manoeuver*. Cambridge, UK: Cambridge University Press.

Helms, L. 2008. 'Parliamentary opposition and its alternatives in a transnational regime: The European Union in perspective'. *Journal of Legislative Studies* 14 (1–2): 213–35.

Hensvik, L., O. Nordström Skans and O. Åslund. 2010. 'Sådan chef, sådan anställd? Rekryteringsmönster invandrare och infödda chefer'. *Ekonomisk debatt* 38 (3): 39–52.

Hermansson, J. 1993. *Politik som intressekamp: Parlamentariskt beslutsfattande och organiserade intressen i Sverige*. Stockholm: Norstedts juridik.

Hix, S. 1999. 'Dimensions and alignments in European Union politics: cognitive constraints and partisan responses'. *European Journal of Political Research* 35 (2): 69–125.

Hjarvard, S. 2007. 'Sprogets medialisering'. In *Språk i Norden 2007*, edited by C. af Hällström-Reijonen, 29–45. Oslo, NO: Nordens språkråd.

——— 2008. 'The mediatization of society: a theory of the media as agents of social and cultural change'. *Nordicom Review* 29 (2): 105–34.

Holgersson C. 2003. *Rekrytering av företagsledare: En studie i homosocialitet*. Stockholm: Handelshögskolan.

Hollis, M. 1988. 'Say It With Flowers'. In *Meaning and Context: Quentin Skinner and his critics*, edited by J. Tully, 135–46. Princeton, NJ: Princeton University Press.

——— 1994. *The Philosophy of Science: An Introduction*. Cambridge, UK: Cambridge University Press.

Holmberg, S. 1974. *'Riksdagen representerar svenska folket': Empiriska studier i representativ demokrati*. Lund, SE: Studentlitteratur.

——— 1989. 'Political representation in Sweden'. *Scandinavian Political Studies* 12 (1): 1–36.

——— 1997. 'Dynamic opinion representation'. *Scandinavian Political Studies* 20 (3): 265–83.

——— 1999. 'Down and down we go: political trust in Sweden'. In *Critical Citizens*, edited by P. Norris, 103–22. Oxford, UK: Oxford University Press.

——— 2000. 'Issue agreement'. In *Beyond Westminster and Congress: The Nordic experience*, edited by P. Esaiasson and K. Heidar, 155–79. Columbus, OH: Ohio State University Press.

——— 2004. 'Polarizing political parties'. *Tidskrift for samfunnsforskning* 45 (2): 355–73.

——— 2011. 'Dynamisk representation'. In *Folket representanter: Om riksdagsledamöter och politisk representation i Sverige*, edited by M. Brothén and S. Holmber, 65–102. Göteborg, SE: Statsvetenskapliga institutionen, Göteborgs universitet.

——— 2014a. 'Representerar riksdagen svenska folket?' In *Svenska politiker: Om de folkvalda i riksdag, landsting och kommun*, edited by D. Karlsson and M. Gilljam, 93–116. Stockholm, SE : Santérus.

——— 2014b. 'Feeling policy represented'. In *Elections and Democracy. Representation and Accountability*, edited by J. Thomassen, 132–52. Oxford, UK: Oxford University Press.

Holmberg, S. and P. Esaiasson. 1988. *De folkvalda: En bok om riksdagsledamöterna och den representativ demokratin i Sverige*. Stockholm: Bonniers.

Hooghe, L. and G. Marks. 2009. 'A postfunctionalist theory of European integration. From permissive consensus to constraining dissensus'. *British Journal of Political Science* 39 (1): 1–23.

Hopkin, J. 2004. 'The problem with party finance: Theoretical perspectives on the funding of political parties'. *Party Politics* 10 (6): 627–51.

Houston, B. 2010. 'The future of investigative journalism'. *Daedalus* 139 (2): 45–56.

Huber, E., J. Huo and J. Stephens. 2016. 'Politics, markets, and top income shares'. Paper delivered at the Council of Europeanists Conference, Philadelphia, PA, April 14–16.

Huber, E. and J. Stephens. 2014. 'Income inequality and redistribution in postindustrial democracies: Demographic, economic, and political determinants'. *Socio-Economic Review* 12 (2): 245–67.

Huber, J. D. and G. B. Powell. 1994. 'Congruence between citizens and policymakers in two visions of liberal democracy'. *World Politics* 46 (3): 291–326.

Hurrelmann, A., A. Gora and A. Wagner. 2013. 'The politicization of European integration: More than an elite affair?' *Political Studies* 63 (1): 43–59.

Hutter, S. and E. Grande. 2014. 'Politicizing Europe in the national electoral arena: a comparative analysis of five West European countries, 1970–2010'. *Journal of Common Market Studies* 52 (5): 1002–18.

Inglehart, R. 1997. *Modernization and Postmodernization: Cultural, Economic, and Political Change in 43 Societies*. Princeton, NJ: Princeton University Press.

Inglehart, R. and H.-D. Klingemann. 1976. 'Party identification, ideological preference and the left–right dimension among Western mass publics'. In *Party Identification and Beyond*, edited by I. Budge, I. Crewe and D. Farlie, 243–73. London, UK: John Wiley.

Inglehart, R. and D. Sidjanski. 1976. 'The left, the right, the establishment and the Swiss electorate'. In *Party Identification and Beyond*, edited by I. Budge, I. Crewe and D. Farlie, 225–42. London, UK: John Wiley.

Inglehart, R. and C. Welzel. 2005. *Modernization, Cultural Change, and Democracy: The Human Development Sequence*. Cambridge, UK: Cambridge University Press.

Isaksson, A. 2006. *Den politiska adeln*. Stockholm, SE: Bonnier Fakta.

Isberg, M. 1999. *Riksdagsledamoten i sin partigrupp: 52 riksdagsveteraners erfarenheter av partigruppernas arbetssätt och inflytande*. Nora, SE: Gidlunds Förlag.

Ivarsson Westerberg, A. and T. Nilsson. 2009. 'De dolda makthavarna – politiska tjänstemän i stad och stat'. *Statsvetenskaplig tidskrift* 111 (4): 323–46.

Iversen, T., D. Soskice and D. Hope. 2016. 'The Eurozone and political economic institutions'. *Annual Review of Political Science* 18: 163–85, available online at: http://www.annualreviews.org/doi/pdf/10.1146/annurev-polisci-022615-113243.

Iyengar, S. and K. S. Hahn. 2009. 'Red media, blue media: Evidence of ideological selectivity in media use'. *Journal of Communication* 59 (1): 19–39.

Janda, K. 1983. 'Cross-national measures of party organizations and organizational theory'. *European Journal of Political Research* 11 (3): 319–32.

Järnbert, M. and J. Olofsson. 2012. *Förtroendevalda i kommuner och landsting 2011*. Stockholm, SE: Statistiska Centralbyrån.

Jensen, T. 1993. *Politik i praxis*. København, DK: Samfundslitteratur.

Jerneck, M., A. Sannerstedt and M. Sjölin. 1988. 'Internationalization and parliamentary decision-making: the case of Sweden 1970–1985'. *Scandinavian Political Studies* 11 (3): 169–94.

Johansson, J. 1999. *Hur blir man riksdagsledamot? En studie av makt och inflytande i partiernas nomineringsprocesser*. Södertälje, SE: Gidlunds Förlag.

Jun, U. 2003. 'Great Britain: from "guilds of notables" to political class'. In *The Political Class in Advanced Democracies*, edited by J. Borchert and J. Ziess, 164–86. Oxford, UK: Oxford University Press.

Kant, I. 1988. 'What Is Enlightenment?' In *Kant: Selections*, edited by L. W. Beck, 462–67. New York: Macmillan.

Karlsson, D. and L. Nordin. 2015. *Riksdagsundersökningen 2014*. Göteborg, SE: Göteborgs universitet.

Karlsson, M. and E. Lundberg. 2015. 'Partimedlemmar'. In *Partier och Partisystem*, edited by M. Hagevi, 91–103. Lund, SE: Studentlitteratur.

Katz, R. S. 1986. 'Party government: A rationalistic conception'. In *Visions and Realities of Party Government*, edited by F. G. Castles and R. Wildenmann, 31–71. Berlin, DE: Walter de Gruyter.

——— 2001. 'The problem of candidate selection and models of party democracy'. *Party Politics* 7 (3): 277–96.

——— 2002 'The internal life of parties'. In *Political Parties in the New Europe: Political and analytical challenges*, edited by K. R. Luther and F. Müller-Rommel, 87–118. Oxford: Oxford University Press.

——— 2014. 'No man can serve two masters: Party politicians, party members, citizens and principal–agent models of democracy'. *Party Politics* 20 (2): 183–93.

Katz, R. S. and P. Mair. 1995. 'Changing models of party organization and party democracy: The emergence of the cartel party'. *Party Politics* 1 (1): 5–28.

——— 1996. 'Cadre, catch-all or cartel? A rejoinder'. *Party Politics* 2 (4): 52–34.

——— 2002. 'The ascendency of the party in public office: Party organizational change in twentieth-century democracies'. In *Political Parties: Old Concepts and New Challenges*, edited by R. Gunther, J. Ramón Montero, and J. J. Linz, 113–35. Oxford, UK: Oxford University Press.

——— 2009. 'The cartel party thesis: a restatement'. *Perspectives on Politics* 7 (4): 753–66.

King, G., R. O. Keohane and S. Verba. 1994. *Designing Social Inquiry: Scientific Inference in Qualitative Research*. Princeton, NJ: Princeton University Press.

Kirchheimer, O. 1957. 'The waning of opposition in parliamentary regimes'. *Social Research* 24 (2): 127–56.

——— 1966. 'The transformation of Western European party systems'. In *Political Parties and Political Development*, edited by J. La Palombara and M. Wiener, 177–200. Princeton, NJ: Princeton University Press.

Kitschelt, H. 1994. *The Transformation of European Social Democracy*. Cambridge, UK: Cambridge University Press.

——— 2000. 'Citizens, politicians and party cartelization: political representation and state failure in post-industrial democracies'. *European Journal of Political Research* 37 (2): 149–79.

———— 2003. 'Landscapes of political interest intermediation: social movements, interest groups, and parties in the early twenty-first century'. In *Social Movements and Democracy*, edited by P. Ibarra, 81–104. New York: Palgrave Macmillan.

———— 2007a. 'Party systems'. In *Oxford Handbook of Comparative Politics*, edited by C. Boix and S. C. Stokes, 521–54. Oxford, UK: Oxford University Press.

———— 2007b. 'Growth and persistence of the radical right in postindustrial democracies: Advances and challenges in comparative research'. *West European Politics* 30 (5): 1176–1206.

Kitschelt, H., P. Lange, G. Marks and J. D. Stephens. 1999. 'Convergence and divergence in advanced capitalist democracies'. In *Continuity and Change in Contemporary Capitalism*, edited by H. Kitschelt, P. Lange, G. Marks and J. D. Stephens, 427–60. Cambridge, UK: Cambridge University Press.

Kitschelt, H. and P. Rehm. 2014. 'Citizens' representation by political parties: Where, if anywhere, in Europe does it still work?' Paper presented at the Annual Meeting of the European Political Science Association (EPSA), Edinburgh, UK, June.

———— 2015. 'Party alignments: Change and continuity'. In *The Politics of Advanced Capitalism*, edited by P. Beramendi, S. Häusermann, H. Kitschelt and H. Kriesi, 179–201. Cambridge, UK: Cambridge University Press.

Kittilson, M. C. and L. A. Schwindt-Bayer. 2012. *The Gendered Effects of Electoral Institutions. Political Engagement and Participation*. Oxford, UK: Oxford University Press.

Koivula, T. and J. Sipilä. 2011. 'Missing in action? EU crisis management and the link to the domestic political debate'. *Cooperation and Conflict* 46 (4): 521–42.

Kölln, A.-K. 2014. *Party Decline and Response: The Effects of Membership Decline on Party Organisations in Western Europe, 1960–2010*. Enschede, NL: Institute for Innovation and Governance Studies and the Department of Public Administration, University of Twente.

Koole, R. 1996. 'Cadre, catch-all or cartel? A comment on the notion of the cartel party'. *Party Politics* 2 (4): 507–23.

Koselleck, R. 2004. *Futures Past: On the Semantics of Historical Time*. New York: Columbia University Press.

Koß, M. 2011. *The Politics of Party Funding: State Funding to Political Parties and Party Competition in Western Europe*. Oxford: Oxford University Press.

Kriesi, H., E. Grande, R. Lachat, M. Dolezal, S. Bornschier and T. Frey. 2008. *West European Politics in the Age of Globalization*. Cambridge, UK: Cambridge University Press.

Krotz, F. 2007. 'The meta-process of "mediatization" as a conceptual frame'. *Global Media and Communication* 3 (3): 256–60.

Krouwel, A. 2012. *Party Transformation in European Democracies*. New York: State University of New York Press.

Ladrech, R. 2002. 'Europeanization and political parties: Towards a framework for analysis'. *Party Politics* 8 (4): 389–403.

———— 2007. 'National political parties and European governance: The consequences of "missing in action"'. *West European Politics* 30 (5): 945–60.

Lakoff, G. and M. Johnson. 1980. *Metaphors We Live By*. Chicago, IL: University of Chicago Press.

Landerer, N. 2013. 'Rethinking the logics: A conceptual framework for the mediatization of politics'. *Communication Theory* 23 (3): 239–58.

Laski, H. J. 1919. *Authority in the Modern State*. New Haven, CT: Yale University Press.

Laver, M. 2005. 'Policy and the dynamics of party competition'. *American Political Science Review* 99 (2): 263–82.

Layman, G. C., T. M. Carsey, J. C. Green, R. Herrera and R. Cooperman. 2010. 'Activists and conflict extension in American party politics'. *American Political Science Review* 104 (2): 324–46.

Lengauer, G., P. Donges and F. Plasser. 2013. 'Media power in politics'. In *Political Communication Cultures in Western Europe: Attitudes of Political Actors and Journalists in Nine Countries*, edited by B. Pfetsch, 171–75. New York: Palgrave Macmillan.

Lewin, L. 2007. *Democratic Accountability*. Cambridge, MA: Harvard University Press.

Lievrouw, L. A. and S. Livingstone. 2009. 'Introduction'. In *Major Works in New Media*, edited by L. A. Lievrouw and S. Livingstone, xxi–xl. London, UK: Sage.

Lijphart, A. 1977. *Democracy in Plural Societies: A Comparative Exploration*. New Haven, CT: Yale University Press.

——— 1984. *Democracies: Patterns of Majoritarian and Consensus Government in Twenty-One Countries*. New Haven, CT: Yale University Press.

——— 1999. *Patterns of Democracy: Government Forms and Performance in Thirty-Six Countries*. New Haven, CT: Yale University Press.

——— 2008. *Thinking About Democracy: Power Sharing and Majority Rule in Theory and Practice*. London, UK: Routledge.

Lipman-Blumen, J. 1976. 'Toward a homosocial theory of sex roles: An explanation of the sex segregation of social institutions'. *Signs* 1 (3): 15–31.

Lipset, S. M. and S. Rokkan. 1967. 'Cleavage structures, party systems, and voter alignments: An introduction'. In *Party Systems and Voter Alignments: Cross-National Perspectives*, edited by S. M. Lipset and S. Rokkan, 1–64. New York: Free Press.

Littré, E. 1956. *Dictionnaire de la langue française, t. 1*. Paris, FR: J. J. Pauvert.

Ljunggren, S. 2010. 'Miljöpartiet De Gröna: Från miljömissnöjesparti till grön regeringspartner'. *Statsvetenskaplig tidskrift* 112 (2): 177–88.

Locke, J. 1993. *Two Treatises of Government*. London, UK: Everyman.

Lovenduski, J. and P. Norris. 1993. *Gender and Party Politics*. London, UK: Sage.

——— 2003. 'Westminster women: the politics of presence'. *Political Studies* 51 (1): 84–102.

Loxbo, K. 2007. *Bakom socialdemokraternas beslut: En studie av den politiska förändringens dilemma – från 1950-talets ATP-strid till 1990-talets pensionsuppgörelse*. Växjö, SE: Växjö University Press.

——— 2009. 'Har den interna demokratin i politiska partier försämrats över tid?' *Sociologisk forskning* 46 (1): 7–27.

———— 2011. 'Att rösta mot systemet'. In *Den svenska väljaren*, edited by M. Hagevi, 165–81. Umeå, SE: Boréa.

———— 2013. 'The fate of intra-party democracy: Leadership autonomy and activist influence in the mass party and the cartel party'. *Party Politics* 19 (4): 537–54.

———— 2014a. 'Europeisering och kartellisering av nationella partisystem? Förändrade konfliktlinjer mellan partierna i riksdagens EU-nämnd mellan 1995 och 2012'. *Statsvetenskaplig tidskrift* 116 (1): 123–48.

———— 2014b. 'Voters' perceptions of policy convergence and the short-term opportunities of anti-immigrant parties: Examples from Sweden'. *Scandinavian Political Studies* 37 (3): 239–62.

———— 2015. 'Sverigedemokraterna: Framgångsrikt enfrågefokus'. *Statsvetenskaplig tidskrift* 117 (2): 169–87.

Loxbo, K. and M. Sjölin. 2016. 'Parliamentary opposition on the wane? The case of Sweden, 1970–2014'. *Government and Opposition*, published online at: http://dx.doi.org/10.1017/gov.2015.39 (accessed 4 April 2017).

Luebbert, G. 1991. *Liberalism, Fascism, or Social Democracy: Social Classes and the Political Origins of Regimes in Interwar Europe*. Oxford, UK: Oxford University Press.

Lukes, S. 1974. *Power: A Radical View*. Houndmills, Basingstoke, UK: Macmillan.

Lundqvist, H. 2011. *Empirical Essays in Political and Public Economics*. Uppsala, SE: Department of Economics, Uppsala University.

Mair, P. 1994. 'Party organizations: From civil society to the state'. In *How Parties Organize: Change and Adaption on Party Organizations in Western Democracies*, edited by R. S. Katz and P. Mair, 1–22. London, UK: Sage.

———— 1997. *Party System Change: Approaches and Interpretation*. Oxford, UK: Clarendon Press.

———— 2000. 'Partyless democracy: Solving the paradox of New Labour?' *New Left Review* 2 (1): 21–35.

———— 2005. 'Democracy beyond parties'. Working paper, Irvine, CA: Center for the Study of Democracy, University of California.

———— 2007. 'Political opposition and the European Union'. *Government and Opposition* 42 (1): 1–17.

———— 2008. 'The challenge to party government'. *West European Politics* 31 (1–2): 211–34.

———— 2009. 'Representative versus responsible government'. MPIfG Working Paper 09/08, Cologne, DE: Max-Planck-Institut für Gesellschaftsforschung, available online at: http://edoc.vifapol.de/opus/volltexte/2010/2121/pdf/wp09_8.pdf (accessed 13 April 2017).

———— 2013. *Ruling the Void: The Hollowing of Western Democracy*. London, UK: Verso.

Mair, P. and R. S. Katz. 1997. 'Party organization, party democracy, and the emergence of the cartel party'. In *Party System Change: Approaches and Interpretation*, edited by P. Mair, 93–119. Oxford, UK: Clarendon Press.

Mancini, P. 1999. 'New frontiers in political professionalism'. *Political Communication* 16 (3): 231–45.

Mansbridge, J. 2003. 'Rethinking representation'. *American Political Science Review* 97 (4): 515–28.

Mansbridge, J. 2011. 'Clarifying the concept of representation'. *American Political Science Review* 105 (3): 621–30.

Marks, G. and C. J. Wilson. 2000. 'The past in the present: A cleavage theory of party responses to European integration'. *British Journal of Political Science* 30 (3): 433–59.

Marks, G. and M. Steenbergen. 2002. 'Understanding political contestation in the European Union'. *Comparative Political Studies* 35 (8): 879–92.

Mattson, I. and K. Strøm. 2004. 'Committee effects on legislation'. In *Patterns of Parliamentary Behavior: Passage of Legislation Across Western Europe*, edited by H. Döring and M. Hallerberg, 91–111. Farnham, UK: Ashgate.

May, J. D. 1973. 'Opinion structure of political parties: The special law of curvilinear disparity'. *Political Studies* 21 (2): 135–51.

Mazzoleni, G. 2008. 'Mediatization of politics'. In *International Encyclopedia of Communication*, edited by W. Donsbach, 3047–51. Malden, UK: Blackwell.

McAllister, I. and D. T. Studlar. 1992. 'Gender and representation among legislative candidates in Australia'. *Comparative Political Studies* 25 (3): 388–411.

McKenzie, R. 1982. 'Power in the Labour Party: The issue of intra-party democracy'. In *The Politics of the Labour Party*, edited by D. Kavanagh, 191–201. London, UK: George Allen & Unwin.

Melki, M. and A. Pickering. 2014. 'Ideological polarization and the media'. *Economics Letters* 125 (1): 36–9.

Michels, R. 1911. *Zur Soziologie des Parteiwesens in der modernen Demokratie.* Leipzig: Klinkhart.

——— 1962. *Political Parties: A Sociological Study of the Oligarchical Tendencies of Modern Democracy.* New York: Free Press.

Miles, L., ed. 2000. *Sweden and the European Union Evaluated.* London, UK: Continuum.

Möller, T. 2015. *Svensk politisk historia: Strid och samverkan under tvåhundra år.* Lund, SE: Studentlitteratur.

Möller, U. and W. Bjereld. 2010. 'From Nordic neutrals to post-neutral Europeans: similarity and change in Finland's and Sweden's policy transformation'. *Cooperation and Conflict* 45 (4): 363–86.

Moring, T. 2006. 'Between medialization and tradition: Campaigning in Finland in a longitudinal perspective'. In *Campaigning in Europe – Campaigning for Europe: Political Parties, Campaigns, Mass Media and the European Parliament Elections 2004*, edited by M. Maier and J. Tenscher, 81–99. Berlin, DE: Lit Verlag.

Moschonas, G. 2002. *In the Name of Social Democracy.* London, UK: Verso.

Mouffe, C. 2000. *The Democratic Paradox.* London, UK: Verso.

Müller, W. C. and K. Strøm. 2010. 'Coalition agreements and cabinet governance'. In *Cabinets and Coalition Bargaining. The Democratic Life Cycle in Western Europe*, edited by K. Strøm, W. C. Müller and T. Bergman, 159–99. Oxford, UK: Oxford University Press.

Narud, H. M. and H. Valen. 2000a. 'Does social background matter?' In *Beyond Westminster and Congress: The Nordic Experience*, edited by P. Esaiasson and K. Heidar, 83–106. Columbus, OH: Ohio State University Press.

Nash, J. 1951. 'Non-cooperative games'. *Annals of Mathematics* 54 (2): 286–95.

Nassmacher, K.-H. 2009. *The Funding of Party Competition: Political Finance in 25 Democracies*. Baden-Baden, DE: Nomos.

Niklasson B. 2005. *Contact Capital in Political Careers: Gender and Recruitment of Parliamentaries and Political Appointments*. Göteborg, SE: Department of Political Science, University of Gothenburg.

Nord, L. 2013. 'Jakten på den perfekta kampanjen: professionaliseringen av de svenska partierna'. In *Kampen om opinionen: Politiskt kommunikation under svenska valrörelser*, edited by J. Strömbäck and L. Nord, 35–63. Stockholm, SE: SNS Förlag.

Norris, P. 1999. 'Recruitment into the European Parliament'. In *The European Parliament, the National Parliaments, and European Integration*, edited by R. S. Katz and B. Wessels, 86–102. Oxford, UK: Oxford University Press.

Norton, P. 2008. 'Conclusion: Making sense of opposition'. *Journal of Legislative Studies* 14 (1–2): 213–35.

Nousiainen, J. 2001. 'From semi-presidentialism to parliamentary government: Political and constitutional developments in Finland'. *Scandinavian Political Studies* 24 (2): 95–109.

Nownes A. J. and G. Neely. 1996. 'Public interest group entrepreneurship and theories of group mobilization'. *Political Research Quarterly* 49 (1): 119–46.

OED: Oxford English Dictionary Online, available at: http://www.oed.com (accessed 16 June 2016).

Öhberg, P. 2011. *Politiker med karriärambitioner – en omöjlig självklarhet: En studie om karriärambitionernas betydelse i den representativa demokratin*. Göteborg, SE: Statsvetenskapliga institutionen, Göteborgs universitet.

Ojanen, H., G. Herolf and R. Lindahl. 2001. *Non-Alignment and European Security Policy*. Helsinki, FI: Finnish Institute of International Affairs.

Olson, M. 1971. *The Logic of Collective Action: Public Goods and the Theory of Groups*. Cambridge, MA: Harvard University Press.

Oskarson, M. 1994. *Klassröstning i Sverige: rationalitet, lojalitet eller bara slentrian*. Stockholm, SE: Nerenius & Santérus.

Oscarsson, H. 1998. *Den svenska partirymden: Väljarnas uppfattningar av konfliktstrukturen i partisystemet 1956–1994*. Göteborg, SE: Statsvetenskapliga institutionen, Göteborgs universitet.

Oscarsson, H. and S. Holmberg. 2013. *Nya svenska väljare*. Stockholm, SE: Norstedt Juridik.

Pålsson, A.-M. 2011. *Knapptryckarkompaniet*. Stockholm, SE: Bokförlaget Atlantis.

Panebianco, A. 1988. *Political Parties: Organization & Power*. Cambridge, UK: Cambridge University Press.

Petersson, O., J. Hermansson, M. Micheletti and A. Westholm. 1997. *Demokrati över gränser: Demokratirådets rapport 1997*. Stockholm, SE: SNS Förlag.

Petersson, O., G. Hernes, S. Holmberg, L. Togeby, and L. Wängnerud. 2000. *Demokrati utan partier: Demokratirådets rapport 2000*. Stockholm, SE: SNS Förlag.

Pfetsch, B., P. Maurer, E. Mayerhöffer, T. Moring and S. Schwab Cammarano. 2013. 'Contexts of the media-politics relationship: Country selection and grouping'. In *Political Communication Cultures in Western Europe: Attitudes of Political Actors and Journalists in Nine Countries*, edited by B. Pfetsch, 31–56. New York: Palgrave Macmillan.

Phillips, A. 1998. *The Politics of Presence*. Oxford, UK: Oxford University Press.

Pierre, J. and Widfeldt, A. 1994. 'Party organizations in Sweden: Colossuses with feet of clay or flexible pillars of government?' In *How Parties Organize: Change and Adaption in Party Organizations in Western Democracies*, edited by R. S. Katz, and P. Mair, 332–56. London, UK: Sage.

Pierre, J., L. Svåsand and A. Widfeldt. 2000. 'State subsidies to political parties: Confronting rhetoric with reality'. *West European Politics* 23 (3): 1–24.

Pitkin, H. F. 1967. *The Concept of Representation*. Berkeley, CA: University of California Press.

——— 1973. *Wittgenstein and Justice: On the Significance of Ludwig Wittgenstein for Social and Political Thought*. Berkeley, CA: University of California Press.

——— 1981. 'Justice: on relating private and public'. *Political Theory* 9 (3): 327–52.

——— 1998. *The Attack of the Blob: Hannah Arendt's Concept of the Social*. Chicago, IL: University of Chicago Press.

Plasser, F. and G. Plasser. 2002. *Global Political Campaigning: A Worldwide Analysis of Campaign Professionals and Their Practices*. Westport, CT: Praeger.

Poggione, S. 2004. 'Exploring gender differences in state legislators' policy preferences'. *Political Research Quarterly* 57 (2): 305–14.

Popper, K. 1989. *Conjectures and Refutations: The Growth of Scientific Knowledge*. London, UK: Routledge.

Przeworski, A. and M. Wallerstein. 1988. 'Structural dependence of the state on capital'. *American Political Science Review* 82 (1): 11–29.

Prior, M. 2013. 'Media and political polarization'. *Annual Review of Political Science* 16: 101–27.

Raaum, N. C. 2005. 'Gender equality and political representation: A Nordic comparison'. *West European Politics* 28 (4): 872–97.

Rådet för främjande av kommunala analyser (RKA). 2012. *Kommun- och landstingsdatabasen*, available online at: http://kolada.se/index.php?page=workspace/nt (accessed 20 May 2012).

Ranney, A. 1954. *The Doctrine of Responsible Party Government: Its Origins and Present State*. Urbana, IL: University of Illinois Press.

Reinfeldt, F. 2015. *Halvvägs*. Stockholm, SE: Bonniers.

Reunanen, E., R. Kunelius and E. Noppari. 2010. 'Mediatization in context: Consensus culture, media and decision making in the 21st century, the case of Finland'. *Communications* 35 (3): 287–307.

Ricoeur, P. 1978. *The Rule of Metaphor*. London, UK: Routledge & Kegan Paul.

Rieker, P. 2004. 'Europeanisation of Nordic security? The EU and the changing security identities of the Nordic states'. *Cooperation and Conflict* 39 (4): 369–92.

Riksdagens utredningstjänst. 2003. *Partistöd.* Dnr 2003: 1196. Stockholm, SE: Sveriges riksdag.

Riksdagens årsbok 2006/07. 2007. Stockholm, SE: Riksdagens tryckeriexpedition.

Riksdagens årsbok 2012/13. 2013. Stockholm, SE: Riksdagens tryckeriexpedition.

Rosenblum, N. L. 2008. *On the Side of the Angels: An Appreciation of Parties and Partisanship.* Princeton, NJ: Princeton University Press.

Sandelin, B. 2005. *Ekonomin i EU.* Stockholm, SE: SNS Förlag.

Sannerstedt, A. 1992. *Förhandlingar i riksdagen.* Lund: Lund University Press.

――― 1996. 'Negotiations in the Riksdag'. *The Bargaining Democracy,* edited by M. Jerneck and L. G. Stenelo, 17–58. Lund, SE: Lund University Press.

Sannerstedt, A. and M. Sjölin. 1992. 'Sweden: Changing party relations in a more active parliament'. In *Parliamentary Change in the Nordic Countries,* edited by E. Damgaard, 89–130. Oslo, NO: Scandinavian University Press.

Sartori, G. 1970. 'Concept misformation in comparative politics'. *American Political Science Review* 64 (4): 1033–53.

――― 1976. *Parties and Party Systems: A Framework for Analysis.* Cambridge, UK: Cambridge University Press.

――― 1984. 'Guidelines for concept analysis'. In *Social Science Concepts: A Systematic Analysis,* edited by G. Sartori, 15–85. Beverly Hills, CA: Sage.

Scarrow, S. E. 2000. 'Parties without members? Party organization in a changing electoral environment'. In *Parties Without Partisans: Political Change in Advanced Industrial Democracies,* edited by R. J. Dalton and M. P. Wattenberg, 79–101. Oxford, UK: Oxford University Press.

――― 2004. 'State subsidies to political parties: Confronting rhetoric with reality'. *West European Politics* 23 (3): 1–24.

――― 2006. 'Party subsidies and the freezing of party competition: Do cartels work?' *West European Politics* 29 (4): 619–39.

Scarrow, S. E. and B. Gezgor. 2010. 'Declining memberships, changing members? European political party members in a new era'. *Party Politics* 16 (6): 823–43.

Scarrow, S. E., P. Webb and D. M. Farrell. 2000. 'From social integration to electoral contestation: The changing distribution of power within political parties'. In *Parties without Partisans: Political Change in Advanced Industrial democracies,* edited by R. J. Dalton and M. P. Wattenberg, 129–53. Oxford: Oxford University Press.

SCB. 2013a. *Undersökningarna av levnadsförhållanden (ULF/SILC),* available online at: http://www.scb.se/Pages/List____257686.aspx (accessed 20 May 2012).

SCB. 2013b. *Arbetskostnadsindex för arbetare och tjänstemän inom privat sektor (AKI),* available online at: http://www.scb.se/Pages/TableAndChart____248029. aspx (accessed 20 May 2013).

SCB. 2015. *Sweden's population by sex and age on 31/12/2014,* available online at: http://www.scb.se/en_/Finding-statistics/Statistics-by-subject-area/Population/ Population-composition/Population-statistics/Aktuell-Pong/25795/Yearly-statistics--The-whole-country/262459/ (accessed 20 March 2015).

Scharpf, F. 2010. 'The asymmetry of European integration, or why the EU cannot be a "social market economy"'. *Socio-Economic Review* 8 (2): 211–50.

Schattschneider, E. E. 1948. *The Struggle for Party Government*. College Park, MD: University of Maryland.

——— 1960. *The Semisovereign People: A Realist's View of Democracy in America*. New York: Wadsworth.

Schmidt, V. A. 2006. 'Democracy in Europe: The impact of European integration'. *Perspectives on Politics* 3 (4): 761–79.

Schulz, W. 2004. 'Reconstructing mediatization as an analytical concept'. *European Journal of Communication* 19 (1): 87–101.

Schwartz, S. H. 2006. 'A theory of cultural value orientations: Explications and applications'. *Comparative Sociology* 5 (2): 137–82.

Schwindt-Bayer, L. A. and W. Mishler. 2005. 'An integrated model of women's representation'. *Journal of Politics* 67 (2): 407–28.

Segerberg, A. 2005. *Thinking Doing: The Politicization of Thoughtless Action*. Stockholm, SE: Department of Political Science, Stockholm University.

Shaw, M. 1979. 'Conclusions'. In *Committees in Legislatures: A Comparative Analysis*, edited by J. Lees and M. Shaw, 361–434. Durham, NC: Duke University Press.

Sjöblom, G. 1968. *Party Strategies in a Mulitparty System*. Lund, SE: Studentlitteratur.

——— 1986. 'Problems and problem solutions in politics'. In *Visions and Realities of Party Government*, edited by F. G. Castles and R. Wildenmann, 72–119. Berlin, DE: Walter de Gruyter.

Sjölin, M. 1993. *Coalition Politics and Parliamentary Power*. Lund, SE: Lund University Press.

Skjeie, H. 1992. Den politiske betydningen av kjønn: En studie av norsk topppolitikk. Oslo, NO: Universitetet i Oslo.

Skinner, Q. 2001. *Visions of Politics,* vol. I, *Regarding Method*. Cambridge, UK: Cambridge University Press.

Sköld, L. and A. Halvarsson. 1966. 'Riksdagens sociala sammansättning under hundra år'. In *Samhälle och riksdag I*, 375–493. Stockholm, SE: Almqvist & Wiksell.

SOM Institute, The. 2014. *SOM Institute Cumulative Data Set 1986–2012*, data file. Göteborg, SE: SOM Institute, University of Gothenburg.

Spivak, G. C. 1998. *In Other Worlds*. London, UK: Routledge.

Staberg, L. 2000. 'Partisammanhållningen – hur stark är den egentligen? En studie av den svenska riksdagen under 1990-talet'. Paper presented for Bachelor Degree, Göteborg, SE: Department of Political Science, University of Gothenburg.

Steensen, S. 2011. 'Online journalism and the promises of new technology: A critical review and look ahead'. *Journalism Studies* 12 (3): 311–27.

Stensöta Olofsdotter, H. 2014. 'Cartel theory from a gender perspective'. *Statsvetenskaplig tidskrift* 116 (1): 73–94.

Stigler, G. J. 1964. 'A theory of oligopoly'. *Journal of Political Economy* 72 (1): 44–61.

Stjernquist, N. 1966. 'Riksdagens arbete och arbetsformer'. In *Samhälle och riksdag IV*, 5–505. Stockholm, SE: Almqvist & Wiksell.

Stoutland, F. 1997. 'Why are philosophers of action so anti-social?' In *Commonality and Particularity in Ethics*, edited by L. Alanen, S. Heinämaa and T. Wallgren, 45–74. New York, NY: St. Martin's Press.

Strøm, K. 1986. 'Deferred gratification and minority governments in Scandinavia'. *Legislative Studies Quarterly* 11 (4): 583–605.

―――― 1990. *Minority Government and Majority Rule*. Cambridge, UK: Cambridge University Press.

Strömbäck, J. 2008. 'Four phases of mediatization: An analysis of the mediatization of politics'. *International Journal of Press/Politics* 13 (3): 228–46.

―――― 2009. *Medier, makt och samhälle. En introduktion till politisk kommunikation*. Johanneshov SE: TPB.

―――― 2011. 'Mediatization of politics: Towards a conceptual framework for comparative research'. In *Sourcebook of Political Communication Research*, edited by E. Bucy and R. L. Holbert, 367–82. London, UK: Taylor & Francis.

Strömbäck, J. and D. V. Dimitrova. 2011. 'Mediatization and media interventionism: A comparative analysis of Sweden and the United States'. *International Journal of Press/Politics* 16 (1): 30–49.

Strömbäck, J. and F. Esser. 2009. 'Shaping politics: Mediatization and media interventionism'. In *Mediatization: Concept, Changes, Consequences*, edited by K. Lundby, 205–23. New York: Peter Lang.

Strömbäck, J. and P. Van Aelst. 2013. 'Why political parties adapt to the media: Exploring the fourth dimension of mediatization'. *International Communication Gazette* 75 (4): 341–58.

Strömberg, L. and Westerståhl, J. 1984. *The New Swedish Communes: A Summary of Local Government Research*. Stockholm, SE: Liber.

Strömblad, P. 2003. *Politik på stadens skuggsida*. Uppsala, SE: Uppsala universitet.

Sundberg, J. 2002. 'The Scandinavian party model at the crossroads'. In *Political Parties in Advanced Industrial Democracies*, edited by P. Webb, D. Farell and J. Holliday, 181–216. Oxford, UK: Oxford University Press.

Svåsand, L. 1991. 'State subventions for political parties in Norway'. In *The Public Purse and Political Parties: Public Funding of Political Parties in Nordic Countries*, edited by M. Wiberg, 119–46. Helsinki, FI: Finnish Political Science Association.

Swedish National Election Studies. 2017. *Swedish National Election Studies Program*, available online at: http://valforskning.pol.gu.se/english (accessed 9 March 2017).

Swedish Parliament, The. 2015. 'Financial support to the parties', available online at: http://www.riksdagen.se/en/How-the-Riksdag-works/The-parties-in-the-Riksdag/Financial-support-to-the-parties/ (accessed 8 April 2016).

Swers, M. 2001. 'Understanding the policy impact of electing women: Evidence from research on Congress and state legislatures'. *Political Science & Politics* 34 (2): 217–20.

Tenscher, J., J. Mykkänen and T. Moring. 2012. 'Modes of professional campaigning: A four-country comparison in the European Parliamentary elections, 2009'. *International Journal of Press/Politics* 17 (2): 145–68.

Teorell, J. 1998. *Demokrati eller fåtalsvälde? Om beslutsfattande i partiorganisationer*. Uppsala, SE: Uppsala University Library.

Therborn, G. 1978. *What Does the Ruling Party Do When It Rules?* London, UK: Verso.

Theriault, S. M. 2008. *Party Polarization in Congress.* Cambridge, UK: Cambridge University Press.

Thesen, G. 2013. 'Political agenda setting as mediatized politics? Media–politics interactions from a party and issue competition perspective'. *International Journal of Press/Politics* 19 (2): 181–201.

Thomassen, J. 2014. 'Representation and accountability'. In *Elections and Democracy: Representation and Accountability*, edited by J. Thomassen, 1–19. Oxford, UK: Oxford University Press.

Thomassen, J. and C. van Ham. 2015. 'Failing political representation or a change in kind?' In *The Role of Parties in Twenty-First Century Politics: Responsive and Responsible?* edited by L. Bardi, S. Bartolini and A. H. Trechsel, 173–92. Abingdon, UK: Routledge.

Tingsten, H. 1966. *Från idéer till idyll: Den lyckliga demokratien.* Stockholm, SE: Norstedts.

Toshkov, D. 2011. 'Public opinion and policy output in the European Union: A lost relationship'. *European Union Politics* 12 (2): 169–91.

Uddhammar, E. 1993. *Partierna och den stora staten: en analys av statsteorier och svensk politik under 1900-talet.* Stockholm, SE: City University Press.

Valmyndigheten. 2015. 'Vad händer efter valet?', available online at: http://www.val.se/det_svenska_valsystemet/partier/vad_hander_efter_valet/ (accessed 8 April 2016).

Van Aelst, P., B. Maddens, J. Noppe and S. Fiers. 2008. 'Politicians in the news: Media or party logic? Media attention and electoral success in the Belgian election campaign of 2003'. *European Journal of Communication* 23 (2): 193–210.

Van Aelst, P., A. Sehata and A. Van Dalen. 2010. 'Members of Parliament: Equal competitors for media attention? An analysis of personal contacts between MPs and political journalists in five European countries'. *Political Communication* 27 (3): 310–25.

Vasigh, B., K. Fleming, and T. Tacker. 2008. *Introduction to Air Transport Economics: From Theory to Applications.* Aldershot, UK: Ashgate.

Verba, S., K. Lehman Schlozman and H. E. Brady. 1995. *Voice and Equality: Civic Voluntarism in American Politics.* Cambridge, MA: Harvard University Press.

Vernersdotter, F. 2014. 'Den nationella SOM-undersökningen 2013'. In *Mittfåra och marginal*, edited by H. Oscarsson and A. Bengtsson, 531–59. Göteborg, SE: SOM Institute, University of Gothenburg.

Volkens, A., P. Lehmann, N. Merz, S. Regel, A. Werner, O. P. Lacwell and H. Schultze. 2016. *The Manifesto Data Collection. Manifesto Project (MRG/CMP/MARPOR).* Berlin, DE: Wissenschaftszentrum Berlin für Sozialforschung (WZB).

Vuksanovic, M. 1979. *Kodbok för 1974 års levnadsnivåundersökning: Dokumentation av ett dataregister för välfärdsforskning.* Stockholm, SE: Institutet för social forskning.

Vuksanovic, V. and M. Vuksanovic. 1992. *68'ans kodbok.* Stockholm, SE: Institutet för social forskning.

Wallin, G., P. Ehn, M. Isberg and C. Linde. 1999. *Makthavare i fokus.* Stockholm, SE: SNS Förlag.

Wängnerud, L. 1998. *Politikens andra sida: Om kvinnorepresentation i Sveriges riksdag*. Göteborg, SE: Department of Political Science, University of Gothenburg.

Wängnerud, L. 2006. 'A step-wise development: Women in parliament in Sweden'. In *Women in Parliament: Beyond Numbers,* edited by J. Ballington and A. Karam, 238–48. Stockholm, SE: IDEA Handbook.

Wängnerud, L. 2009. 'Women in parliaments: Descriptive and substantive representation'. *Annual Review of Political Science* 12: 51–69.

Wängnerud, L. 2015. *The Principles of Gender-Sensitive Parliaments*. London, UK: Routledge.

Wängnerud, L., P. Esaiasson, M. Gilljam and S. Holmberg. 2012. *Swedish Parliamentary Survey*. Göteborg, SE: Department of Political Science, University of Gothenburg.

Weber, M. 2008. 'Politics as a vocation'. In *Max Weber's Complete Writings on Academic and Political Vocations*, edited by J. Dreijmanis, 155–207. New York: Algora Publishing.

Wenzelburger, G. 2014. 'Parties, institutions and the politics of law and order: How political institutions and partisan ideologies shape law-and-order spending in twenty Western industrialized countries'. *British Journal of Political Science* 45 (3): 663–87.

Westerståhl, J. and F. Johansson. 1981. *Medborgarna och kommunen: studier av medborgerlig aktivitet och representativ folkstyrelse*. Ds Kn 1981: 12. Stockholm, SE: Kommundepartementet.

Widfeldt, A. 1997. *Linking Parties with People? Party Membership in Sweden 1960–1994*. Göteborg, SE: Department of Political Science, University of Gothenburg.

Wiberg, M., ed. 1991. *The Public Purse and Political Parties: Public Financing of Political Parties in Nordic Countries*. Helsingfors, FI: Finnish Political Science Association.

Wolinetz S. B. 2002. 'Beyond the catch-all party: Approaches to the study of parties and party organization in contemporary democracies'. In *Political Parties: Old Concepts and New Challenges*, edited by R. Gunther, J. Ramón Montero and J. J. Linz, 136–65. Oxford, UK: Oxford University Press.

World Economic Forum. 2015. *Global Gendergap Index 2014*, available online at: http://reports.weforum.org/global-gender-gap-report-2014/rankings/ (accessed 6 June 2015).

Index

Note: Page numbers for figures and tables are italicized.

accountability, 3, 25, 46, 58, 190, 192, 193, *194*, 196, 205
Alliance parties (Sweden), 160

Ball, T., 40
Bartolini, S., 99
Best, H., 72
Björklund, J., 174
Blyth, M., 28, 34–36, 41n4
Borchert, J., 75, 76, 77
Borg, A., 173, 175
Brommesson, D., 201
Bunce, A., 128

cartel: conceptual history/analysis of, 29–33, 37–41; use of term, 22, 27–28, 29–32, 33, 39, 41. *See also* collusion; co-operation; depoliticisation
cartel-like behaviour, concerted action in, 32–33, 34, 38
cartel party ideal type, 27, 30
cartel party theory: basic assumptions/ hypotheses in, 16, 22, 23, 43–46, 68, 164, 207–9; democracy, view of in, 68, 189–91, 192, 195–203, 205–6; depoliticisation in, 23, 28, 33–34, 44, 59, 97, 208; economic theory, use of in, 28–29, 34–36, 37; left–right dimension in, 43, 45, 59–60, 99, 155, 207, 208; media logic in, 119, 121; metaphor in, 28, 32, 37; normative implications of, 25, 39, 40, 189–90, 195, 208; principal-agent question in, 5, 8. *See also* depoliticisation; issue congruence; mediatisation of politics; party membership decline; party organisational culture; party policy convergence; Sweden, cartelisation thesis
Casas-Zamora, K., 212
catch-all parties, 1, 2, 3, 6, 16, 214
Centre Party (Sweden) party culture analysis, 164, *165*, 169, 170, 177–79, 181, 183–84, 185
Christian Democrats (Sweden) party culture analysis, 164, *165*, 169, 170, 181–83, 184, 186, 200
citizenship, 191
civil society: disempowering of, 45, 207; and party elite withdrawal, 16, 22, 26, 43, 44, 46–47, 77, 93, 199, 200, 207

collusion, 28, 30–32, 34, 35, 36, 37, 38, 39, 41, 44, 45, 68, 100, 159, 190–91, 196, 200, 208, 209
Comparative Manifesto Project (CMP), 22, 54, 104
convergence, 28, 31, 213; cartel theory, use in, 33, 37–38, 54, 55, 123, 191, 209, 214; dynamics of, 33. *See also* party policy convergence
co-operation, 28, 30, 31, 34, 37, 38, 39–40, 201; cartel party distrust of, 195; and interdependence, 35; inter-party, 32, 33, 36, 196
co-ordination, 32–33, 36; as covert, 31, 32
Cotta, M., 72
culture, concept of, 162–63; in party politics, 163. *See also* party organisational culture

Dahl, R., 100, 190, 191–92
Dahlerup, D., 146
democracy: cartel party concept of, 68, 189–91, 192, 195–203; consensus model, 192, 193–95, 196, 197; decline of, 44, 46, 49, 50, 52, 66, 67, 68, 100–101; disempowerment in, 3; liberal, 192, 195; media exploitation in, 201; normative criteria in (Dahl's polyarchy), 190, 191–92; particularisation in, 201; party government model, 192–94, 195, 196, 197; Swedish consensus model, changes in 197, 200. *See also* intra-party democracy; political trust; representative democracy
depoliticisation, concept of, 28, 214; in cartel theory, 33–34, 37–38, 59, 99; and political conflict, 99. *See also* Swedish European Union Affairs Committee study; Swedish Riksdag
Donges, P., 135
Downs, A., 2, 209, 213. *See also* median voter theorem

Duverger, M., 29–30, 40

Ekengren, A.-M., 201
electoral-professional party, 26, 214
electoral volatility, 121, 123
employment, 9–10; IT advances, effect on, 9, 10
Erlingsson, G. Ó., 211
Esaiasson, P., 80–81, 128
European integration, 8; convergence in, 9, 44, 207; depoliticisation effect of, 97, 99–100, 101, 105, 114; and national politicisation, 97, 101, 114; and partisan polarisation, 9, 45; and positive/negative integration, 114
Europeanisation, 21, 23, 97–98, 117n1; and cartel party theory, 99, 101; depoliticisation hypothesis in, 97, 99–100, 101, 109, 114; and elite collusion, 100, 101, 113. *See also* Swedish European Union Affairs Committee study
European Parliament, 18; policy congruence study, 58
European Union: democratic accountability in, 3; depoliticisation of, 34; migration issues in, 9

financial crisis (2008), effects of, 11–12
Finland, 24; and EU membership, 132; parliamentary system in, 134, 137; political culture in, 127, 134, 137
Finland, mediatisation perception study, 24, 121, 133–35, 136–37, 138, 206; consensus/continuity findings in, 127, 131–32, 134, 135, 137, 138, 206; foreign policy, use of in, 126–27, 131, 133–34, 138; homogenisation in, 127, 131, 132, 134–35, 138; limited role of media in, 131–32, 134, 135, 136–37, 138
Finnish Foreign Affairs Committee, 126, 127, 133–34, 137, 138
Freidenvall, L., 146

Geertz, C., 162–63

gender representation, 7, 21, 143–57; and cartel party theory, 24, 143, 155; and new issues politicisation, 143, 145, 146; in Nordic countries, 146; political conflict, increase in, 24, 143, 144, 146, 147, 155–56. *See also* women's representation

gender representation, Swedish study, 146–57; conflict measurement in, 147–48; gender equality in, 144; parliamentary conflict, impact on, 144, 146, 151–55, 206; standing committees, involvement in, 149–51, 152–55, 156

Germany: cartel parties (1887), 30, 37; social-democracy in, 4

Gezgor, B., 77

Gidlund, G., 47

globalisation, 8, 9, 17, 45; democracy, effect on, 3, 21, 23; depoliticisation effect of, 99, 105, 112

Greece, 12, 13n3

Green Party (Sweden), 18–19, 148; party culture analysis, 25, 50, 160, 164, 165, 169, 175–76, 177, 178, 181, 183, 185, 186

Guest, G., 128

Hagevi, M., 22, 23, 50, 198

Hägglund, G., 182

Håkansson, N., 135

Halvardsson, A., 81

Holmberg, S., 58, 61–63, 80–81

Iceland, 144

immigration, 10, 12, 64, 166

income inequality, 8

individualisation theory, 210–11, 212

intra-party democracy, 5, 30, *194*; decline of, 45, 49–53, 67, 210; and elite control, 45, 49, 53, 67; and individualisation theory, 210–11; media coverage, effect on, 51–52. *See also* mediatisation of politics; Sweden, party system in

Isaksson, A., 74

issue congruence, 58–59, 60–61, 68, 69nn8–9; Swedish analysis, 59–64, 205; use of left-right indicators in, 59–63

Johnson, L., 128

Juholt, H., 179

Kant, I., 197

Katz, R. S., 1, 2, 3, 5–8, 15, 16, 27–41, 43–47, 58, 71–72, 76, 99, 101, 113–14, 116, 119–20, 127, 159, 161, 189, 190–91, 195–96, 197, 200–201, 202, 205, 206, 208–13. *See also* cartel party theory

Kinberg Batra, A., 173

Kirchheimer, O., 1, 2, 3–4, 8, 100, 109. *See also* catch-all parties

Kitschelt, H., 24, 26, 33, 38, 41n4, 58, 68, 123, 125, 138

Koole, R., 30

Koß, M., 47

Krouwel, A., 163, 185

labour market challenges, 9–10; IT, effect on, 9, 10

Left Party (Sweden), 19, 50, 110, 112; party culture analysis, 160, 165, 168–69, 170, 173–74, 176, 177, 178, 182, 184, 185, 186

left–right dimension: in cartel party theory, 43, 45, 59, 99, 155, 207, 208; issue congruence indicators of, 59–63; in Swedish parliamentary conflict, 112–13, 114, 115–16, 208, 209; Swedish party divisions on, 15–21, *20*, 54, 55, *56*, *57*, 59–64, 67, 147–48, 152, *153*, 160, 170, 205, 207

Lengauer, G., 135

Liberals (Sweden), 113; party culture analysis, 165, 168, 169, 170, 174–75, 177, 184–85, 186

Lijphart, A., 193, 196, 197, 213

Linde, H., 173, 174

Lipset, S. M., 145
Locke, J., 40
Loxbo, K., 22, 23, 50, 198

Mair, P., 1, 2, 3, 5–8, 15, 16, 17, 27–41, 43–47, 58, 71–72, 76, 97, 99–100, 101, 113–14, 116, 119–20, 127, 159, 161, 189, 190–91, 195, 196–97, 199, 200–201, 202, 205, 206, 208–13. *See also* cartel party theory
Marx, K., 76
mass party, 24, 50, 54, 66, 72–73; party leader dominance in, 51, 53, 207; view of democracy in, 189, 207
median voter theorem, 2; and policy convergence, 209
mediatisation, concept of, 120
mediatisation, perceived effects study, 124–42; foreign policy, use of in, 126, 127, 129; fragmentation in, 125–26, 128, 135; homogenisation in, 125–26, 128, 129; interviews, used in, 127–28, 139–40
mediatisation of politics, 21, 23–24, 119–42; in cartel party theory, 119–22, 123, 125, 126, 133, 138; as force for fragmentation, 121, 123–24, 125, *126*, 127, 135–36, 137–38; individualisation, effect on, 123; media advisors, role in, 119, 121–22, 125, 129–30; media logic in, 119, 120, 122, 133, 140n1; party elite control of, 121–22, 125, 130, 137; perceived effects analysis, 125, 126–42; personalisation of politics in, 122, 125; policy homogenisation in, 119, 120, 121, 122, 125, *126*, 127, 133, 137; political culture, role in, 138–39; Swedish analysis, 24, 26, 51–52, 124–42
mediatisation perception, Swedish study, 24, 121, 127–31, 132–33, 135–36; foreign policy, use of in, 126, 127, 128, 130, 133, 138; fragmentation in, 127, 128, 130,

131, 132–33, 136, 138, 206; homogenisation in, 127, 128, 130–31, 132, 136, 138. *See also* Finland, mediatisation perception study
Michels, R., 1–2, 3, 4, 8, 40; iron law of oligarchy, 43, 49, 68
Moderates (Sweden), 113, 115; party culture analysis, 162, 164, 165, 168, 169, 170–73, 177, 179, 180, 183, 184, 186–87

Nash equilibrium, 35
NATO, 132
New Democracy (Sweden), 19, 102, 107, 148
New Labour (UK), 196–97
Nordic Defence Cooperation (NORDEFCO), 132
Norris, P., 71
Norway, 146

Ohly, L., 174
opposition, political, 23, 114, 191, 193, 194; 'opposition in principle', 109, 117n5
opposition parties, 102, *194*

Panebianco, A., 162
parliamentary systems, 192, *194*; conflict in, 100, 101, 105, 195; committees in, 19, 21; politicisation/depoliticisation hypotheses in, 100–101. *See also* Swedish Riksdag
participation, political, 191
parties: democratic role of, 190, 192, 207, 211; dissatisfaction with, 6, 11–12, 13, 208; individualisation, effect of on, 210–11, 212; new parties, formation of, 211–12; organisational cultures in, 159–60, 161–62; and policy convergence, 7, 8, 22, 45, 53–57, 209; policy polarisation and conflict in, 213–14; public financing, effect on, 23, 43, 44, 47, 67, 73, 76, 77, 83, 207,

208, 211–13; representativeness of, 6–7, 43, 46, 71; responsiveness of, 190, 192, 193, *194*, 195, 196. *See also* catch-all parties; democracy; intra-party democracy; party policy convergence; political trust, decline in; professionalisation of politics
partisanship, 196, 201; necessary tension in, 202
party activism, 4–5, 45
party identification/loyalty, 18, 24, 210
party membership decline, 4–5, 16, 38, 69n2, 84, 208; individualisation, effect on, 67, 210–11; joining incentives/threshold, changes in, 77–78, 83; social composition and exclusivity in, 78, 93; in Sweden, 26, 44–45, 46–47, 67
party organisational culture, 23, 159–87; in cartel party theory, 159–62, 163, 164–65, 207, 208; definition of, 159; ends–means rationality conflict in, 160, 162, 163; as individualistic/collective, 164–65, 167–68; as pragmatic/ideal, 25, 164, 165, 167; professionalism in 25, 164; as restraint on cartelisation, 25, 159, 160, 161–62, 166
party organisational culture, Swedish analysis, 159–60, 164–87; idealism/pragmatism dimension in, 169–70, 172, 173, 174, 175, 176–77, 180, 181, 183–85; individualism/collectivism dimension in, 169–70, 172, 173, 174, 177–78, 179, 180, 183–85; interviews used in, 166–67; logic of cartelisation in, 160, 164, 165, 166, 176, 177, 183–85, 208; MP autonomy, effect on, 160, 167–68, 169–70, 172, 173, 174, 176, 177, 179–80, 182–83; 1998–2002 data, 164–65, 166, 168–69, 183, 185; party collaboration, effect on, 160, 165, 172, 175, 177, 207; political events, effect on, 166; political

responsibility dimension in, 166, 167, 168–69, 171, 173–74, 175, 176, 178, 180, 181, 183; 2012–2013 data, 166, 183, 185. *See also* Sweden, party system in
party policy convergence, 7, 8, 22, 38, 44, 54, 55, 58–59, 60, 190, 207, 213–14; median voter theorem explanation, 209; mediatisation, role in, 119; party competition, role in 209; Swedish analysis of, 26, 54–58, 59–64, 67, 205, 207, 209
party voter loyalty, 44, 47
personalisation of politics, 122, 123, 125. *See also* mediatisation of politics
Persson, G., 180
Petersson, O., 74
Phillips, A., 143
Pitkin, H., 202
pluralism, 201
policy polarisation, and degree of conflict, 213–14
political campaigning, 73, 119
political class, concept of, 76, 77
political cleavages theory, 143
political logic, concept of, 120
political party, notion of contract in, 40
political trust, decline in, 46, 58, 64–66, 67, 205
politicisation, concept of, 98–99; in parliament, 100–101, 114. *See also* Europeanisation; Swedish European Union Affairs Committee study
polyarchy, 190, 191–92
populist radical-right parties, 2, 7, 13, 98, 102
power, critique of, 197
professionalisation of politics, 21, 71–96, 164, 190, 200; careerism in, 75, 78–79; cartelisation, effect on, 23, 25, 47, 67, 71–73, 76, 190; elite dominance in, 73, 93, 190, 196; and homosociality recruitment, 79–80; media use in, 125; membership

influence on, 72–73; public financing, role in, 23, 43, 44, 47, 67, 73, 76, 77, 83, 207, 208, 211; recruitment pool in, 72, 73, 77–78, 79, 83; social homogeneity in, 71, 72, 73, 80; Swedish analysis of, 26, 72–74, 79, 80–94, 206. *See also* party membership decline
professional politician, concept of, 74–77, 80
proportional representation systems, 73

Raaum, N., 146
Reinfeldt, F., 170–71, 173
representative democracy: basic values of, 190, *194*, 195; as 'hollowed out', 43, 46, 58, 100, 112; and issue congruence, 58, 59, 68; mediatisation, effect on, 120. *See also* gender representation; mediatisation of politics; party policy convergence; political trust, decline in
Rokkan, S., 145, 146
Rosenblum, N., 201, 202

Sahlin, M., 179
Sannerstedt, A., 198
Sartori, G., 37, 40, 202
Scarrow, S., 77, 212
Scharpf, F., 114
Schattschneider, E. E., 98–99, 114
Sjölin, M., 198
Sköld, L., 81
social democracy, 3; financial crisis of 2008, effect on, 12; Scandinavian form of, 4
Social Democrats (Sweden), 15, 19, 50–51, 54, 55, 102, 109, 110, 111–12, 113, 115, 116; party culture analysis, 160, 164, 169, 170, 174, 177, 179–81, 183, 184, 186–87
socialism, 12; shift from capitalism to, 3–4
SOM Institute, University of Gothenburg, 81

Steensen, S., 124
Stigler, G., 34–35, 37, 41n3
Strömbäck, J., 120
Surveyinstitutet, Linnaeus University, 59
Sweden: December Agreement (2014), 15–16, 26nn1–2, 200; party activism in, 49, 50, 51–52; party public financing in, 47–49, 66; political culture in, 18, 127
Sweden, cartelisation thesis, 44–69, 195, 197–203, 205–14; causal relationships, absence of, 206–8; consensual democracy analysis, 197–203, 205; elite collusion in, 199–200, 209; elite ideological convergence analysis, 45, 53–57, 59, 66, 67, 213; intra-party democracy analysis, 45, 49–53, 66; issue congruence analysis, 58–64, 67, 205; mediatisation in, 24, 26, 51–52; party conflict increase in, 112–13, 114, 115–16, 208, 209, 213; party government model, shift to, 199, 200; policy conflict in, 198–99, 200; political trust analysis, 46, 58, 64–66, 67, 69n9, 205. *See also* gender representation; mediatisation of politics; party organisational culture
Sweden, party membership analysis, 4–5, 18, 47–49, 66; gender differences in, 84–86; public financing/membership decline, 44–45, 46–49, 66, 78, 206, 207; social composition analysis, 78, 80, 83, 93. *See also* gender representation, Swedish study; party organisational culture, Swedish analysis
Sweden, party system in, 7, 15, 17, 18–19, 50, 56, 209, 211; fragmentation in, 211; intra-party democracy analysis, 5, 45, 49–53, 66, 197, 207; left/right divide in, 54, 55, *56, 57*, 59–64, 67, 147–48, 152, *153*, 160, 170, 205, 207; media influence in, 51–52; membership influence

in, 50, 51–53, 82; new parties in, 212; opposition party distinctions in, 56; part-time/full-time politicians data, 82; political blocs in, 160, 209; professionalisation analysis, 72–74, 76–77, 79, 80–94, 206; public funding in, 212–13; selective incentives/economic rewards focus, 82–83. *See also individual Swedish parties*; party organisational culture, Swedish analysis

Sweden Democrats, 7, 15, 19, 102, 105, 107, 110, 111, 148, 166, 180

Swedish Association of Local Authorities and Regions, 81

Swedish European Union Affairs Committee study, 98, 101–18, 147, 207; consensus/conflict measurement in, 103–4; content analysis, 1970–2014, 102–3, 104, 108–10, 114; Euroscepticism in, 107, 110, 113; government–opposition dynamic in, 104, 114, 208; interviews used in, 104–5, 111–13; left/right conflict increase in, 112–13, 114, 115–16, 208, 209; manifesto data in, 98, 114–15; policy area differences in, 110–11, 113, 205, 207; politicisation/depoliticisation results in, 105–18; welfare/labour market political conflict in, 113

Swedish Foreign Affairs Committee, 127, 135, 153, 155

Swedish National Election Study, 64–65

Swedish Parliamentary Survey, 59, 80–81

Swedish Riksdag: bloc voting in, 199; committees in, 21; depoliticisation analysis, 23, 98, 101–18, 206, 207–8; extra-parliamentary recruitment, 79, 81–83, 87–89, *90–91*, 92–93; gender differences in, 84–86, 89, 92, *94*; homosociality recruitment in, 79, 92; MPs social composition analysis, 72–74, 76–77, 79–80, 82–87, 89, 93; MP social homogeneity analysis, 72–74, 80, 88–96; party convergence analysis, 1970–2014, 54–57, 207–8; party seat distribution, 1970–2014, 19, *20*. *See also* party organisational culture, Swedish analysis

Uddhammar, E., 198

Van Aelst, P., 120
Verba, S., 78, 84
voting equality, 191

Weber, M., 74–75
welfare state, 8, 12, 67; globalisation, effect on, 50; Swedish analysis, 18, 50, 81, 88, 113
women's representation, 143–57; as substantive and symbolic, 144–45; and women's interests, 143, 145. *See also* gender representation; gender representation, Swedish study
World Economic Forum, 144

About the Contributors

Katarina Barrling is a researcher at the Department of Government at Uppsala University, Sweden. Her research interests include parliamentary party groups, party organization and political culture. Aside from many publications in Swedish, international publications include 'Exploring the Inner Life of the Party: A Framework for Analysing Elite Party Culture', *Scandinavian Political Studies* 36 (2), 2013, and, with Jean-Pascal Daloz, 'Représentation politique et modestie ostensible en Europe du Nord', *Nordiques* 4, 2004.

Douglas Brommesson is an associate professor in political science at Lund University, Sweden. His research interests include foreign policy analysis, party politics, and religion and politics. His work within party politics has mostly focused on the relationship between media and parliamentarians, including the mediatization of politics, as well as ideological change within political parties. He has previously published in outlets such as *Cooperation and Conflict, International Review of Sociology, Journal of International Relations & Development, International Politics and the Oxford Handbook on Swedish Politics*. He has also edited and contributed to *Global Community? Transnational and Transdisciplinary Exchanges* (2015).

Ann-Marie Ekengren is a professor in political science at the University of Gothenburg. Her main research areas are foreign policy decision-making, international relations and party politics. Ekengren is the author of nine books, mainly in foreign policy making, and has published articles in *Cooperation and Conflict, International Review of Sociology, International Studies Quarterly, Party Politics, Scandinavian Political Studies* and *Scandinavian Journal of History*.

Henrik Enroth is an associate professor in political science at Linnaeus University, Sweden, with a special interest in social and political theory. His recent work has appeared in journals such as *International Political Sociology*, *Party Politics*, *European Journal of Social Theory*, *Contemporary Political Theory* and *Transnational Legal Theory*, as well as in *The SAGE Handbook of Governance* and *The SAGE Encyclopedia of Political Theory*. He has also edited and contributed to *Global Community? Transnational and Transdisciplinary Exchanges* (2015).

Magnus Hagevi is a professor in political science and leader of *Surveyinstitutet* at Linnaeus University, Sweden. His research interests focus on political parties and political behavior at mass and elite levels. Hagevi is the author of several books, mainly about political behavior, legislative behavior and political parties. His recent work has appeared in *West European Politics*, *International Review of Sociology*, *Review of Religious Research* and *Journal for the Scientific Study of Religion*.

Anna Högmark attended University of Göteborg, earning her master's degree in political science. She also served as a research assistant on the project 'Party Government in Flux'. She now works at the Immigration Authorities in Sweden.

Herbert Kitschelt is a professor in political science and the George V. Allen Professor of International Relations at Duke University. He specializes in comparative political parties and elections in established and new democracies, comparative public policy/political economy, and twentieth-century social theory. His continued interest in the theory of party system dynamics is documented in recent contributions to edited volumes and journal articles, such as the piece on the cartel theory in *European Journal of Political Research* (2000), and in *Comparative Political Studies* (2000). Moreover, he has published a number of articles on the interaction between democratic party competition and political economic reform strategies, such as in the co-edited volume by Kitschelt, Peter Lange, Gary Marks and John Stephens, *Continuity and Change in Contemporary Capitalism* (1999), Paul Pierson (editor), *The New Politics of the Welfare State* (2000).

Karl Loxbo is an associate professor in political science at Linnaeus University, Sweden. His research interests focus on the transformation of partisan conflicts and the success of radical right parties in Western Europe, intra-party democracy and the impact of ethnic diversity on social trust. His research has been published in journals such as *Party Politics*, *Scandinavian*

Political Studies, Local Government Studies, Journal of Elections, Public Opinion and Parties, Journal of Trust Research and *Acta Sociologica.*

Helena Olofsdotter Stensöta, PhD, is an associate professor in political science at the University of Gothenburg. Her research focuses on gender, ethics, public policy and administration. Her most recent publication is an edited volume by Palgrave Macmillan (w. Lena Wängnerud) *Gender and Corruption. Historical Roots and New Avenues for Research.* She further has published in *Administration & Society* (w. Marie Østergaard Møller, 2017); *Governance*, (w. Lena Wängnerud, 2015); *Ethics and Social Welfare* (2015); *Child Indicators Research* (w. Erica Nordlander, 2014); *Journal of Public Administration Research and Theory* (2012); *Social Politics* (w. Daniel Engster, 2011) and *Public Administration Review* (2010), among other journals.

Mats Sjölin is a professor in political science at Linnaeus University. He has led the research project from which this volume has evolved, as well as projects on public corruption and political ethics. His research has been published in journals such as *Local Government Studies* and *Scandinavian Political Studies* and in several books.

www.ingramcontent.com/pod-product-compliance
Lightning Source LLC
Chambersburg PA
CBHW021813270326
41932CB00007B/164